GORBACHEV

GORBACHEV

ON MY COUNTRY

AND THE WORLD

Translated from Russian by George Shriver

COLUMBIA UNIVERSITY PRESS

NEW YORK

COLUMBIA UNIVERSITY PRESS
Publishers Since 1893
New York
Chichester, West Sussex

Copyright © 2000 Columbia University Press
All rights reserved
Library of Congress Cataloging-in-Publication Data

Gorbachev, Mikhail, 1931–
[Razmyshleniia o proshlom i budushchem.   English]
On my country and the world / Gorbachev.
p.   cm.
Includes index.
ISBN 0-231-11514-8 (cloth)
1. Soviet Union—History—Philosophy.   2. Russia (Federation)
—History—1991– —Philosophy.   3. World politics—1989–
4. Gorbachev, Mikhail Sergeevich, 1931–   —Political and social
views.   I. Title.   II. Title: Gorbachev—on my country and the world.
DK49.G6713   1999
947.085′01—dc21
99–31273
CIP

Two quotations on p. 40, one from Woodrow Wilson in early 1919 and one from a
document reportedly approved by him on October 30, 1918, are retranslated from
Russian. We were unable to find the original English wording. It is not, as best we
can determine, in the 69-volume Papers of Woodrow Wilson, published by
Princeton University Press.
The quotation from Victor Gordon Kieman on p. 43 is retranslated from the Rus-
sion. We were unable to locate the original English wording.
(In almost all cases we have been able to verify the accuracy of the author's quotations, and have used original English wording wherever available.)—Trans.

CONTENTS

PART THREE

The New Thinking: Yesterday, Today, and Tomorrow

169

GORBACHEV

Part One

THE OCTOBER REVOLUTION: ITS SENSE AND SIGNIFICANCE

More than eighty years have passed since the event which in our country, until recently, was generally called the Great October Socialist Revolution. Today debates about its character, content, and consequences are intensifying and often sound just as irreconcilable as the positions taken by the participants in the revolution who found themselves in opposing camps.

But then, what is surprising about that? More than two hundred years have passed since the great French revolution of the eighteenth century, but to this day that revolution inspires sharply conflicting judgments and opinions. This is all the more true of the October revolution—not only because it is closer to us in time but because, just as the French revolution shaped the entire course of the nineteenth century, the Russian revolution, whatever one might say about it, largely determined the course of the twentieth century. *And this century has proven to be a turning point for all humanity.*

A contemporary of the revolution, the celebrated American journalist and writer John Reed, called his eyewitness account of the revolution *Ten Days That Shook the World.* A contemporary of ours, the Englishman Eric Hobsbawm, a historian and sociologist whose name is no less well known than John Reed's, considers the October revolution to have been a "global constant in the [twentieth] century's history."

Both these men were right.

Today we know much more about the October revolution than did its participants, and more than the heirs of the revolution in our country were allowed to know. Glasnost and perestroika have given us the opportunity to learn many fundamental facts about the revolution which had been classified or falsified—and about the decades after it. The disclosure of the truth that was begun under glasnost— even though it caused shock and aroused protest on the part of many people, and for many different reasons—became a stimulus toward reviving the moral health of our society.

Today, incidentally, a system of secrecy is being revived—not in relation to October but toward many subsequent events, including quite recent ones. Lies and half-truths have again become an essential part of politics. As in the past, this is a symptom of the unhealthy moral character of the regime.

The policy of glasnost in the perestroika era and its continuing, unstoppable momentum allow us to look at ourselves with open eyes, providing us with new knowledge about the many-sided nature of October and its consequences, and enabling us to reflect on various aspects of post-October developments in their true dimensions and significance.

How, then, does the October revolution present itself to our view today, more than eighty years later?

CHAPTER I

A Blunder of History, Accident, or Necessity?

THIS CHAPTER'S TITLE states three of the various explanations for the October 1917 revolution and its place in history. Discussion and disagreement over these different versions continue, with virtually endless variations on these themes. Everything or anything can be found here—from the assertion that October was merely a successful putsch by a handful of revolutionaries headed by Lenin to the claim that it was the result of a secret plan by the German General Staff.

Today, after eight decades, with the enormous amount of material available to researchers, one thing may be stated absolutely and definitively: *In the specific situation that arose in Russia and around it, the October revolution was historically inevitable.*

Russia was pregnant with revolution from the beginning of the twentieth century. This does not mean that the revolution necessarily had to take such a destructive, and veritably apocalyptic form.

We need to go back a little at this point and ask what Russia was like before World War I. There is a commonly encountered opinion—it was virtually the official line in the Soviet era—that, back then, Russia was a slumbering, backward, savage or semisavage country, one that was vast and powerful but at the same time impoverished and miserable. That is not true—or to put it more precisely, that is not the full truth.

The phenomenal growth of Russian industry during the decade and a half before World War I, especially after 1906, would today be called an "economic miracle." The gross national product increased by 220 percent. The most advanced types of production were introduced as industry was rapidly modernized. Russia outpaced the West in the degree of concentration found in the primary sectors of its economy. Fixed capital was expanding three times faster than the rate of such expansion in America. The growth of savings bank deposits was indicative. In 1914 they had reached 1,704 million gold rubles. The internal market was expanding swiftly, not only in the production of producers' goods but in items of mass consumption, such as sugar, butter, kerosene, footwear, and clothing.

The cooperative movement in the countryside was the second largest in the world, second only to the movement in Great Britain where this form of organization had originated. Siberia was being colonized at a furious pace. Its population doubled during the nine-year period between the Russo-Japanese War and World War I. Agricultural production increased more than threefold, and agricultural exports rose tenfold. Siberia had entered a genuinely "American" period of economic and cultural development.

In the eight years before World War I there was an increase of 12,000 versts of railroad track, bringing the total to 64,500 versts of track for the country as a whole. The profitability of the railroads tripled in a period of three years, reaching a level of 449 million gold rubles in 1912.

Preparations for the introduction of a system of compulsory public education had begun. Before war broke out in 1914 there were 122,000 primary public schools in Russia with eight million pupils. Each summer, school teachers had the opportunity to travel to Italy, France, Germany, and other European countries to gain wider experience and learn about setting up a system of secondary education for Russia.

In the prewar years, especially under the impact of the 1905 revolution, Russian society acquired the features of a distinctly organized system. Political parties and elections to the Duma raised the level of political consciousness. The court system, which began to operate more and more independently, attained a level of authority that was unusual for Russia. There were significantly expanded opportunities to exercise freedom of speech, to criticize the authorities, and to criticize government policies, not only in the Duma. Newspapers were sprouting like mushrooms after rain.

There was still, of course, a great deal of lawlessness and arbitrary rule. But from the point of view of social activism and the involvement of large numbers of people in public activity, Russia was no longer what it had been.

As for culture, this was the time of the celebrated "Silver Age" in Russia, when our country played a vanguard role in world art and literature, creating new schools and trends that lasted for decades.

All the testimony of people at that time tells us that no one was thinking about having a war. No one wanted it, up to and including a significant portion of the higher imperial aristocracy. Until the last moment no one knew that the rulers in St. Petersburg had become entangled in a web of military intrigue. The tsar himself, for a period of several days, a long time under the circumstances, hesitated on whether to respond with a military mobilization to the ultimatum issued by the tsar's relative and "friend" Kaiser Wilhelm II.

This look backward at Russia before World War I is not out of place, I think, as a confirmation of the thesis that objectively it was not necessary for Russia to become involved in World War I. It could have remained on the sidelines, as the United States did. It was only as the curtain was falling, in 1917, that the United States entered the war.

Nevertheless, we should not allow anything said here to lead us astray in our image of Russia at the turn of the century. At the time of the revolution it was by no means a country of "prosperous capitalism." It was true that Russian capitalism, which began its journey belatedly in comparison with the West, was moving ahead at an intense pace. But society as a whole remained semifeudal, with an archaic sociopolitical system that gave rise to very sharp class antagonisms. From the beginning of the twentieth century Russia found itself in a condition of profound crisis. The need for change was felt tangibly in all strata of society. Attempts at reform were undertaken in the last years of the nineteenth century and the early twentieth century, but they went nowhere because they did not dare infringe on the power of the autocracy, the rule of the tsar. History teaches us, however, that when the times are ripe for change and the government refuses or is unable to change, either society starts to decay or a revolution begins.

Something further should be added on this point. A crisis-filled or critically explosive potential had built up almost everywhere in the world by the beginning of the twentieth century. The tension in social relations was reflected in a rising wave of strikes by workers, protest actions by farmers, and the increased influence of socialist parties in many countries. The first anticolonial revolutions in the outlying areas of the world capitalist system had already taken place. In relations between the most powerful countries the time had grown ripe for a redivision of spheres of influence around the world. Germany had made a great leap forward in economic development, and its military potential was being promoted openly, including in the realm of naval power. An increasingly aggressive German foreign policy resulted in tough and knotty international crises, one after the other.

World War I laid bare the crisis of international relations in all its intensity. The contradictions that had built up erupted in a tremendous explosion, and during the war these contradictions continued to develop new modifications, which varied with the changing fortunes of war. For Russia, the war into which the tsarist government plunged our country, flying in the face of its real national interests, when it could have stayed on the sidelines, soon provoked an internal explosion that spread through the entire nation.

The beginning of 1917 saw the spontaneous outpouring known as the February revolution. For a long time in our country it was customary not to acknowledge the full significance of this revolution, to dismiss it merely as a prologue to the October revolution. In fact it was a major event in and of itself. The "great empire of the tsars" was overripe for change on a colossal scale, and the February revolution made the breakthrough toward the changes that were needed. At the time that this revolution succeeded, the further course of events was by no means fatally predetermined.

February was a revolution of the masses in the full sense of the word. The people of Russia, its citizens, who were yearning for freedom, peace, and bread, made this revolution. Hunger protests by the women of Petrograd were the spark that ignited the flame. As John Reed wrote, "it was the masses of the people, workers, soldiers, and peasants, which forced every change in the course of the Revolution." The political groups were caught off guard. Today the unfalsified documents of the Russian political parties of that time are being published—ranging from the left to the extreme right—and it is evident how unprepared the politicians were for the actions of the masses. On the very eve of February 1917, Lenin, who was then in Zurich, said that the present generation was not fated to see the revolution. Confusion and dismay are the most appropriate words with which to characterize the attitudes prevailing in the headquarters of the various political parties at that time. February was a proclamation of freedom. The three-hundred-year-old monarchy collapsed. A republic came into being, and the possibility of democratic change emerged. For a short time Russia became the freest of all the countries in the war.

But the February revolution quickly played itself out. Those who came to replace the tsar proved to be helpless, cowardly, and self-seeking; they were unable to rise to the historical needs of the time. Consequently the war continued, although it was universally hated. Neither peace nor relief from hunger and economic dislocation was granted to the people. Even democratic liberties began to erode. Antigovernment demonstrations were dispersed by force of arms. Troublesome newspapers were simply closed down. Political opponents of the government were persecuted and arrested. It was at that time, not only after the October revolution, that there appeared food-requisitioning units, which took grain from the peasants.

Russian democracy—which had great diversity but was fragmented and divided—was unable to take realistic action toward resolving all the problems that had come to a head. It was unable to bring the country out of crisis and back to normalcy.

The Provisional Government proved incapable of implementing fundamental change. Expectations were left hanging. Under these conditions October was inevitable. Of course the February revolution and its subsequent development deserve continued study. But taking into account everything we know today, certain conclusions seem evident.

One of the main conclusions is this: *The October revolution undeniably reflected the most urgent demands of the broadest strata of the population for fundamental social change.* The central slogans of the revolution, which arose from below and were not manufactured by anyone, were for freedom, for peace to all, for the factories to go to the workers, for the land to go to the peasants, for bread to go to the hungry. These slogans concisely stated the basic demands of the people.

A question arises: Was there, could there have been, an alternative to October? Could events have developed differently?

A democratic alternative, in the form of a positive development of the February revolution, as we have said, was buried as the result of the weakness of the post-February regime. It was not possible to go back to the first days of the February revolution, and the tsarist regime had completely discredited itself. Only one alternative remained—as many even in monarchist circles admitted—and that was a new, more radical revolution.

Nevertheless, another variant potentially existed—that of an extreme, right-wing, reactionary military dictatorship. I will cite the authoritative testimony of General Denikin, who was, of course, a leader of the Whites. Referring to the attempt by General Kornilov to carry out a coup d'état in August 1917, Denikin wrote: "By his own firm and sincere conviction and under the influence of public opinion, Kornilov saw in a dictatorship the only way out of the situation created by the spiritual and political prostration of the [Provisional] government." Denikin stated further: "Kornilov, and especially those in his immediate entourage, were inclined toward a one-man dictatorship." It must be said that this kind of "solution" to the problem was regarded as virtually the optimal solution by many on the right and even by some liberal bourgeois politicians. The Bolsheviks presented their variant in opposition to these plans for a coup and in opposition to the helplessness of the Provisional Government. And they were victorious.

This, of course, created a tremendous rift in Russian society, one fraught with civil war. Could that kind of war have been avoided? Let us turn to the authority of Vladimir Lenin. Here is what he wrote on this question: "If there is one absolutely indisputable lesson of the revolution, one absolutely demonstrated by the facts, it is that only and exclusively an alliance of the Bolsheviks with the Socialist Revolutionaries and Mensheviks and exclusively an immediate transfer of all power to the soviets could have made a civil war in Russia impossible" (Lenin, *Collected Works* [Russian ed.] 34:222). No such alliance, however, was formed. One may scrupulously follow the course of events day by day and hour by hour to determine who bore the responsibility for this failure. The general conclusion will be that all those to whom Lenin referred were responsible—that is, the Bolsheviks, the Mensheviks, and the Socialist Revolutionaries.

A certain parallel suggests itself here, or if not a parallel, at least a consideration. The February revolution did not produce the expected and possible results, because Russian democracy was weak and fragmented. Rivalry and ideological prejudice proved to be stronger than the need for unification of all democratic forces on a national basis to win peace and land and to combat hunger and economic ruin. After October the civil war broke out for the same reason. In the years since October—in other countries and in other situations—has it not been true that the inability to come to agreement has prevented leftist and democratic parties, including Communists, from uniting to forestall a negative course of events—as, for example, in Germany before Hitler's rise to power?

I will go further. During the years of perestroika the fragmentation of the democrats, the back-biting among them, the attempts by each group to show that it was "more democratic" than the others, ultimately became one of the reasons for the undermining of democratic change and then the interruption of perestroika as a result of the August 1991 coup attempt. The same has happened in Russia since 1991. Our country has not accepted Yeltsin's reforms nor does it wish to return to the past, but a democratic alternative has not been created among the divided and fragmented democratic forces, and a destructive rivalry among leaders of tiny parties disrupts the democratic part of the spectrum in Russia.

This is a lesson for everyone who is seriously concerned about the future prospects of their own country and of the world community. Even today the wearing of ideological blinders, adherence to abstract schemes, and egoistic concern exclusively with gaining advantage for one's own party in many cases prevent a genuinely democratic choice. Yet history, with rare exceptions, contains many possible variants and is by no means lacking in alternatives.

There is, of course, another aspect of the truth regarding the civil war in Russia. It would unquestionably have been less savage, and would not have lasted so long, if not for foreign military intervention. In seeking to prevent the spread of the "Bolshevik infection" (and that was standard terminology among leaders of the Entente), the West did not hesitate to send interventionist forces from fourteen different countries. This was in response to the Bolshevik calls for, and practical actions promoting, the bonfire of world revolution. That is all true, but it had far-reaching consequences.

The goal that was openly proclaimed in the West at that time was to strangle the infant Soviet republic, and this goal persisted even after the civil war. In later times this allowed Stalin and the government subordinated to him to portray any opponent of his regime, any political opposition, even those who simply disagreed with him within the ranks of the Communist Party, as "foreign agents" and to whip up the "patriotic wrath of the masses" against them. Actually it can be said that the West lowered an iron curtain against Russia long before Churchill's speech in Fulton, Missouri. Indirectly this provided powerful nourishment for the Stalinist dictatorship and helped to preserve it, enabling it to justify not only errors but crimes as well.

The civil war, without question, was a colossal tragedy for our country and our people. The human losses were enormous. More than two million citizens emigrated, creating a "second Russia" outside our country. The question remains: Was the civil war inevitable?

The harsh and embittered feelings of that time are understandable of course. Maxim Gorky, in his *Thoughts Out of Season*, wrote that "war brought out naked, bestial instincts." A huge number of people lost everything they had. Hundreds of thousands were left without a shred. From then on they had nothing to lose. Others took up war as a profession. And all this—on both sides—was reinforced and illuminated by ideology, with colorful and dramatic slogans used to stir up frenzied passions. Also, there were vast quantities of weapons, and it became an everyday affair to put them to use for almost any reason. Physical losses were not the only result. The moral damage was tremendous. Our people suffered a psychological degradation that left a very deep imprint on the whole subsequent history of our country.

The Reds, who were defending the cause of the revolution, were fighting for Russia and for its future. But the Whites, who preached a different set of ideals, were also fighting for Russia, for what they considered its salvation. In this case patriotism did not unite but separated the two sides. In fact, however, ideological fanaticism suppressed true patriotism. Our country reached the brink of destruction as a result of this double-headed "patriotism." And our population found itself fragmented and divided for decades afterward.

I am not in any way questioning the feelings or motivations of Red Army fighters—they were sincere. The "Soldiers of October" believed in the rightness of their cause. Their exploits deserve to be honored and memorialized. But the soldiers on the other side, the Whites, also believed in their cause.

During the Great Patriotic War [the Nazi-Soviet phase of World War II, from 1941 to 1945], many White émigrés sided with the Soviet Union against Nazi Germany. Thousands of them perished. They did not (in most cases) give up their faith in Russia, although they had lost their country, nor did they give up their views. Their feelings for their native land took precedence.

Is this not a lesson for the present time and for the future—in Russia but not only in Russia? Ideological and political intolerance, even with the best and most sincere intentions, produces results that are the direct opposite of those intended.

The outcome of the civil war was, of course, the victory of the Bolsheviks. Why? Let us listen to someone who was by no means "Red"— Leonard Shapiro. In his book *The Russian Revolutions of 1917*, he wrote:

> . . . the people as a whole, in spite of the unpopularity of the Communists, preferred the Soviet regime to the available alternatives. The peasants disliked both sides and wanted above all to be left alone; but when it came to the choice, they preferred the Communists who gave them land to the Whites who took, or threatened to take, it away.

Despite an element of oversimplification, this explanation goes to the heart of the matter.

The slogans of the October revolution, especially those that were put into practice in the early period of the revolution, were decisive in bringing victory to the Bolsheviks. The historical necessity embodied in these slogans is confirmed by this fact; that is, there was a necessity for a profound transformation of the country along the lines indicated by the slogans calling for bread, peace, land, and so forth. This has enormous significance in and of itself, not only for Russia. Nevertheless, in reflecting on the revolution, its course of development, and its gains in comparison with its losses—and in comparison with the experience of other revolutions—one is drawn to the conclusion that the general question of the role of revolutions in history needs further, serious study.

Marx's formula that revolutions are the locomotives of history was very much in vogue for a long time and remains so even today. Nevertheless this formula is worth rethinking. Have revolutions really been the locomotives of forward or upward movement by society? Or have they been extreme solutions to situations in which the ruling powers were incapable of solving problems that had come to a head while the masses were no longer able to endure the existing situation?

Revolutions have undeniably been the sources of great change in the life of society. But they have also been very costly. Revolutions have been referred to as festivals of the oppressed and exploited masses. But haven't these same masses suffered great losses as a result of revolutions? Moreover, revolutions have often been followed by retrogressive movements. The term *Thermidor* has entered the vocabulary of political science as a kind of symbol for such retrogressive movements, which have sometimes been quite painful and unhealthy.

At the very height of perestroika I, as general secretary of the Central Committee of the Communist Party of the Soviet Union, stated publicly from the highest public platform in the Soviet Union: "I renounce revolution as a means of solving problems," although our country was ripe for change to such a profound extent that it was truly in need of a revolution. My concern was that a new revolution might cause destructive upheavals as in the past—or worse, since this is the atomic age.

In my view, the optimum form of social development, corresponding to the interests of all citizens, is *evolutionary reform*. When the necessity for change arises, the pace at which reforms take place, as experience has shown, depends on many factors. But it depends primarily on the level of maturity of civil society, the degree of responsibility among the ruling circles, and a general agreement to renounce intolerance and extremism.

What has been said is not intended to deny the unquestionably great significance of, let us say, the French revolution or the October revolution. They occupy an unshakable place in history. The main question is this: Did these revolutions, especially the October revolution, set an example as the optimal way of resolving the social problems which had come to a head at that time? Did such revolutions provide the most suitable and advantageous means for resolving the actually existing conflicts and contradictions? Did these revolutions in fact bring about what they had promised?

CHAPTER 2

Was Socialism Built in the Soviet Union?

THE OCTOBER REVOLUTION was termed a socialist revolution, and the Soviet Union was proclaimed a socialist state and even held up as a model. Later it was argued that what we had in our country was "developed socialism." Was it really a socialist revolution that took place in October 1917, and was the system created by that revolution a socialist one? This is a valid and important question from the point of view of history and historical truth and from the standpoint of the future for all who continue to profess socialist ideas.

Let me quote a statement by Lenin: "Our revolution up until the summer of 1918 and even until the autumn of 1918 was, to a significant degree, a bourgeois revolution" (*Collected Works* [Russian ed.] 38:143). What did Lenin mean here? Certainly he himself never renounced the socialist aims of the revolution.

Lenin had in mind one very simple circumstance or fact of life. The revolution accomplished in October 1917 was obliged objectively, before all else, to carry out the tasks of a bourgeois revolution. In Russia in 1917 such tasks as reorganizing the structure and character of the government, making a fundamental transformation in the system of land ownership, and resolving the nationalities question were all problems that had not been solved despite the great progress in the last years before World War I. Without their being solved it was impossible to move forward.

In October 1917 the victors in the revolutionary struggle confronted a society shaken to its foundations by the unprecedented slaughter and destruction of the world war.

After the revolution many Social Democrats, both in the West and in Russia (Plekhanov, for example), said that in a society like Russia there could be no talk of socialism. The material basis for socialism had not yet been created by capitalism. The Menshevik author Sukhanov wrote: "Russia has not reached that height of development of the productive forces under which socialism would be possible." In Lenin's last writings he answered his opponents—writings that are referred to as his political testament. What was his reply to Sukhanov in particular? Lenin agreed that Sukhanov's was "an undeniable argument" that had to be considered (45:380). Lenin continued:

> If for the creation of socialism a certain level of culture is required (although no one can say exactly what that level of culture should be, for it is different in every Western European state), why could we not begin with the conquest by revolutionary means of the prerequisites for such a particular level of culture and then, on the basis of workers' and peasants' power, move toward catching up with other countries. (45:381)

Here the question is presented in a sober, well-reasoned way.

But it was not until the years 1921–23 that policies based on such a reasonable approach made their appearance. In the first days and years of the revolution the Bolsheviks pursued a line of direct introduction of communist principles. The Kronstadt revolt and peasant uprisings, especially in Tambov province in 1921, signaled the defeat of this policy line. Lenin acknowledged this when he said, among other things: "You can't leap over the people."

Nevertheless it must be said that the October revolution did carry out the first part of the tasks facing it—those Lenin characterized as the tasks of the bourgeois revolution. It destroyed the autocratic machinery of state and put an end to the legacy of feudalism in the countryside. It opened up a certain opportunity for national development in what was called the "borderlands," the outlying colonial areas of the Russian empire. The cooperative movement also grew—not the kind that was later identified with all-out collectivization in the countryside but the civilized kind that had arisen earlier, before 1917. In addition, basic principles for industrial development were sketched out in the State Plan for the Electrification of Russia (GOELRO). Of course this was only a beginning, but one full of promise. What happened then?

After Lenin's death, and up to the end of the 1920s, a struggle went on in Russia between differing conceptions of how to move forward into the future. By the beginning of the 1930s Stalinism had triumphed in the Soviet

Union. The term *Stalinism* of course is a conditional one, although its usage has become customary. The one-sidedness of the term tends to flatten out the entire Soviet past, to paint it a single, uniformly dark color. In fact it was a multicolored, profoundly contradictory, and multilayered phenomenon.

Today in Russia, and also outside our country, a debate is going on. What was the nature of the system built in the Soviet Union? The most varied of answers are given to this question. Here, some say: Yes, it was socialism, if not outright communism, and it was very nearly a model system. Others object: No, it wasn't socialism; it was either state capitalism or even feudal capitalism or something of that kind. Still others disagree with both these views. They say: Yes, it was socialism but not a full-fledged kind of socialism; it was distorted, deformed, and incomplete.

A similar variety of views may be found in the West. But one other point of view is held in the West to which I would like to call particular attention. Proponents of this view hold that indeed socialism was built in the USSR. They argue that thanks to the Soviet experience we now know what socialism is and therefore can reject and write off this kind of antihuman system once and for all and forget about it.

This argument is false. My view is that in the Soviet Union a harsh and even cruel totalitarian system triumphed. It underwent an evolution to be sure; after Stalin's death its harshness and cruelty were modified and blunted somewhat, but in essence it remained the same.

Totalitarianism in the Soviet Union cannot of course serve as a model for anyone. That is indisputable. But it is also true that the kind of system that triumphed in the Soviet Union in the 1930s cannot be an argument against the socialist idea. I will return to this question below. For now there are other questions to consider.

The first of them is this: How was it possible for Stalinism to triumph? A complete answer to this question would require quite an extensive discussion in the course of which it would be necessary to review almost the entire history of the past eight decades. That is beyond the scope of the present work, but it is necessary to touch on some aspects of the matter.

We have already discussed one aspect—the particular features or characteristics that had developed in tsarist Russia, its social, economic, and political backwardness. Because of this backwardness the Russian people were not prepared to accept genuinely democratic ideals. Stereotyped ideas about "our good father, the tsar" had taken deep root in the mass consciousness, the idea of an omniscient, all-knowing leader who was always right. In the Stalin era wide use was made of such stereotyped thinking, and this was the psychological soil in which Stalinism was able to grow. Alas, such stereotypes have not been overcome even today.

It also cannot be forgotten that the Bolsheviks inherited a country in the depths of chaos. Harsh measures were required to overcome this—especially because, even after the end of the civil war, the resistance of the former ruling classes continued to make itself felt. Of course inexperience, even ignorance and fanaticism, among the revolutionaries themselves also played a role. Many of them considered the power they had won to be a carte blanche, that anything was permitted. The personal qualities of the leaders were also a very important factor that must be taken into account, especially those of Stalin, whom Lenin proposed to remove from the leadership. To me, Stalin was a cunning, crafty, cruel, and merciless individual, and a morbid suspiciousness was an innate part of his character.

In Russia today one can hear people saying at times: "We need a new Stalin." Such slogans tell us, first, that our population is still not living in genuinely democratic conditions, still has not lived in a genuinely human way: second, such slogans reflect the profound disillusionment and despair people feel regarding the existing order in Russia today. The majority of Russians, nevertheless, do not support such slogans. They favor freedom and liberty.

One of the reasons for what happened (that is, the rise of Stalinism)—and the chief error the Bolsheviks made even before Stalin—was the "model" of socialism they chose, the conception of socialism that took shape in the minds of the Bolsheviks and in their writings even before the revolution.

As is generally known, Marx and Engels did not work out a detailed blueprint of the future socialist society. And this was no accident. They were both opponents of "recipes." They stressed the need to take specific conditions into account, the particular changes needed in one or another country, and the mutability of circumstances in which change was to be implemented.

We must also recall that the views of Marx and Engels evolved. Thus, toward the end of his life, Engels came to the firm conviction that a democratic republic is the best form of government for the construction of socialism.

On the eve of October, during his last period in the underground, Lenin wrote the booklet *State and Revolution* (which remained uncompleted). This was in fact a systematic presentation, with commentary, of selected ideas about a socialist system drawn from his teachers, Marx and Engels. Lenin's work, however, remained utopian and schematic, and the experience of the first few years of the revolution refuted that document.

In the spring of 1918 Lenin published an article entitled "The Immediate Tasks of the Soviet Government." This was a more or less realistic program of action adapted to the conditions that had developed at that time. In this work, incidentally, the first hints of ideas that later developed into the New Economic Policy may be detected. Later those ideas were set aside in favor of the policy of so-called war communism. After the civil war Lenin returned to those ideas and worked out the full program of the New Economic Policy. He admitted that major mistakes had been made during the previous four years. This was a serious matter. To me, it is obvious that Lenin, a man of tremendous intellect, analyzed the postrevolutionary experience with the maximum of candor and rigor. He rejected a great deal and called much into question. In his article of early 1923, "On Cooperation," he uttered the celebrated phrase that it was now necessary to "acknowledge a fundamental change in our entire point of view toward socialism" (45:376). This indicates the direction in which he was searching. But many enigmas remain regarding his point of view.

It is clear that Lenin wanted to promote pacification and reconciliation both in Russian society and in international relations, to bring people back together who had been divided by cruelty and hatred so they could jointly engage in constructive work and activity for the sake of the future. It is worth emphasizing that Lenin at that time paid attention not only to the economic side of things. In his "Letter to the Congress" he wrote about the problems of democracy. He began his thoughts on this question with these words: "I would strongly recommend that a number of changes in our political structure be undertaken at this congress" (45:343).

His plans had not only a tactical aim but a strategic one as well. He did not have time to give full and final shape to his strategy. But knowing all of Lenin, not just bits and pieces quotable for one or another propagandistic purpose, I can state that his strategy excluded the revival of anything like war communism. Nevertheless Stalin imposed a new variation of war communism on our country.

I do not think that the New Economic Policy was just a tactical retreat in Lenin's view, as is often said. Serious and objective study is required on this point. What was involved evidently was a search for an approach to rethinking the place of the October revolution and of the new Russia in relation to the destiny of world civilization as a whole. Several propositions in Lenin's last writings speak along these lines, although various shadings and nuances can be found in these writings. Were these shadings not a reflection of the disputes within the Communist Party about the New Economic Policy? After all, many party members were accusing Lenin of revisionism at that time, of retreating, of betraying the cause of the revolution.

What I see in Lenin's last writings is a different person—a person who, after leading the country into and through the revolution, understood that mistakes had been made. This was a dramatic moment for the revolution. I understood this, and it influenced me greatly. These ideas of Lenin's and his New Economic Policy, however, were completely cast aside by Stalin.

What was it that was defective in the Bolshevik model of socialism?

First, it was a crudely schematic model based on ideological principles and standards that could not withstand close examination. Stalin's interpretation of these principles and standards deepened their harsh and dogmatic character. His version became a quasi-religious doctrine based on intolerance and ruthless suppression of all who in any way did not fit on this bed of Procrustes.

Second, the most generalized principle of the Bolshevik "model" was the "dictatorship of the proletariat." Borrowed from Marx, this idea was carried to the point of absurdity.

Before the revolution Lenin wrote that the proletariat cannot conquer power in any way except through democracy, that it cannot construct a new society in any way except democratically. In fact the proletarian dictatorship in Russia almost from the beginning, and especially under Stalin, represented a complete break with democracy. The dictatorship of the proletariat was said to be nothing less than the highest form of democracy. Yet there was not a true dictatorship of the proletariat in the sense of a mass movement, based on a major stratum of society. It was a dictatorship by a small ruling group at the top and by the hierarchical apparatus (the nomenklatura) that served it.

The banning of non-Communist parties after the revolution and the curtailment of freedom of speech were an obvious sign of a break with democracy. Such measures may be taken in conditions of extreme emergency but only as temporary measures. Also, the introduction of a one-party system and "unanimity of opinion" as a principle inevitably led to the distortion of the natural course of events. It inevitably led to arbitrary rule and ended with very severe consequences.

No matter what arguments were used to justify the need to suppress and disperse other parties in Russia after 1917, I think that the final establishment of a one-party system was perhaps one of the most serious errors. It prevented the October revolution from becoming a source for powerful democratic development and prevented our country from truly flourishing.

By the end of the 1920s Soviet society was completely monopolized by the party and its ideology. A repressive and essentially totalitarian system was solidly established. Different figures are given for the number of Soviet citizens who were destroyed or became victims of the Gulag system. At any rate, they number in the millions.

The question is often asked: Did the Soviet people understand what Stalin's "purges" really were—or to put it more simply—what the terror of the 1930s and 1940s really was? There is no easy answer. Not many knew the full extent of the "purges." A great many people considered them justified. The closed nature of our society, the aggressive and obsessive anti-Western propaganda, and the deeply rooted awareness that we were in a "besieged fortress" (which incidentally was a result of Western policy)—all this made it possible for repression to be justified as a necessary defense against foreign and internal enemies.

Quite a few people had their doubts about the repression and condemned it, although of course not openly. I must remind readers that the majority of Soviet citizens had long become accustomed to the situation of so-called doublethink. When speaking aloud in public they supported the actions of the authorities, but at home among themselves or in a circle of close friends they would express doubts and even indignation. Not until perestroika was this system of doublethink overturned.

Another fact is even more surprising. People arrested for nonexistent crimes, unbreakable Bolsheviks, who had many times looked death in the eye while fighting for their ideas, in this new situation ended up broken. They slandered and denounced themselves and their comrades, confessed to being "enemies of the people," criminal evildoers! What an amazing turn of events. Yet today this is not so much a problem for historians—historically everything has basically been explained—as it is for psychologists.

Stalin destroyed virtually the entire Leninist old guard. Moreover, he sought to erase from memory all the revolutionary merits and distinctions of those who had made the October revolution. He robbed others of their achievements and attributed them to himself. Indeed the entire history of our country after October was rewritten until it was unrecognizable. Stalin's aim in all this was solely to consolidate his absolute personal power.

Some of my relatives were among those affected by the repression of the 1930s. And although I surely did not know everything that had happened in our country, nevertheless—through my relatives and as a result of the fate they had suffered—I learned a lot. My mother's father supported the revolution, became a Communist and organizer of a collective farm, and never questioned the Soviet government or its policies. In fact he felt, being a peasant, that Soviet power had given him the land he farmed and had thereby saved his family. In the thirties he was arrested and sentenced to death. The story he related to me once (only once—he never took up the subject again) was horrifying. Over the course of fourteen months he was tortured many times in very cruel ways. By chance he survived. An assistant prosecutor in a higher judicial body, apparently someone with a conscience, did not consider his "case" grounds for execution or for any charges whatsoever. My grandfather was released. But his strength had been undermined, and he died at the age of fifty-nine.

My other grandfather was arrested for not fulfilling the plan for the sowing of crops. In 1933 in the Stavropol region, as in the Ukraine and indeed the entire southern part of the Soviet Union, there was a fierce drought; its consequences were worsened by the harsh government policy toward the peasants. Half my paternal grandfather's family died, and, sure enough, he was unable to complete the plan for the sowing of crops. He was exiled to Siberia. Later he was able to return to his home where he joined the collective farm and labored conscientiously into his old age.

I wish to make a special point: to speak about the tragedy of the Russian Orthodox Church. Even before the revolution the Bolsheviks regarded the Church as an ideological opponent. From the realm of belief and conscience, religion was transferred to the realm of politics. This laid the foundation for the terrible drama of the future. On the other hand, when the civil war deeply divided our society, it was the former ruling classes who began the resistance to the revolution, and the Church became a refuge for them; it entered politics on their side. Understandably the Bolsheviks regarded the Church as a political opponent against which it was necessary to struggle.

Certainly this was understandable during the acute phase of internal conflict. But later, after the civil war had ended, in time of peace, they continued to tear down churches, arrest clergymen, and destroy them. This was no longer understandable or justifiable. Atheism took rather savage forms in our country at that time. During perestroika a firm course was taken toward freedom of conscience. I based this on my belief that religious people are worthy of respect. Religious faith is an intensely private matter, and each citizen should have the unqualified right to his or her own choice.

Of course the totalitarian regime disguised itself with democratic decorations: a constitution, laws of various kinds, and "representative" bodies of government. In fact all the life activity of society was dictated and guided—from beginning to end—by the party structures, by the resolutions, decisions, and orders of the top echelons of the party. Even the legislative and executive bodies of the various union republics existed in fact in a state of lawlessness, even though under the constitution they were proclaimed to be sovereign states with full powers of their own. Only in rare cases in history has such a concentration of power, such supercentralization, ever been encountered. Most important was that, for all practical purposes, the citizens of the USSR were deprived of any real opportunity to influence the government or have any control over it.

The monopoly of power rested on a monopoly of state ownership. Collective farm property and the property of cooperatives was in fact government property. Peasants and members of cooperatives in general could not take a single step without the permission of the local and central authorities. I am familiar with all this from my own personal experience, and I myself made broad use of the peculiar features of this system in my activities.

The backbone of the system that took shape in the USSR was, of course, the Communist Party. The Bolshevik party was formed in special circumstances—it operated in the underground, constantly harassed and persecuted by the tsarist authorities. This determined not only its structure, which was adapted to working illegally, but also the forms and methods of its functioning. During the revolution and civil war these methods demonstrated their effectiveness, and they were kept intact when peace was restored.

While Lenin was alive the party still maintained strong democratic traditions. The stenographic records of the party congresses of that time contained sharp debates and criticism without regard to persons and indicate that real voting took place when resolutions were adopted. Later, all that disappeared. Secrecy, rejection of dissidence of any kind, intolerance, and iron discipline—all that was revived and magnified by Stalin, who described the party as a crusading order. In this way he sought to conceal his own power-hungry designs.

In combination with the "model" of society discussed previously, all this developed into a system of totalitarian rule in which the following became typical: rejection of political pluralism, a "party-state," harsh, all-encompassing, and supercentralized administration of the country based on the monopoly of state ownership.

In the post-Stalin period much changed, but the party remained inviolable. Khrushchev's attempt to relax the party's tight hold on everyone and everything by granting a larger role to the government apparatus cost him the post of general secretary of the party.

During perestroika a policy was adopted of fundamentally reorganizing party activity, democratizing it internally, and later changing its very role in society. However, the structure of the Communist Party of the Soviet Union (CPSU) and its methods of work, even the composition of its personnel (the bureaucrats of the nomenklatura), were so thoroughly instilled with old habits, traditions, and standards, as though set in concrete, that reforming the party and transforming it into a normal political organization proved to be an extremely difficult task. This difficulty marked the entire process of change, which took place in contradictory fashion, engendering sharp resistance and conflict between the reform forces and the conservative forces.

We must be precise and fair in our assessment of the party during perestroika. The fact is that the CPSU began the reforms when leaders who were adherents of reform were in its leadership. Moreover, those changes would not have begun at all if the initiative for them had not come from the CPSU. And it is not just a question of the reform group at the head of the party. A large section of the rank-and-file party membership favored change in our society. In the last analysis, it was the Central Committee of the CPSU that spoke in support of democracy, political pluralism, free elections, the creation of a mixed economic system, reform of the system of federated states, or republics, belonging to the Soviet Union, and so forth. In 1990, at the Twenty-eighth Congress of the CPSU, all these changes were approved by that body.

Nevertheless the CPSU did not fully pass the test. It never truly became a party of reform. And it condemned itself by its own action in supporting the August coup in 1991; that is, the majority of the Central Committee and many local and provincial committees supported the coup.

In the end, the "model" that came into existence in the USSR was not socialist but totalitarian. This is a serious matter to be reflected on by all who seriously aspire to progress for the benefit of the human race.

A natural question arises: How could people put up with all this, this cruelty, this complete alienation from property and power? Did they fear repression? Were they kept down by this fear? Or were they convinced by propaganda that everything was all right? The answer to these questions reveals the profoundly paradoxical nature of Soviet society.

Undeniably there was fear. Millions of people had heard about the Gulag, and it was a rare family that had not felt its deathly grip to one extent or another. Propaganda was also able to achieve its aims under the conditions of a closed society, singing the praises of the existing system in every possible way as the best in history. And of course all the so-called educational work from kindergarten to the university, and in factories and offices, also played a role. But it is impossible to explain everything just by these facts, and it would be wrong to try.

For a considerable number of people, probably the majority, the Soviet system was a product of a great and glorious people's revolution. Millions of people believed in the ideals proclaimed by the revolution, and they considered the principles of Soviet society to be just. They were sincerely convinced that this society was better than other, bourgeois societies, and for a long time they kept their faith and hope that socialist ideas would be realized—ideas that in fact are quite noble and lofty. That is how they were presented to us in the schools and in Soviet literature, and that is how they appeared in films, the art form with the greatest mass appeal. These hopes and beliefs were reinforced by certain realities of Soviet life.

To demonize all Soviet "leaders" at all levels, to portray them as unqualified villains and evildoers, unprincipled self-seeking scoundrels who were indifferent to the interests and needs of the people—that is a shallow and frivolous approach. Of course there were villains, quite a few of them. But most of those who came to power had the intention of serving the "toiling masses" from which they themselves had come. That the system rendered their aspirations useless, reduced their efforts to nothing, and ultimately snuffed out their finer impulses—that is a separate question.

The upper echelons of the party and government sought to maintain in the mass consciousness the conviction that it was necessary to pursue the ideals of October and that no deviation was permissible from the choice made in 1917. At the same time, those at the top understood that society could not be ruled by fear alone. Therefore the economic development plans, whose main purpose was in fact to strengthen the Stalin or post-Stalin regimes, did provide for the satisfaction of the minimum necessary economic and social development of the population.

The aims and ideals of the Soviet revolution inspired the patriotic enthusiasm of millions of people in the 1930s, during World War II, and in the postwar reconstruction period.

This explains the Soviet Union's great leap forward, the achievement of a high level of industrial capacity in a very short time, the transformation of the Soviet Union into a major power in terms of science and culture. The historic victory in the Great Patriotic War against Nazism, which was a surprise not only for Hitler but also for the Western democracies, is also explained by what we have said above.

All this is true. But the historical truth is also that the regime and the system abused the faith of the people in these high ideals, turning them to its own advantage. Rule by the people, equality, justice, and the promise of a happy future—all these ideas were utilized for the sake of maintaining and strengthening totalitarianism. The essence of these methods was outlined accurately by Alexander Solzhenitsyn in his speech accepting the Nobel Prize: "Violence has no way to conceal itself except by lies, and lies have no way to maintain themselves except through violence. Anyone who has proclaimed violence his method inexorably must choose lying as his principle."

Dissatisfaction with the existing situation always existed among Soviet people. Many refused to be reconciled with the cruel system imposed on them. Over the course of time the level of education and culture of the Soviet people rose, and that contributed to the number who refused to accept the cruel system. The system needed skilled personnel, but these very cadres, once they had been trained, entered into confrontation with the system, which denied people a great many things, above all, freedom.

When the ineffectiveness of the system became obvious and the promises of a better life proved deceptive, people lost confidence in the government and the party. The growing gap between the government and its citizens was the fundamental cause of the weakening of the system. Of course the system could have continued to rot away slowly for many more years, but the denouement was approaching faster and faster. Conditions had ripened—not only economically but also politically and psychologically—for a fundamental change in the entire vector of development. Conditions had grown ripe for perestroika.

CHAPTER 3

Let's Not Oversimplify!
A Balance Sheet of the Soviet Years

I HAVE ALREADY mentioned the debates going on in Russia over social-ism—whether it existed or not. There are also disputes, which are no less sharp and sometimes even sharper, over what balance sheet to draw on the decades since October, during the existence of the totalitarian system.

Here, too, we find viewpoints that are polar opposites, ranging from total rejection (it was a "black hole" in the history of Russia) to unstinted praise and calls for a return to the past. Reflected in these disputes is the complexity and intensity of present-day political battles over the question of what path our country should take in its further development. These debates also reflect the disastrous situation in which the people find themselves. Yes, the path that our country and people have traveled has been complex in the extreme. The results are also not all of one kind. However, the more com-plex the past has been, the more cautious, careful, painstaking, and objective we must be in approaching the assessments of that past.

The task that faced Russia at the time of the October revolution was to break free of the fetters of feudalism and absolutism, to make a leap forward in economic development, to pull the country out of backwardness and onto the road of progress and modernity.

The ruling circles in prerevolutionary Russia did not believe in the pos-sibility of even posing such a task, let alone solving it. Here, for example, is what Kokovtsev, the head of the tsarist Cabinet of Ministers, said in a speech to the Duma in May 1913: "To propose that in the space of some twenty years and a little more that we could catch up with states that have cultures centuries old, this is the kind of demand that should not be made."

Here is another piece of evidence. In 1925 a Russian émigré by the name of A. Kaminka, a former big shot in banking in tsarist Russia, took up the task of outlining the Russian economy of the future as he envisaged it. "Over the course of decades, several decades at least," he wrote, "the course of development of our economic life will be such that agriculture and raw materials will be the main source of exports for us, in exchange for which we will restore the riches that have been destroyed, and in the field of industry, as a general rule, we will be in a position to carry out only the simplest tasks."

In fact, however, in the Soviet era, and in a very short time at that, former tsarist Russia was transformed into what for those times was a leading industrial power. That is a generally recognized fact. *A civilizing turn of events took place—instead of a backward agricultural country, Russia became an industrial-agrarian power comparable to the advanced countries of the world.* This cannot be denied.

While fully appreciating this achievement today, we cannot help but see another aspect as well. The modernization of Russia over the course of the entire Soviet period had the character of catching up. The official slogan was "overtake and surpass the West." But the question was how to do that and in what respects.

In terms of quantitative indexes, for example, the amount of steel produced or the number of combines, the Soviet Union actually did catch up, even with America. But the quality of production in the overwhelming majority of cases was not high. The efficiency of production was incomparably lower than in the Western countries, and energy consumption and the consumption of raw materials was incomparably higher. People attempted to pass over all this in silence. Frank and public discussion of the real situation in our country took place for the first time only in the summer of 1985, that is, after perestroika had begun.

To be sure, the task of going from extensive to intensive development of the economy was posed in the 1970s, but nothing was actually accomplished along these lines. Our country continued to develop extensively, and in the final years before perestroika was able to exist only by virtue of oil and gas exports.

Ideological blinders—the dogmas of Stalinist ideology—did great harm to the development of our society. Let me recall, if nothing else, the persecution of geneticists and the rejection of advanced methodology in many other spheres of science and technology. Cybernetics was declared to be false, a pseudoscience, even though Soviet scientists achieved quite a bit in working out some of the principles in this field and some practical solutions. Our country was closed to contacts with foreign science and technology; yet worldwide experience shows that a country's isolation, its being closed off and turned inward upon itself, results in backwardness. So then, if we evaluate our country's great leap forward in industrial development as it deserves to be evaluated, we cannot forget that there was a certain limited character to our industrialization, an unjustified delay in passing over to intensive development, development that would outstrip and leave behind the previous phase.

There is another, very important aspect of the matter—the price paid for what was achieved. We understand that in the very short time allowed to us by history, creating the industrial potential that would enable us to withstand the war with Nazi Germany could not have been accomplished without extraordinary measures. The question is, What kind of measures should those have been?

Unquestionably during those years there was a great enthusiasm for this labor among our people, a mass willingness to sacrifice the present for the sake of the future. And it is useless for people today to try to deny this, as many do.

Unfortunately enthusiasm was not the only factor in industrialization. Under Stalin, industrialization was also carried out with reliance on forced labor, using the prisoners in the Gulag. Industrialization was accompanied as well by the ruination of the peasantry, for whom collectivization was in fact a new form of serfdom.

Collectivization can be compared to the "fencing off" process in England in the period when capitalist relations were first coming into existence. The expulsion of the English yeomen from the land was not in any way a voluntary process; in similar fashion, almost everywhere in the Soviet Union peasants were forced to join the collective farms; they were simply driven into them like cattle. The local authorities used the cruelest methods, fulfilling quotas set by the central government. Many peasants who had received land as a result of the October revolution had grown stronger, that is, they had improved their economic status; they had become what in the Soviet Union was called "middle peasants." They did not want to give up what they had earned by honest labor. The cruelty with which collectivization was carried out is astonishing. People who were able to produce better than others, the competent and industrious, were destroyed. A terrible blow was dealt to the countryside, the consequences of which have not been outlived to this day. This had its effect on all the rest of the country.

Alternatives were possible (for example, the variant proposed by Bukharin). But those alternatives were condemned and cast aside. Yet experience in other countries has shown that the modernization of agriculture creates new resources and lays the basis for the development of the economy as a whole.

In the USSR, methods used in collectivization were justified by the argument that the country had to be quickly raised to a higher level; otherwise, as Stalin said, "they will wipe us out." But who could say that our country could not have been raised to a higher level using a different approach, one of respect for working people, a democratic approach? The "rules of the game" might have been harsh, but there should have been rules, not utter barbarism, not complete inhumanity. Collectivization and the Gulag together destroyed the human potential of our nation; both drained the blood from the most important and vital base of our economy—agriculture—and they strengthened the dictatorial regime.

Much of what happened afterward and much of what is going on in Russia today has roots in the Stalin era. It is clear that the choice of a path of development for the USSR had been made in the late 1920s, but it was flawed. That is the essence of the matter. The excessively high cost for the successes achieved cannot be justified. On the other hand—and this is of great importance—the heroic feats accomplished by our people cannot be rendered valueless by reference to this excessively high cost. The high cost of what was achieved was because of the system. The results achieved were because of the self-sacrificing labor of our people.

In evaluating the results of the Soviet period, we cannot limit ourselves, of course, simply to the economic aspect. Especially because, from the social and cultural point of view, the Soviet Union made astonishingly great achievements in the decades after October 1917.

From 1930 on, employment was guaranteed for the entire able-bodied working population. For the people of the Soviet Union, income increased slowly but steadily. During the entire period of the Soviet government's existence since the civil war, with the obvious exception of World War II, there was not a single year in which income fell. The statistics for urban housing by 1985 had increased from 180 million square meters to 2,561 million square meters. Before the revolution, three-quarters of Russia's population was illiterate. By the mid-1980s, 70 percent of the population as a whole and 88.3 percent of the employed population had had primary and secondary education, which was free of charge. As the American historian Melvin S. Wren has written, "One of Communist Russia's most outstanding achievements has been the conquest of illiteracy."

Another American professor, George Z. F. Bereday, wrote in the book *Transformation of Soviet Society*: "The provision of libraries, the advances of the theater arts and the film industry, the development of sports, the activism of youth organizations—these are among the most successful and most obvious of Soviet achievements."

I should add that one of the major social achievements of Soviet power was the establishment of a public health system and of other social protections. These are all undeniable achievements, but on a purely material level the standard of living in the Soviet Union remained significantly lower than in most developed countries. Payment for labor was minimal, and the social benefits that were provided free of charge or for a very small sum did not supplement people's incomes to a very great degree. Be that as it may, Soviet citizens generally felt confident about their future: Things would not get worse and perhaps would even get better.

The colossal changes that took place in our country did not just affect Russia. The so-called borderlands—the outlying regions of the former empire—also experienced tremendous changes, especially regarding literacy, education, public health, industrialization, and urban construction, and in the sense of being linked up with world culture. The non-Russian areas developed their own intelligentsia. For dozens of nationalities of the former Russian empire this was a time when nations were formed and state systems came into existence. The prominent American historian Frederick L. Schuman commented, "The forgotten men of Transcaucasia, Turkestan, and remote Siberia not only learned how to read and write their own tongues but came into possession of schools, libraries, hospitals, and factories, with resulting living standards far above those of other Asian peoples beyond the Soviet frontier."

To put it briefly, October played a civilizing role in the vast expanses of Asia and southeastern Europe. As in the other areas of social life, these processes affecting the non-Russian nationalities proceeded in a highly contradictory way. To the extent that totalitarianism became entrenched in our country, the particular cultural life of each nationality was squeezed into an alien ideological framework. Revolutionary changes imposed from Moscow were, to a considerable extent, an artificial superstructure alien to the traditions and mentality of the bulk of the population. After Stalin's theory of "autonomization" was implemented, even the union republics such as Ukraine, Kazakhstan, and Georgia were treated merely as parts of a unitary state, although formally, under both the Soviet constitution and the constitutions of the Soviet republics, they remained "separate countries." The term *union republic* was supposed to mean that they were part of a *union*, together with other republics, not that they were mere provinces to be administered by the central government.

The reforms of the perestroika era were aimed at a qualitative renewal of society and at overcoming the totalitarian structure blocking the road to democracy. Fundamental reforms were begun under very complex conditions, but they were cut short by the August coup attempt and the Belovezh agreement that dissolved the Soviet Union.

In the period of "shock therapy" reforms, which began in 1992, the historical achievements of the Soviet period were lost to a large degree. Social rights were constricted. The material well-being of the people was reduced nearly by half. More than one-third of the population now lives below the poverty line. And how many are just on the edge of that line! Unemployment has become a reality, the health care system is being destroyed, science and education are in a bad way: There is not enough money to address these problems, and, above all, there is no government responsibility for the future of the country.

To return to our original topic, I must say that in economic and social respects the Soviet Union achieved a great deal. On the political level, it kept retreating further and further from the original ideals of October. The Soviet period was a time in which democracy was suppressed and systematically denied in practice. I draw this conclusion knowing the figures in this regard: There were 2.3 million deputies (elected representatives) in Soviet institutions at all different levels. There were more than 6 million members of permanent "production conferences," almost 8 million trade union activists and more than 10 million participants in so-called committees of popular control, and so on.

It would be a mistake to think that all this meant nothing. Certain elements of democratism existed in the functioning of these organizations, especially at the grass-roots level. On the whole, though, the entire gigantic system functioned only for one purpose: to consolidate and strengthen the power of the party-state. The government bodies that were called instruments of popular rule did not have genuinely democratic rights or powers. They were controlled by the party leadership. And on all essential questions of policy and power, no one had the possibility of choosing an alternative. The orders were handed down from above. Pluralism of thought or deci-

sion making was considered a retreat from the principles of so-called socialist democracy.

Russia had more than enough capable people. They could have accomplished a great deal had they been given freedom and rights, but they were
paralyzed by the dictates of the party, by the narrow and rigid framework of
party directives, by the rules of the system of command from above.
Decades of existence under conditions of totalitarianism and the personality cult inevitably resulted in apathy, anemia, loss of initiative, and the extinguishing of social energy in our country.

Of course there were periods during the Soviet era when society seemed
to straighten up and throw its shoulders back. One of the high points, iron-
ically, was during World War II. It was a very difficult experience. Our victory in the war was later attributed to the stability and effectiveness of the
system. That was true only in the sense that it was able, through the methods of harsh dictatorship, to concentrate all the country's resources, above
all, material resources. The true victor, however, was the people, the Russians first of all, but also the many other nationalities who sincerely considered the Soviet Union to be their fatherland.

The people displayed the most powerful and impressive qualities in that
difficult time. Despite Stalin's terror, which on the very eve of the war
mowed down thousands of talented generals and officers of the Soviet
army, that army nevertheless was victorious in the war, as was the Soviet
military school that produced the army. World-class leaders were forged in
the heat of battle.

On the home front, the workers and peasants, engineers and scientists,
women and teenagers learned to create the necessary military equipment in
a very short time, equipment that in many respects was superior to that of
the enemy. This despite the fact that a large number of industries had to be
relocated hundreds, even thousands of kilometers away from the front lines
and away from the occupied zones, to safe rear areas where essentially an
entirely new military system of production was built up.

This tremendous victory aroused great expectations among the Soviet
people, but these expectations were not fulfilled. Frightened by a population
that had grown proud as the result of its victory, that felt itself to be free and
sovereign because of that victory, the system cruelly intensified ideological
and political pressures. Millions of people, beginning with former prisoners
of war, were made victims of repression. A new wave of terror swept the

country. Official anti-Semitism was added to the arsenal of government techniques, and a shameful campaign against so-called cosmopolitanism was unleashed. Totalitarianism made use of every means possible, every lever of power, to shield itself from the slightest possible encroachment by the people.

This trend altered after Stalin's death, a change connected, above all, with the activities of Nikita Khrushchev. He was without doubt an outstanding public figure. The overthrow of the "personality cult" of Stalin as a result of the Twentieth Party Congress, in 1956, and other ideas proclaimed at that congress, such as the firm determination to travel the road of peaceful coexistence with the West, renunciation of the idea that war between socialism and capitalism was inevitable, and the idea of equal rights among so-called socialist countries and among Communist parties, promised a fundamental change in the life of our country and in international relations. Change began, and the entire social atmosphere was transformed. While this was the first step toward emancipation from totalitarianism, it must be said that the decisions of the Twentieth Congress did not meet with a uniform reaction in our society.

Khrushchev's report on the personality cult was distributed to all local areas, so that people could become familiar with it. Many were confused and would not accept the decisions of the Twentieth Congress. I remember this from my own experience. I had the chance to participate in explanations of the essence of the congress's decisions in a rural district of the Stavropol region. The speeches, given in large auditoriums, simply were not accepted. When I began to hold meetings with small groups of people, some discussion began. Nevertheless quite a few remained silent, and from some you could hear remarks such as, "Stalin's reprisals were against those who forcibly drove the peasants into the collective farms." That was how reality was refracted in some people's minds.

In fact this kind of reaction was not surprising. After all, the Stalin "personality cult" had essentially consisted in the myth that Stalin was a man of genius, the leader and father of all the peoples. This myth had been instilled in people's minds by an all-powerful propaganda machine with no alternative sources of information. The effectiveness of this propaganda, backed up by repression, the reality of a deeply rooted delusion bordering on mass psychosis—these were impressively confirmed by the feelings of shock that affected millions of people when Stalin died.

I was a university student at the time, and I remember that, for the majority, Stalin's death was a tremendous shock. Etched in my memory are the words spoken with great emotion by my recently deceased friend Zdenek Mlynar, who was my fellow student at Moscow University and who later became one of the organizers of the Prague Spring. Mlynar said to me: "Mishka, what will become of us now?"

I never saw Stalin when he was alive. The desire to say farewell to him in his casket was a very intense one. For days on end people came in huge crowds to the Hall of Columns where his body was lying in state. People wept, even sobbed.

Today, after so much has become clear and comprehensible, my ideas about Stalin naturally have changed. If they had not, I obviously would not have begun perestroika. To set about making reforms meant, above all, overcoming the Stalin within. And not only Stalin but the entire subsequent experience of the era of stagnation. During perestroika we acquired a very clear idea of what Stalinism meant, what Stalinism represented in people's consciousness. And this still makes itself felt even today.

There are many contradictions in Khrushchev's record. These had to do with the specific circumstances of his career, the road he traveled in life. (Politically and ideologically he was a product of the Stalin school, and some of the crimes of the Stalin regime were on his conscience.) His contradictions are also related to aspects of his individual character. He would take one step forward and two steps back. He would rush this way, then that, back and forth. Khrushchev gave our society a taste of freedom and then turned off the tap himself. In his memoirs, incidentally, he stated rather clearly his reason for this. "When we decided to allow a period of thaw and consciously moved in that direction," he wrote, "the leadership of the USSR, including myself, at the same time feared doing this: What if the thaw gave rise to a flood that would sweep over us and with which it would be difficult to deal?" Fear of democracy is the product of a totalitarian regime and an obstacle to any serious progress.

Nevertheless I would like to stress that Khrushchev was a precursor of perestroika. He gave the first impetus to a reform process that could develop further and only succeed as a democratic process. In principle, his was an important precedent in our history.

The most important event remaining from Khrushchev's legacy is his denunciation of Stalinism. The attempts undertaken in the Brezhnev era to turn the clock back in this respect failed. They could not restore the Stalin system. That was one of the conditions that made the beginning of perestroika possible. Thus I recognize a definite connection between perestroika and what Nikita Khrushchev accomplished. In general, I have a high regard for the role he played historically.

After revolutionary enthusiasm had subsided and receded into history (which is only natural), after the patriotic upsurge inspired by the war had been quickly curtailed, after the euphoria of the Twentieth Party Congress had been stifled in short order by its own initiator, our society seemed to become ossified. The incentive to work efficiently disappeared, as did people's desire to participate in a socially conscious way in public affairs or to take any kind of initiative aside from criminal activity. Political conformism and a primitive leveling psychology took deep root. The stagnation in society was fraught with serious consequences that actually began to make themselves felt in literally all areas. During the era of stagnation our country was creeping toward the abyss.

My understanding of the depths to which totalitarianism had brought our country impelled me to make a decisive and irreversible choice in favor of democracy and reform. To be sure, democratic methods of leadership and openness are much more complicated than totalitarian methods of rule. Here everything is transparent and leaders are fully subject to public scrutiny. They can be criticized, just like any other citizen. It has already become a cliché that despite all its insufficiencies democracy is superior to other forms of rule. Nevertheless it, too, needs to be renewed, but we will discuss that in the final section of this book.

For now, returning once again to our theme, I wish to say something about the Social Democratic leaders of the 1920s and 1930s. The bulk of them took a hostile attitude toward October and toward what came after the revolution. The division in the working-class movement, the atmosphere of hostility between Communists and Social Democrats, prevented mutual understanding and often blocked objectivity in approaching any problem. Nevertheless, on the whole, the most outstanding representatives of the Second International tried to make an honest assessment of what was going on in Russia from their standpoint as proponents of socialism. While criticizing Soviet power, they did not deny its achievements. What is fundamental for me is that coinciding assessments come to light regarding the main point: Lack of freedom and democracy can destroy the cause of the revolution, or, to a certain extent, had already destroyed it.

One of the most prominent theoreticians of the Second International, Friedrich Adler, in his book *Socialism and the Stalinist Experiment* (1932), said the following:

> In the first phase of war communism the dictatorship served the purpose of destroying feudal ownership, distributing the land, and rooting out the capitalists; in short, eliminating the former ruling classes. They no longer exist ... *But the dictatorship persists just as powerfully, ruthlessly, and cruelly as before. What are its social functions now? There is only one: to suppress the workers themselves, in order to carry through industrialization at their expense, and in order to crush in the egg any attempt by the workers to resist the sacrifices they are forced to endure* ... What has happened and is happening in Russia will never be recognized by us as a necessary experiment for the sake of constructing a socialist social order.*

It is common knowledge that Karl Kautsky supported the Bolsheviks before the revolution, but afterward he made a sharp break with them, above all, once again, over the question of democracy. In 1920 he wrote:

> The last bourgeois revolution has apparently become the first socialist one, which has had a tremendous impact on the revolutionary proletariat in all countries. From that revolution, however, the proletariat can take only its *goals*; its *methods* are applicable only to the unique circumstances in Russia; they are not applicable in Western Europe. The contradiction between methods and goals in the final analysis is bound to affect the revolution itself.

Today, half a century later, it is quite obvious that Kautsky was right. Totalitarianism undermined itself with its own methods.

Finally, let us quote from Otto Bauer, the father of the Austrian school of Marxism, so-called Austro-Marxism, one of the leaders of Social Democracy who sincerely sought to get to the root of what had happened in our country. "If that is socialism," he wrote in his work entitled *Bolshevism or Social Democracy*,

> then it is socialism of a unique kind, a *despotic* socialism. Inasmuch as in this case socialism does not mean that the working people themselves control the

---

* Emphasis in original.

means of production, they do not direct the labor process themselves, and they do not distribute the product of their labor. On the contrary, in this case socialism means that *the state power, separated and estranged from the people, and representing only an insignificant minority of the people, which has raised itself up over the mass of the people*, has control over the means of production and over labor power, over the process of labor and the products of labor, and it subordinates to its own labor plan all the living forces of the people using the methods of force and violence, and involves them in its own way of organizing labor.*

Bauer, while seeing everything from the point of view of Social Democracy, did not lose hope. In the same work quoted above he expressed an interesting thought: "The dictatorship of the proletariat in Russia is . . . a phase of development toward democracy . . . it is more of a transitional phase in the development of Russia which in the best of cases will last only until the mass of the Russian people have become ripe for democratic government." Otto Bauer's optimism, as subsequent history was to show, was solidly based.

Even today, after the democratic breakthrough of perestroika, Russia's progress toward democracy is going very slowly and with difficulty. Here the past has its effect; it holds people tightly in its embrace. There is no alternative except to train oneself every day to live under democratic conditions. In the West this process took centuries.

Another issue is perhaps more important: The present authoritarian regime is putting the brakes on Russia's development toward democracy. For this regime, democracy is becoming more and more of a burden. The political forces that came to power on the democratic wave have been removed from power or have removed themselves from power today. A bureaucratic-oligarchic regime has taken shape, and under the disguise of democratic phraseology it has imposed a neoliberal course of so-called reforms on our society.

In trying to achieve its aims, it does not consider the price that ordinary citizens have to pay, and it has not hesitated to attack the democratic gains of perestroika. The Russian parliament is paralyzed and can do little under these circumstances. The mass media are controlled by the government and the oligarchy. The courts and the public prosecutors are not free to act. A

---

* Emphasis in original.

new wave of reforms is being attempted whose aim is by no means the well-being of the citizenry but satisfaction of the interests of bureaucratic finance capital.

What nevertheless inspires us with hope for the future is the attitude of Russian citizens toward the rights and freedoms they have gained. A recent poll of twelve thousand Russians, covering virtually every region of the country, showed 82 percent supporting the statement: "We want to live in a free country"; that is, people who find themselves in the most difficult of circumstances nevertheless want freedom. The greater part of those who voted for Boris Yeltsin in the 1996 presidential elections did so in order that the Communists would not win. People do not want to go back to the past.

This means that today it is no longer possible to turn Russia back to totalitarianism.

CHAPTER 4

October and the World

ONE OF THE BASIC features of the twentieth century has been the division of the world community into two opposing camps, East and West. By this I mean the dividing line drawn, first, between the Soviet Union and the West and, later, after other states began taking the road first traveled by the Soviet Union, between the countries of the so-called socialist camp and the developed Western countries.

This division has fundamentally determined the whole course of world history since 1917. It did not, however, have an equal effect on both sides. The negative consequences are obvious and have been much studied. The positive consequences—and there were some—have so far remained in the realm of propaganda. I think that historical science still has a long way to go toward making a genuinely objective and dispassionate analysis of all the ups and downs of the century now drawing to a close.

It is not of course a question of speculating on what the world might have been like if the October revolution had not happened. There is no basis for scientific analysis in that. But to try to weigh the actual effect of the USSR on the course of international relations—that would be an important undertaking.

Let us ask a question: While it was impossible to prevent the division of the world into two opposing systems after the victory of the revolution in Russia, might it not have been possible to avoid those extreme consequences that ultimately resulted in an endless series of confrontations culminating in the Cold War?

Reasoning theoretically, one might say: Yes, it would have been possible if both sides, immediately after the civil war in Russia and the failure of Western military intervention, had taken the road of recognizing each other's right to exist. In the real world, however, it proved impossible. Especially because, not only in Russia but to a considerable extent in what one might call the popular consciousness worldwide, the victory of October was seen as the beginning of a "new era." The division of the world into two opposing social systems was depicted by Communist ideologists as a good thing. Lenin spoke of it as final and irreversible. This is fully understandable in view of the "model" of social development the Bolsheviks were seeking to put into effect.

They took as their starting point the view that October was the beginning of a worldwide revolution. Following their example, similar revolutions would be victorious in Western Europe, then in other countries, and finally the whole world would "go socialist." But the world revolution did not happen. "Soviet" revolutions (or insurrections) were defeated in several countries. At the end of his life Lenin admitted this fact and proposed that a new course be taken, oriented toward the prolonged existence of the Soviet state under "capitalist encirclement." A new policy was proclaimed—"peaceful coexistence" (Lenin's own term) with the capitalist world.

First, the West had no confidence in this "new course." Although the West recognized the USSR diplomatically and economically, it continued its attempts by various means to overthrow the Bolsheviks. Second, the Soviet leadership—both secretly and openly—continued to support revolutionary forces whose aim was to overthrow capitalism.

The Twentieth Congress of the CPSU renounced the idea that a new world war was inevitable and spoke in favor of "peaceful coexistence." Yet five years later the party's new program, adopted at its Twenty-second Congress, declared peaceful coexistence to be "a form of the class struggle." This formula was not renounced until 1986, when a new version of the party program was adopted at the Twenty-seventh Congress.

Until that time the old orientation remained in force. In the name of an ideology that placed the peoples of the Soviet Union in hostile opposition to most of the world, our country increased its participation in the arms race, exhausting its resources and turning the military-industrial complex into the primary factor governing all politics and public consciousness in the USSR. We were feared, and we considered this to our credit, because the enemy should be afraid. And it was not just a question of our immense nuclear arsenal but also the provocative actions in which the Soviet Union engaged, such as the invasion of Czechoslovakia and intervention in Afghanistan.

All this is true, but the responsibility for the many decades of tension cannot be laid solely at Soviet feet. In the West, from the very beginning of the Russian revolution, a policy was adopted of trying to suppress that revolution.

In December 1917, for example, Leonido Bissolati, a minister of the Italian government, stated: "The influence of the Bolsheviks has reached proportions that are not without danger for us. If in the near future the Russian government does not fall, things will go badly for us. O Lord, punish the Bolsheviks!" In March 1918 Arthur Balfour, summing up the results of the London Conference of prime ministers and foreign ministers of France, Italy, and Britain, wrote the following in a dispatch to U.S. President Woodrow Wilson: "What is the remedy? To the Conference it seemed that none is possible except through Allied intervention. Since Russia cannot help herself [!], she must be helped by her friends." In early 1919 President Wilson also spoke in very definite terms: "We must be concerned that this [Bolshevik] form of 'rule by the people' is not imposed on us, or anyone else."

Wilson's "concern" was expressed in the deployment of armed expeditionary forces on the territory of Soviet Russia. And it must be acknowledged that this was not done merely to prevent "rule by the people" from spreading to other countries. The intentions of the Western powers went much further, as historical documents show.

On October 30, 1918, President Wilson approved a document (not for publication of course!) with commentary on the famous Fourteen Points, the American peace program. In this document the recommendation was made that Russia not be regarded as a unitary state. The document suggested that separate states, such as Ukraine, should arise on Russian territory. The Caucasus region was seen as "part of the problem of the Turkish empire." Another suggestion was that one of the Western powers be authorized to govern Central Asia as a protectorate. As for the remaining parts of Russia, the idea expressed in this document was to propose to Great Russia and Siberia that a government "sufficiently representative to speak in the name of these territories be created."

All this happened eighty years ago. But to judge from certain lightly tossed-off phrases and the highly "selective" diplomacy pursued by some Western countries, one gets the impression that even today "nothing has been forgotten."

I will not pursue this theme further. The documents and facts on this issue are numerous. The main point is to recognize that both sides, over the course of all the years since the revolution, have engaged in rough confrontation, sometimes openly, sometimes secretly. After World War II this was expressed in the arms race, above all, the nuclear arms race (although both sides feared it and neither side wanted a head-on military clash, especially not with weapons of mass destruction). This struggle was also expressed in rivalry on other continents (a race to see who could win more supporters or allies). Only after perestroika began did the situation start to change. Both sides altered their approach and, to a certain extent, sought to meet each other halfway. This led to the end of the Cold War.

I should note that surviving elements of that era of confrontation have not been eliminated to this day. Most of the "holdovers" are found in the West, but in Russia, too, not all the prejudices and habits of that era have been overcome. That, however, is a separate topic.

It was apparently not possible to avoid the world's many decades of confrontation and division. But it is important to draw lessons from the past for future use. This mutually confrontational approach to international relations does no one any good; everyone has to pay the price. It should not be forgotten, moreover, that a hostile, confrontational attitude by each side toward the other only embitters both and intensifies all the dangers that may arise.

More than seventy years of confrontation, as we have said, left their mark on the entire course of world history. Even under these conditions, and despite all the contradictory aspects of the Soviet past, in which tragedy and heroism were interwoven, giving rise to totally unexpected situations, the existence and development of the Soviet Union had an enormous impact on the rest of the world.

At first, in the years right after October 1917, this impact took the outward form of mass movements that swept like waves across many countries. October inspired hope in a great many people, especially working people, that improvement in the conditions of their lives was possible. That was when the Communist movement was born, the best organized of all mass movements known to history.

We cannot close our eyes of course to the fact that Soviet Russia was a bulwark of decisive support and aid to these movements, but we also cannot keep quiet about the main consideration: What was involved was a spontaneous reaction by working people to the example set by October, on whose banners were inscribed the same kind of slogans for which they themselves had been fighting for decades in their own countries.

As Karl Kautsky wrote in 1920:

If the low level of economic development in Russia today still rules out a form of socialism that would be superior to advanced capitalism, still the Russian revolution has performed a truly heroic feat, freeing the peasantry from all the consequences of feudal exploitation from which it had been suffocating. No less important is the fact that the Russian revolution instilled the workers of the capitalist world in a consciousness of their own power.

After World War II there emerged a large group of countries (the so-called socialist camp), representing nearly one-third of the human race. These countries not only took up the ideas of October; they also borrowed forms of government from the Soviet Union. The question of the nature of the revolutions that took place in Eastern Europe and East Asia deserves further study, particularly regarding their origins: What was the "balance" between the native popular movements in those countries and Soviet policy in bringing them into existence?

The creation of democratic, antifascist regimes was the natural result of the defeat of fascism in World War II and of the fact that the forces that had collaborated with the fascists were completely discredited. The subsequent stage, however, in which for all practical purposes one-party systems were established on the Soviet model (or something close to it), was not such a natural result. It was the result of open or secret pressure from Moscow. This also had to do with the Stalinist conception of proletarian internationalism and ideological unity among all Communist parties. Those parties, too, bear their share of responsibility for what happened. In addition, we cannot forget about the Cold War—that is, the responsibility the West also had for the policies Moscow pursued in relation to its allies.

When we began perestroika, one of the first steps we took was to declare an end to intervention in the internal affairs of our allies, to what was known as the Brezhnev doctrine. It could not have been otherwise. Having charted a course toward freedom, we could not deny it to others. Reproaches are often directed at me today, asking what I "gave up" or who I "gave it up" to. If such terminology is to be used, then we "gave up" those countries to their own people. We "gave up" that which did not belong to us. In general, I consider freedom of choice indispensable for every nation and one of the most meaningful principles in politics today.

In the opinion of George F. Kennan, the Russian revolution unquestionably accelerated the disintegration of the European colonial empires. Here, too, it was not a question of "exporting the Russian revolution." The anticolonial revolutions unfolded as a reaction to the emancipation of the nationalities of Russia, to the transformations that began to take place in the former borderlands of the tsarist empire. It was precisely the presence of the Soviet Union as part of the world balance of forces, and the attractive force of the Soviet example for the people in the colonies, that forced the colonial powers in a number of cases to make concessions to the liberation movements and grant independence to the colonies. From this point of view it is interesting to hear the opinion of a respected specialist Victor Gordon Kiernan, a professor at Edinburgh University. He wrote: "The fear that India would start to lean too far toward Moscow and socialism explains, in many respects, the granting of independence to India in 1947. Fear of the expansion of Soviet influence in the final analysis forced the West to take the road of decolonization in general."

Even from the point of view of sober-minded Westerners who are not socialists, this aspect of Soviet influence cannot be underestimated. What was involved here was a genuine quickening of the pace of social progress on a world scale.

The existence of the Soviet Union had an impact on the capitalist world itself, on everyday life in the West. As many Westerners have admitted, social policy in the Soviet Union acted as a stimulus toward the introduction of similar social programs in the West, the granting of social benefits that had not existed before October or that had generally been considered unacceptable. It turned out to be simply impossible, even dangerous, to lag behind "Communism" in such matters.

I will cite testimony from sources connected with two quite different ideological tendencies. In a Belgian socialist magazine, *Le Socialisme*, we find the following: "There is no question that the Russian revolution of 1917 and the general rise of the revolutionary movement after World War I forced the capitalists to make numerous concessions to the workers, concessions that otherwise would have required much greater effort to extract." Here, on the other hand, is a statement by Walter Lippmann, the well-known columnist, who for several decades was one of the chief molders of opinion in American society: "But we delude ourselves if we do not realize that the main power of the Communist states lies not in their clandestine activity but in the force of their example, in the visible demonstration of what the Soviet Union has achieved."

Both statements come from the period before the dissolution of the Soviet Union. Have opinions changed since then? In 1997 I had an interview with Arrigo Levi, a prominent Italian writer and commentator. Our conversation dealt with the eightieth anniversary of October. The interview was later shown on television. I can recall verbatim much of what was said, especially Levi's comment: "Communism was unquestionably a powerful catalyst for progress in other countries."

Yes, that was so. Now, on the other hand, with Russia in its present condition of crisis, when the power of its social example has faded, a new policy is gaining strength in many Western countries, a policy of cutting back on people's social rights and benefits, a desire to solve all problems connected with intensified global competition by making cutbacks in social programs at home. The French authors Jean Francois Kahn and Patrice Picard have written in this regard:

> The pathetic fiasco of the collectivist utopia had the inevitable result of spurring on the savage race for individual success, a race that of course proceeds on unequal terms. If the illusory successes of Communism contributed at first to a rejuvenation of capitalism, there is no question that the downfall of the Soviet system hastened the emergence of ultraliberal tendencies.

These are "tendencies" that in the final analysis can prove to be extremely dangerous.

In this part of the present work it seems appropriate to share my thoughts on the experience of various countries, because the entire world is changing before our eyes and an intensive search is under way for roads to the future.

We need the experience of the past as a lesson, as the source of all that is best in the cumulative achievements of the human mind, the creative product of many nations and populations. The eighty years that have passed since October demonstrate this—and they do so in two ways. The fruitful exchange of experience has truly enriched life, enriched every nation that took part in this exchange. But artificial self-isolation, the refusal to make use of the experience of others, places a brake on development and reduces the range of possibilities for every nation that takes or has taken the isolationist path. The example of the Soviet Union, which barricaded itself not only from the social experience of the West but also from its scientific and technical progress, is highly instructive. Japan and Southeast Asia provide the opposite example. Energetically assimilating the experiences of other countries and enriching them with their own contributions, they were able in a very short time, historically speaking, to break through to the high ground of contemporary progress.

The same experience shows, however, that simply to copy from others' achievements in a mechanical way, especially in socioeconomic respects, to make one's own country over in the image of other models—even if those were very successful models—is dangerous and counterproductive. Sooner or later a high price must be paid for such a mistake.

Testifying to this in the most obvious and dramatic way is the example of Russia in the last few years. The Russian leadership has been warned many times against copying others in a formalistic way, against following outside advice that is by no means unselfish or disinterested. An important book was published in Russia in 1996: *Reformy glazami amerikanskikh i russkikh uchenykh* [The reforms seen through the eyes of American and Russian scholars]. Among the authors were several recipients of the Nobel Prize in economics. This book called attention, among other things, to the inadmissibility of mechanically applying a general "model" to the very specific conditions in Russia.

Also, of course, the history of past decades has shown quite clearly that the *imposition* of any recipes or "models" from the outside, especially with the use of forcible measures (economic or political) is, without question, ruinous. That is what happened to the Eastern European countries on which the Soviet Union imposed its model. The results are well known. Incidentally, wherever local leaders tried in some way to correct or revise the "advice from their (Soviet) elder brother," taking into account their own national traditions and conditions, things went better.

Today the whole world is watching as Washington attempts to impose on others its model of how to approach major political, economic, and social problems. It is necessary to study the American experience; there definitely is much of interest in that experience. But to copy everything that is done across the ocean is unproductive and dangerous. This is well understood in Europe. It was no accident that at a recent G–8 summit in Denver the European leaders displayed no inclination whatsoever to follow the American president's exhortations on how to stimulate economic development and solve social problems.

The natural interaction and mutual influence of different experiences, the study and utilization of whatever corresponds to one's own interests—that is another question altogether. Today that kind of interaction has become an imperative necessity not only for international progress but for national progress as well.

In recent years, especially after the dissolution of the Soviet Union and the changes in Eastern Europe, some people have triumphantly proclaimed that everything has returned to the way it should be. (This was done particularly by Francis Fukuyama in *The End of History?*) But to take this approach is a profound error. Today's world is an entire solar system in which the West is only one of the planets. The influence of October has been very great, as seen in the fact that the world has changed so strikingly and irreversibly. A process of change on a world scale began in October 1917. The world continues to change. And it is in no one's provenance to turn back the course of history.

The many years' experience since October allows us to consider matters more broadly and to draw lessons from the past for the sake of the future.

CHAPTER 5

One More Balance Sheet:
Something Worth Thinking About

LET ME CITE a certain episode. In the summer of 1991 a regular session was held in Prague by the Interaction Council, an organization founded by the former German premier Helmut Schmidt to bring together a number of highly qualified and experienced men who had formerly been presidents or prime ministers of their countries. A copy of the concluding declaration adopted at this session was sent to me. It proved to be quite interesting, and I asked the newspaper *Pravda* to print it in full. The responses we received to this document were quite varied. But most of the discussion and debate it provoked centered on a passage in the document stating something we were not at all accustomed to hearing, because it contradicted a notion that had been instilled in us for decades—that the Soviet system was superior in all respects. The passage in question stated: "Neither the capitalist market system nor the socialist command economy has proved that it can satisfy both individual and collective needs or that it can distribute income fairly."

This conclusion was completely justified. Indeed, neither the Western socioeconomic system nor the system created under the name of socialism has been able to solve many of the fundamental problems of the twentieth century. We could go further and state that neither system has been able to avoid acute contradictions, crises, and social or national upheavals. Neither has been capable of making progress toward solving global problems, beginning with ecological problems, the severity of which threatens the very existence of civilization.

Of course the balance sheet on the two existing social systems is not uniform. On the economic plane, the Western countries undeniably have achieved significant results in terms of production efficiency and the quality and quantity of goods produced. In the Soviet Union, in a number of areas connected with the development and application of high technology, above all, military technology, impressive achievements were made. It is enough to mention the field of space exploration. But in most other areas—in production efficiency, the quality and quantity of goods produced, and, above all, consumer goods and technology applied to civilian use—the Soviet Union obviously lagged behind the West.

Until the mid-1970s (mainly in quantitative respects) the gap between the two systems was reduced somewhat, but subsequently it began to increase again. The phenomena of stagnation made themselves felt in our country with growing force.

In making this comparison and analyzing it, we cannot help but conclude that the key to Western success was the utilization of the advantages of the market economy. The Soviet Union ignored those advantages and lost the incentive toward development. The administrative-command system, that is, the supercentralized administration of the economy, deprived the Soviet Union of flexibility and maneuverability. The economic mechanism was geared toward willful types of decisions that did not take into account economic and ecological considerations, decisions that in many cases were harmful immediately or later on.

The experience of the past eighty years, however, reveals something else as well. On the social level, and on the environmental level, even the most advanced market economy has not proved very effective.

The efficiency of the market economy results from its central law, that of profits and the maximization of profits, but it proved incapable of eliminating poverty for millions of people. As a result, the global "North-South" problem has arisen and remains a terrible menace hanging over the entire world community.

In the most highly developed countries the market has greatly improved productivity, but it has imposed a harmful consumer mentality on the population and created a situation in which unemployment has steadily increased, affecting many millions with all its dramatic social and moral consequences.

Unemployment is one of the basic defects of the market-based system. This defect should be overcome or at least minimized in terms of its consequences for working people. But how? The answer is by means of a rational social policy. But this requires revision of some of the present-day dogmas, which many "experts" have raised to the level of "indisputable laws of development." If development makes masses of people superfluous, removes them from a life of useful activity, and throws them on the scrap heap, does it not follow that either the content or the direction of development (or both) must be changed? The same can be said about the environmental consequences of market economics. The present system of economic management based on the pursuit of profits is destroying nature. In the West, measures are being taken to make production safer ecologically. But this occurs only when the situation reaches extreme limits, or it happens under pressure from public opinion. In many cases, attempts to "solve" environmental problems are made by exporting harmful production to other countries. Thus, in the final analysis, improving environmental conditions in one place is accomplished at the expense of worsening the world ecological situation in general.

All these considerations, which have become quite evident, have had the result that in recent times the market economy is being criticized more and more in the Western countries themselves. A report by the Interaction Council, entitled "In Search of a Global Order," noted:

> The market mechanism has demonstrated that it is not a panacea for solving intractable world problems nor for achieving fundamental social aims. On the one hand, there is no better system than the market economy for achieving economic growth and prosperity. On the other hand, a market in and of itself cannot ensure a satisfactory distribution of income and tends to result in the exclusion of the weak, the unorganized, and the vulnerable. . . . The market has demonstrated that it is not capable of solving the fundamental problem of the environment which it regards as 'external.' There are no market solutions for such problems as poverty, hunger, and population growth.

An equally sharp expression of views has been heard from the Nobel Prize-winning U.S. economist James Tobin, who wrote:

> The Invisible Hand deserves two cheers, not the three or four proposed by its zealot ideologues. Individual self-interest can be a motivation for actions of great benefit to society, but only if disciplined and channeled . . . the Invisible Hand theorem has to be modified by recognizing externalities and public goods, where individual and societal interests diverge. These require treatment by governments to protect collective interests.

We have spoken above about the advantages and flaws of the centralized planned economy in the Soviet Union as far as the social sphere was concerned. Without repeating what has been said, it should be noted that despite its weaknesses the system that was called socialist gave people (at least the majority of working people) a minimal income necessary for life and confidence in the future, which working people in the West as a rule do not know. But on the ecological plane, this system did not pass the test.

The lesson, it seems, is obvious: There needs to be a search for solutions that would provide for active utilization of market mechanisms, but these would have to be combined without fail with measures of social and ecological protection. In my view, the search for these solutions is not being conducted seriously except by a few left-wing parties.

Meanwhile the market economy, which has been established solidly throughout the world, faces a new test. The economy has become a global one, and of course so has the market. Under these conditions, all the virtues of the market as well as all its shortcomings are likewise being globalized, and both positive and negative qualities are emerging more and more strongly. This is especially true since the market economy currently has no "rival" in the form of an opposing system in the East, which previously prevented the West from ignoring the social aspects of the economy. The problem of combining social and ecological imperatives is becoming acute.

A comparative analysis of the results of the competition between the two systems could be continued. There is a vast amount of material here, but it is a subject for a separate book. What we would like to do now is to think about a way out of the *general crisis* of world development, a crisis that confronts the world community with the need for radical transformation flowing in one common channel as a new civilizing process in order to provide salvation for all. Here there arises, first, the question of the role of government. I do not think there are any grounds for removing government from all consideration, as proponents of the invisible hand theory do. Incidentally, the role of government as a key regulator of economic and social life is recognized by numerous foreign authors who belong to the most varied shadings on the political spectrum. We have already quoted James Tobin on the need for government action when individual and social interests diverge. Tobin also noted that "Adam Smith himself was quite aware of government's role."

It is impossible not to notice that even in countries where liberal, even ultraliberal, views prevail, the role of government has by no means disappeared. The forms this role takes are of course changing. For example, government-owned property is being qualitatively reduced as a result of several waves of privatization, and direct intervention by government agencies in solving economic problems is being restricted. But government continues as a major source of purchasing orders for businesses, and it regulates economic development through tax policies and other financial devices, distributing quite a large part of the national income through the budget.

As for the experience of the Soviet Union, it showed that when government assumes the role of the sole or primary property owner, it is transformed into an instrument for unrestricted domination by a bureaucracy, while the producers are deprived of the opportunity to display initiative and cultivate the spirit of enterprise. These qualities find no room for expression under conditions in which government dictates economic policy. In the final analysis, this system acts as a brake on progress and a deadening influence on those forces that provide dynamism in the national economy and give it the capacity for modernization and innovation. Incidentally, in some countries that belonged to the so-called socialist camp there existed a fairly well-developed cooperative sector of the economy (for example, in Hungary and East Germany), and this sector demonstrated its capability and efficiency. Of course certain national traditions played a role here, too, but this simply confirms that even limited attempts to optimize the role of government in the economy can produce substantial results.

A conclusion suggests itself: Finding the optimal correlation between the role of government and that of private "actors" in the economy, with self-management by those "actors," that is, finding an appropriate combination of the role of government and that of the market—this is a task that remains unresolved. This applies as well to Russia today, where the idea of separating the government from the economy and the social sphere during a transitional period has had distinctly disastrous results. It seems that there have been recent attempts in Russia as well to find the necessary balance between the role of the market and that of government. But so far these are only attempts.

Generally speaking, an ideal solution to this problem is unlikely ever to be found. In each country, each society, at any given time, it takes on its own particular features, its own special twists and turns. The search for an ideal solution will probably continue. But the extent to which it is successful depends in large part on democracy in the economy, in politics, and in the society as a whole.

This is one of the most important lessons of our history. *The Soviet Union, in the final analysis, experienced its tragedy because democracy was suppressed as a matter of principle over a long period of time.* On the other hand, the signs of a revival in public life, the restored ability of citizens to display initiatives—these began with the revival of democracy that is linked with perestroika. Recent years—especially since 1993, after the dissolution of the Russian parliament and the shelling of the parliament building, and the adoption of a new constitution granting authoritarian powers to the executive branch—have been marked by the constriction of democracy, distortion of it, and the depreciation of its most vivifying aspects. This is dangerous. A feeling of hope rises, nevertheless, because in spite of everything, the majority of Russian citizens consciously and voluntarily have refused to go along with the antidemocratic choice.

Today the development of democracy in the West is held up as an example for the future. While acknowledging what has been achieved there, we cannot help noting that Western democracy is not well: It is in a crisis. Democratic institutions persist, but the citizenry seem more and more alienated from those institutions, which are simply degenerating. Vitally important decisions are made behind citizens' backs, without their participation and beyond their control. These decisions are made by political elites and are the result of political trade-offs that often serve the interests of narrow groups. As a result, the political activity of most people has lessened and the gap between government and society has increased. Thus, even in the most-developed Western countries, democracy itself needs to be renewed; it needs, if I may say so, a democratization.

Of course the situation varies from country to country. But the chief political question for the present and the future is to find up-to-date forms of democracy and to fine-tune them in their most essential aspects—while of course taking into account the unique evolution of each society. This problem is further discussed below.

In the light of the entire Russian post-October experience, we have solid criteria for evaluating the potentials of one or another economic system or sociopolitical regime. And thus we can hope to obtain useful solutions in our search for the road to the future.

In drawing the balance sheet on the past eighty years, we cannot fail to touch on a key question for the future, namely, "Who won the Cold War?"

The Cold War ended as a result of the interaction of various factors. We must be honest about this. If there had not been a change in Soviet policy, if the new thinking had not emerged, the Cold War might have continued for much longer. That point deserves emphasis.

It is customary for Westerners to claim that the West was victorious in the Cold War and that the East—above all, the Soviet Union—was defeated. This analysis of the issue is very convenient for those who would like to impose conditions on the so-called losing side, to bend it to their will. True, quite a few people in Russia admit they were defeated, but they also seek to avoid any serious analysis of what actually occurred. What happened is this: In the rivalry between the two social systems—the one that was established in the Soviet Union and other countries allied with it, and the other that existed and still exists in the West—the positions held by the Western system turned out to be superior. In what respect, and why, are the questions at issue. As discussed above, the responsibility for this lies in the "model" of social development established by the Bolsheviks and the policies pursued throughout their years in power, especially after Lenin's death.

The system founded by the Bolsheviks has now passed from the historical scene. Although I emphasize that fact, it would be a major mistake to consider the "Russian experiment" useless, as though it had made no contribution to humanity. Since that is surely not the case, certain conclusions need to be drawn not only by the successor governments of the former Soviet Union but also by the West. Both Soviet developments and those in the West have posed many problems that remain unresolved. In seeking solutions to these problems, everything must be taken into account, both the experience of the USSR and that of its former opponents. To ignore any part of our common world experience would be irresponsible and would not bring us closer to solving the problems before us.

As for who won the Cold War, the answer, in my opinion, lies simply in rephrasing the question. We should ask, Who gained by the termination of that war? Here the answer is obvious: Every country, all the peoples of the world, benefited. Because the confrontation has been overcome, we have all been delivered from a terrible danger, the threat of nuclear catastrophe. We all have a unique opportunity—the first in many centuries—to organize a truly peaceful coexistence among people of different nations and governments all over the planet. We can engage in development under conditions of cooperative and constructive activity.

Of course simply because such a possibility exists does not mean these prospects will be realized. It is evident thus far that not much has been achieved. There is a saying, "The dead hand of the past lays hold of the living." The legacy of the past is so heavy, with so many layers, that the world has not yet been able to free itself from that legacy. Moreover, pressing new problems confront us that were previously unforeseen.

The lessons of the past nevertheless encourage us to do all we can to rid ourselves from the burdens of that legacy so that we may transform the future, if not into a golden age (probably an exaggerated hope), then into a period of humane progress corresponding to the interests of all humanity.

CHAPTER 6

October and Perestroika

THERE HAS BEEN a continuing debate over when reform actually began in our country. Politicians and journalists have been trying to locate the exact point at which all our dramatic changes began. Some assert that reforms in Russia did not really begin until 1992.

The basis for reform was laid by Khrushchev. His break with the repressive policies of Stalinism was a heroic feat of civic action. Khrushchev also tried, though without much success, to make changes in the economy. Significant attempts were made within the framework of the so-called Kosygin reforms. Then came a long period of stagnation and a new attempt by Yuri Andropov to improve the situation in our society. An obvious sign that the times were ripe for change was the activity of the dissidents. They were suppressed and expelled from the country, but their moral stand and their proposals for change (for example, the ideas of Andrei Sakharov) played a considerable role in creating the spiritual preconditions for perestroika.

Of course external factors were also important. Thus the Prague Spring of 1968 sowed the seeds of profound thought and reflection in our society. The invasion of Czechoslovakia, dictated by fear of the "democratic infection," was not only a crude violation of the sovereignty and rights of the Czechoslovak people. It had the effect, for years, of putting the brakes on moves toward change, although change was long overdue both in our country and throughout the so-called socialist camp. I should also acknowledge the role of such phenomena as Willy Brandt's "Eastern policy" and the search for new avenues toward social progress by those who were called Euro-Communists. All this contributed to deeper reflection in our country, reflection on the values of democracy, freedom, and peace and the ways to achieve them.

Thus we see that attempts at change were made, quite a few of them in fact. But none of them produced results. This is not surprising: After all, none of these attempts touched the essence of the system—property relations, the power structure, and the monopoly of the party on political and intellectual life. The suppression of dissidence continued in spite of everything.

Clearly what was needed was not particular measures in a certain area, even if they were substantial, but rather an entirely different policy, a new political path. Since early 1985, especially after the April plenum of the CPSU Central Committee, this kind of policy began to be formulated. A new course was taken.

Today, in retrospect, one can only be amazed at how quickly and actively our people, the citizens of our country, supported that new course. Apathy and indifference toward public life were overcome. This convinced us that change was vitally necessary. Society awakened.

Perestroika was born out of the realization that problems of internal development in our country were ripe, even overripe, for a solution. New approaches and types of action were needed to escape the downward spiral of crisis, to normalize life, and to make a breakthrough to qualitatively new frontiers. It can be said that to a certain extent perestroika was a result of a rethinking of the Soviet experience since October.

The vital need for change was dictated also by the following consideration. It was obvious that the whole world was entering a new stage of development—some call it the postindustrial age, some the information age. But the Soviet Union had not yet passed through the industrial stage. It was lagging further and further behind those processes that were making a renewal in the life of the world community possible. Not only was a leap forward in technology needed but fundamental change in the entire social and political process.

Of course it cannot be said that at the time we began perestroika we had everything thought out. In the early stages we all said, including myself, that perestroika was a continuation of the October revolution. Today I believe that that assertion contained a grain of truth but also an element of delusion.

The truth was that we were trying to carry out fundamental ideas that had been advanced by the October revolution but had not been realized: overcoming people's alienation from government and property, giving power to the people (and taking it away from the bureaucratic upper echelons), implanting democracy, and establishing true social justice.

The delusion was that at the time I, like most of us, assumed this could be accomplished by improving and refining the existing system. But as experience accumulated, it became clear that the crisis that had paralyzed the country in the late 1970s and early 1980s was systemic and not the result of isolated aberrations. The logic of how matters developed pointed to the need to penetrate the system to its very foundations and change it, not merely refine or perfect it. We were already talking about a gradual shift to a social market economy, to a democratic political system based on rule of law and the full guarantee of human rights.

This transition turned out to be extremely difficult and complicated, more complicated than it had seemed to us at first. Above all, this was because the totalitarian system possessed tremendous inertia. There was resistance from the party and government structures that constituted the solid internal framework of that system. The nomenklatura encouraged resistance. And this is understandable: Since it held the entire country in its hands, it would have to give up its unlimited power and privileges. Thus the entire perestroika era was filled with struggles—concealed at first and then more open, more fully exposed to public view—between the forces for change and those who opposed it, those who, especially after the first two years, simply began to sabotage change.

The complexity of the struggle stemmed from the fact that in 1985 the entire society—politically, ideologically, and spiritually—was still in the thrall of old customs and traditions. Great effort was required to overcome these traditions, as mentioned above. There was another factor. Destroying the old system would have been senseless if we did not simultaneously lay the foundations for a new life. And this was genuinely unexplored territory. The six-year perestroika era was a time filled with searching and discovery, gains and losses, breakthroughs in thought and action, as well as mistakes and oversights. The attempted coup in August 1991 interrupted perestroika. After that there were many developments, but they were along different lines, following different intentions. Still, in the relatively short span of six years we succeeded in doing a great deal. The reforms in China, incidentally, have been going on since 1974, and their most difficult problems still remain unsolved.

What specifically did we accomplish as a result of the stormy years of perestroika? The foundations of the totalitarian system were eliminated. Profound democratic changes were begun. Free general elections were held for the first time, allowing real choice. Freedom of the press and a multiparty system were guaranteed. Representative bodies of government were established, and the first steps toward a separation of powers were taken. Human rights (previously in our country these were only "so-called," reference to them invariably made only in scornful quotation marks) now became an unassailable principle. And freedom of conscience was also established.

Movement began toward a multistructured, or mixed, economy providing equality of rights among all forms of property. Economic freedom was made into law. The spirit of enterprise began to gain strength, and processes of privatization and the formation of joint stock companies got under way. Within the framework of our new land law, the peasantry was reborn and private farmers made their appearance. Millions of hectares of land were turned over to both rural and urban inhabitants. The first privately owned banks also came on the scene. The different nationalities and peoples were given the freedom to choose their own course of development. Searching for a democratic way to reform our multinational state, to transform it from a unitary state in practice into a national federation, we reached the threshold at which a new union treaty was to be signed, based on the recognition of the sovereignty of each republic along with the preservation of a common economic, social, and legal space that was necessary for all, including a common defense establishment.

The changes within our country inevitably led to a shift in foreign policy. The new course of perestroika predetermined renunciation of stereotypes and the confrontational methods of the past. It allowed for a rethinking of the main parameters of state security and the ways to ensure it. I will return to this subject.

In other words, the foundations were laid for normal, democratic, and peaceful development of our country and its transformation into a normal member of the world community.

These are the decisive results of perestroika. Today, however, looking back through the prism of the past few years and taking into account the general trends of world development today, it seems insufficient to register these as the only results. Today it is evidently of special interest to state not only *what* was done but also *how* and *why* perestroika was able to achieve its results, and what its mistakes and miscalculations were.

Above all, *perestroika would have been simply impossible if there had not been a profound and critical reexamination not only of the problems confronting our country but a rethinking of all realities—both national and international.*

Previous conceptions of the world and its developmental trends and, correspondingly, of our country's place and role in the world were based, as we have said, on dogmas deeply rooted in our ideology, which essentially did not permit us to pursue a realistic policy. These conceptions had to be shattered and fundamentally new views worked out regarding our country's development and the surrounding world.

This task turned out to be far from simple. We had to renounce beliefs that for decades had been considered irrefutable truths, to reexamine the very methods and principles of leadership and action, indeed to rethink our surroundings entirely on a scientific basis (and not according to schemes inherited from ideological biases).

The product of this effort was the new thinking, which became the basis for all policy—both foreign and domestic—during perestroika. The point of departure for the new thinking was an attempt to evaluate everything not from the viewpoint of narrow class interests or even national interests but from the broader perspective: that of giving priority to the interests of all humanity with consideration for the increasingly apparent wholeness of the world, the interdependence of all countries and peoples, the humanist values formed over centuries.

The practical work of perestroika was to *renounce stereotypical ideological thinking and the dogmas of the past. This required a fresh view of the world and of ourselves with no preconceptions, taking into account the challenges of the present and the already evident trends of the future in the third millennium.*

During perestroika, and often now as well, the initiators of perestroika have been criticized for the absence of a "clear plan" for change. The habit developed over decades of having an all-inclusive regimentation of life. But the events of the perestroika years and of the subsequent period have plainly demonstrated the following: *At times of profound, fundamental change in the foundations of social development it is not only senseless but impossible to expect some sort of previously worked out "model" or a clear-cut outline of the transformations that will take place. This does not mean, however, the absence of a definite goal for the reforms, a distinct conception of their content and the main direction of their development.*

All this was present in perestroika: a profound democratization of public life and a guarantee of freedom of social and political choice. These goals were proclaimed and frequently reaffirmed. This did not exclude but presupposed the necessity to change one's specific reference points at each stage as matters proceeded and to engage in a constant search for optimal solutions.

An extremely important conclusion follows from the experience of perestroika: Even in a society formed under totalitarian conditions, democratic change is possible by *peaceful evolutionary means*. The problem of revolution and evolution, of the role and place of reforms in social development, is one of the eternal problems of history. In its inner content perestroika of course was a revolution. But in its form it was an evolutionary process, a process of reform.

Historically the USSR had grown ripe for a profound restructuring much earlier than the mid-1980s. But if we had not decided to begin this restructuring at the time we did, even though we were quite late in doing so, an explosion would have taken place in the USSR, one of tremendous destructive force. It would certainly have been called a revolution, but it would have been the catastrophic result of irresponsible leadership.

In the course of implementing change we did not succeed in avoiding bloodshed altogether. But that was a consequence solely of resistance by the opponents of perestroika in the upper echelons of the nomenklatura. On the whole the change from one system to another took place peacefully and by evolutionary means. Our having chosen a policy course that was supported from below by the masses made this peaceful transition possible. And our policy of glasnost played a decisive role in mobilizing the masses and winning their support.

Radical reforms in the context of the Soviet Union could only have been initiated from above by the leadership of the party and the country. This was predetermined by the very "nature" of the system—supercentralized management of all public life. This can also be explained by the inert condition of the masses, who had become used to carrying out orders and decisions handed down from above.

From the very beginning of the changes our country's leadership assigned primary importance to open communication with the people, including direct disclosure in order to explain the new course. Without the citizens' understanding and support, without their participation, it would not have been possible to move from dead center. That is why we initiated the policies of perestroika and glasnost simultaneously.

Like perestroika itself, glasnost made its way with considerable difficulty. The nomenklatura on all levels, which regarded the strictest secrecy and protection of authorities from criticism from below as the holy of holies of the regime, opposed glasnost in every way they could, both openly and secretly, trampling its first shoots in the local press. Even among the most sincere supporters of perestroika, the tradition over many years of making everything a secret made itself felt. But it was precisely glasnost that awakened people from their social slumber, helped them overcome indifference and passivity and become aware of the stake they had in change and of its important implications for their lives. Glasnost helped us to explain and promote awareness of the new realities and the essence of our new political course. In short, without glasnost there would have been no perestroika.

The question of the relation between ends and means is one of the key aspects of politics and of political activity. If the means do not correspond to the ends, or, still worse, if the means contradict the ends, this will lead to setbacks and failure. The Soviet Union's experience is convincing evidence of this. When we began perestroika as a process of democratic change, we had to ensure that the means used to carry out these changes were also democratic.

In essence, glasnost became the means for drawing people into political activity, for including them in the creation of a new life, and this, above all, corresponded to the essence of perestroika. Glasnost not only created conditions for implementing the intended reforms but also made it possible to overcome attempts to sabotage the policy of change.

We are indebted to glasnost for a profound psychological transformation in the public consciousness toward democracy, freedom, and the humanist values of civilization. Incidentally, this was one of the guarantees that the fundamental gains of this period would be irreversible.

Perestroika confirmed once again that the normal, democratic development of society rules out universal secrecy as a method of administration. Democratic development presupposes glasnost—that is, openness, freedom of information for all citizens and freedom of expression by them of their political, religious, and other views and convictions, freedom of criticism in the fullest sense of the word.

Why, then, did perestroika not succeed in achieving all its goals? The answer primarily involves the question of "harmonization" between political and economic change.

The dominant democratic aspect of perestroika meant that the accent was inevitably placed on political reform. The dialectic of our development during those years was such that serious changes in the economic sphere proved to be impossible without emancipating society politically, without ensuring freedom—that is, breaking the political structures of totalitarianism. And this was accomplished. But economic change lagged behind political change, and we did not succeed in developing economic change to the full extent.

In recent years I have often had occasion to refute criticism to the effect that we should have begun with economic changes and held tightly to the political reins, as was done in China. There was no lack of understanding of economics on our part, still less scorn or disregard for it. To dispute that line of criticism it is sufficient to examine the chronology of events of perestroika. From the very beginning most plenary sessions of our Central Committee were devoted precisely to restructuring the economy. This aspect of the process occupied nearly three-quarters of my time and effort as general secretary, as well as the work of my colleagues and our government agencies. However, the state monopoly ownership that prevailed in our economy for decades, the administrative-command system that had left its mark on our economic personnel and party leaders, most of whom had been trained in economic management, indeed the very character of our economic system which had been functioning over such a prolonged period—all these factors contributed to *incredibly powerful inertia*, which made the task of switching over onto new tracks, the tracks of a real market economy, tremendously difficult. Even if all our economic ideas and decisions during perestroika had been flawless (and I cannot say they were), that inertia would have been present.

Change had begun, but we were searching for an optimal way of making a peaceful transition from a totalitarian economy to a democratic one. The search was long and drawn out. Moods of disillusionment and disappointment, loss of faith in perestroika, dissatisfaction with the worsening material situation—all these forces began to rise among the people (although the material conditions at that time cannot be compared to those that resulted from the "shock therapy" of Gaidar and Yeltsin). Support for the reforms in our society grew distinctly weaker, and populist demagogues took advantage of this, promising to correct matters in the course of one year, which was sheer balderdash. But people wanted a quick change for the better. The society's dissatisfaction over market conditions was thoroughly exploited by the opponents of reform inside the CPSU.

Another factor that threatened perestroika was the delay in solving the nationalities question, transforming the USSR from an actual unitary state to a truly multinational federation and thus, in the last analysis, bringing the situation into correspondence with the relevant clauses of the Soviet constitution. Nationalist elements and the ruling circles in the [non-Russian] republics, deciding that the moment had come to weaken control from the center, took advantage of this.

The negative processes began to gain strength after Yeltsin's group came to power in Russia and issued a declaration of sovereignty for the Russian Federation. The intention behind this was in fact to eliminate the union of republics (although nothing was said about that at the time). They were able to counter that destructive policy line with the line of preserving the union and reforming it fundamentally. By July 1991 the various republics had agreed on a new union treaty. The attempted coup by the opponents of reform thwarted the signing of that treaty. And although those opponents were defeated, the events of August 1991 gave a powerful impetus to the processes of disintegration, and the position of the central government of the Soviet Union was greatly undermined. The leadership of the Russian Republic took advantage of this. It had already been attempting constantly to assume the right to make decisions that would affect the entire union. Thus the process of estrangement and disunification among the republics was intensified, and all this resulted, in December 1991, in an agreement between Russia, Ukraine, and Belarus to dissolve the USSR.

These are some of the lessons of perestroika. Of course I have only indicated the most important and fundamental ones. These lessons, it would seem, have a definite importance not only for historians. Today when the entire world is in flux, when the need for change has arisen in many countries as a result of the many new challenges of the approaching new century, any experience of change and reform takes on a significance that is not limited by national borders.

I can say this without fear of error: The experience of the transition from totalitarianism to democracy in my country, for all its uniqueness, contains much that may be of interest to democratic reformers in other countries. Especially if we keep in mind the intensified tendency toward decentralization and the rising new wave of nationalism. What about for Russia itself? What might be useful for its further development? The continuing crisis in Russia is explained in many respects by the fact that it departed from the evolutionary road of reforms and yielded to the influence of the proponents of "shock therapy." It retreated from genuinely democratic standards in public life, scorned the social imperative, and failed to resolve the question of establishing proper federated relationships. We can be sure that the future of Russia as a democratic, peace-loving, humane country can be assured only if it continues to move along the path of genuinely democratic renewal, which was begun by perestroika—of course taking into account in the process all the new elements that have emerged.

In concluding this chapter let us once again recall October. The revolution of 1917 was victorious under the banner of ultrademocratic slogans. These slogans were not merely demagogic, not just a means of winning power. They expressed a profound basis for the transformation of our country, a country that used to be called the Russian empire. However, the Bolsheviks, and after them Stalin, demonstrated to their country and to the world in the most convincing way that democracy cannot be built on principles of hatred, hostility, or elimination of one part of society, or of the world, by another. Today in Russia, in the final analysis, we have come to understand democracy as a universal human value, and the task we face is not to end up once again in the position of serving as a "negative model."

Thoughts about perestroika naturally encompass the entire complex of problems of the new thinking, including, in foreign policy, the international aspect. The road to a new foreign policy was a long one.

The first decree adopted after the October Revolution was the decree on peace. It proposed an immediate end to World War I on all fronts—but it did not call for a separate peace, as was sometimes claimed in later literature. The Entente countries rejected this appeal. Only then did Russia leave the war separately, concluding the Brest-Litovsk Treaty with Germany. This was a humiliating treaty, a treaty of servitude. But it released our tortured and exhausted country from the worldwide slaughter. And at the same time it served as a stimulus toward ending the war as a whole. The effect of the peaceful signal Russia had given was felt everywhere in the world, by the masses of soldiers in combat and by the populations of the warring countries. Its impact was enormous, and for the Entente rulers this made Russia a more dangerous and hated enemy than even Germany itself. They were forced to draw other conclusions as well, however, from what had happened in Russia.

President Woodrow Wilson noted that the Bolsheviks had successfully influenced world public opinion by their use of a most effective weapon—a policy of peace. If the U.S. were to counter that influence successfully, it would have to seize that weapon from them. There soon appeared Wilson's famous Fourteen Points—the American program for peace, which definitely reflected and took into account the peaceful challenge made by October and its impact on the world.

Soviet foreign policy after October was not irreproachable from the point of view of consistency in pursuing a peaceable line in the international arena. If nothing else, the attempts to implement the idea of world revolution, the activities of the Communist International, directed from Moscow, were sufficient to make the West distrust the peace initiatives of the USSR. But actually, from 1922 on, Soviet Russia and the Soviet Union were not inclined to initiate or engage in wars. Peaceful relations with the West, and mutually advantageous, businesslike economic ties [with the West], became a question of self-preservation for Russia.

The activities of Soviet diplomats in the 1930s, in the context of the overall democratic movement against fascism and war, are well known. This policy was dictated by the needs of the Soviet people, although the Kremlin had its own hidden agenda in this process. I believe that Stalin made a gross error in the rapprochement with Germany in 1939, an error that cost our country and the world dearly. However, the so-called Western democracies, which at the time were operating in the spirit of the Munich agreement, committed an error of no less significance.

It was natural for the USSR to join the anti-Hitler coalition with those who might have seemed to be its irreconcilable ideological opponents. This alliance was the determining factor for victory in a war that affected the destinies of all humanity. If this alliance had been maintained after the war, in a different form of course, the peace toward which we are now moving just at the end of the century could have been ours much earlier. But the former allies rushed headlong into the Cold War. Each side bears its share of responsibility for this. Which side bears the greater responsibility is a question that has not yet been answered by honest, objective historians in a sufficiently convincing way.

We cannot say that the Soviet Union's entire postwar foreign policy brought only harm to our country and had nothing positive to offer to the outside world. It is enough to recall the ideas of the Twentieth Party Congress and some of Khrushchev's specific actions, as well as the policy of détente under Brezhnev and the attempt to limit the nuclear arms race. The flaw in Soviet foreign policy, however, consisted in the fact that all its energy came from an ideological source. A hard core of ideological constructs ultimately determined the behavior of the USSR on decisive questions of international relations and nourished an atmosphere of confrontation toward the West, which was of course also partly a response to the no less confrontational policy pursued by the West toward the Soviet Union. In thinking about these problems at length, I have come to the conclusion that the policy pursued by both sides was dictated by mutual fear and was ideologically driven. As a result, by the mid-1980s the world was approaching a boundary line beyond which there loomed a universal nuclear catastrophe.

In beginning perestroika, we understood that if nothing was changed in our country's foreign policy, we would get nowhere with the internal changes we had in mind. An analysis of the world situation and our country's place in it had begun even before 1985. With the start of perestroika the work in this area moved forward energetically, and it was no longer kept secret but proceeded in full view of the broadest public. What was being discussed? We sought to define in a new way the true national interests of our country, the real parameters and imperatives for national security. We strove to examine soberly the condition of the world community and the main trends in world development. And on this basis, we tried to work out a well-considered program of specific actions in the main areas of foreign policy.

We understood of course that everything did not depend on us: Confrontational thinking and a combative political "culture" were characteristic phenomena on both sides of the Iron Curtain. But we realized that a great deal depended on us. During the years of discord with the West we in the USSR, with our nuclear arsenal and by some of our actions, had inspired distrust not only in official circles but among the broader public. Therefore it was necessary first to change our behavior in practical terms in our relations with other governments. The decisive element was to devise foreign policy conceptions that would be new in principle, to develop fresh criteria and principles for all Soviet policy in the international arena. As described above, the fruit of this effort was the new thinking—a philosophy and methodology of new approaches toward world affairs.

The new thinking was not developed all at once. It was enriched and refined as changes took place in our world outlook; it was checked and verified through our experiences in dealing and communicating with the outside world. All this, as well as the results of our changed policies, will be discussed in greater detail in part 3 of this book.

CHAPTER 7

Does Socialism Have a Future?

ONE OF TODAY'S most fashionable clichés both in Russia and the West is to speak of the total collapse of the socialist idea. Socialism has been anathematized. All the misfortunes suffered by the Soviet people and others who pursued that same chimera, or on whom it was imposed—all their sufferings are attributed to socialism. This is a false conclusion. The socialism about which many great minds in the history of humanity have written and about which millions of people have dreamed never did exist—neither in the Soviet Union nor in Eastern Europe, Asia, or Cuba. And if that is true, then it simply flies in the face of history as well as logic to assert that socialism was defeated.

Nevertheless what happened in those countries that for a long time were called socialist, even "communist," has given us greater knowledge about socialism than any theory could. We now know what is incompatible with socialism and what it cannot permit. We also know what requirements must be met by any policy aimed at making the socialist idea a reality. Let me emphasize, we know this both from the experience of the Soviet Union and from that of Western countries, where elements and processes of socialization of the productive forces have also developed to a considerable extent.

My own opinion is quite definite: *The socialist idea has not lost its significance or its historical relevance.* This is so not only because the very idea of socialism, which includes such concepts as social justice, equality, freedom, and democracy, is one that can never be exhausted but also because the entire development of the world community confirms, with new urgency every day, that we need justice, equality, freedom, democracy, and solidarity. That need has not been extinguished but continues to grow. The popular movements that arise and develop in the most varied parts of our planet testify to this, do they not? What is it that Russia's citizens are dissatisfied with today?

It is social injustice, namely, the deepening division of society into the poor (more than half the population) and the super rich (less than 2–3 percent of the population). Russians are dissatisfied with existing limitations on democratic freedoms, violations of human rights, and subordination of the mass media to the dictates of a handful of men with deep pockets.

What are the citizens of the European Union demanding? They want unemployment brought under control. They want action to stop impoverishment and marginalization. They want the rights and powers of cities, towns, regions, and local government bodies increased and respected. They yearn for a political system that reflects the genuine interests and needs of the people, that protects their identity in the present context of globalization.

What about the countries that still lag behind the modern world? Don't their requirements for a normal life, for economic development, for overcoming hunger and poverty, illiteracy, and a primitive existence come within the framework of the socialist idea? Let me stress that I am speaking of that idea outside any particular party context.

True, the criteria differ everywhere, as do the various approaches to specific questions. But there is a common denominator: a demand for social justice, equality, freedom, and democracy—in all things, from politics to economics to everyday life.

Therefore I am convinced, first, that *the socialist idea is inextinguishable*. It will continue to inspire people to take action in the name of everything contained in that idea, namely, *natural* human rights and freedoms. (The term *natural* is entirely appropriate here.) Second, I believe that the question of implementing the socialist idea must be approached in a modern way, that is, taking into account the actual current situation, the experience that has been accumulated, and the real challenges and requirements of the near future.

Let us consider the matter. A development of any kind is possible only given the existence of an inner diversity. Achieving an "ideal" through the victory of one of the existing trends in society and the elimination of all others inevitably results in the destruction of the system so created.

Thus, for example, the suppression of political pluralism in the USSR, the forcible elimination of all non-Communist parties, and then of all differing shades of opinion within the Communist Party itself—those actions essentially amounted to the first step toward the establishment of totalitarianism, and at the same time toward all the subsequent dramatic turns of events. In other words, those actions led the way toward the emasculation of the socialist idea, toward a deformation of the principles of socialism to the point of their complete negation.

That is why it seems *hardly correct or productive over the long term to pose the question of building a society in which socialist ideology would be completely dominant, a society with socialist features only, with socialist forces having exclusive sway.*

Previous conceptions of socialism were constructed as antipodes to the "model" of capitalist society (and in many cases such concepts continue to exist today). But our times have demonstrated the relativity of all social structures. They are all historical, in flux, changeable, especially in our dynamic age. The very terms *capitalism* and *socialism* in their ordinary and accustomed interpretation no longer offer much in the way of describing and understanding reality. The contemporary world is not a dichotomy; it is a multiplicity. Capitalist society has everywhere been highly variegated, and future societies will likewise be anything but copies of one another.

I think that any attempt to "construct" a single universally applicable "model" for implementing the socialist idea, relying on certain constants that would be identical in all cases—such an approach is fruitless. Isn't a different approach required, one in which socialism will be regarded *not as a closed social formation but as a set of values*, whose implementation would create the conditions for the free development of all people as a condition for the development of each individual?

It seems to me that the cornerstone of the socialist idea, as understood at the present time, consists, above all, in the optimal solution to two problems. The first is efficiency of production, provision of the material bases for the fully rounded development of all people. The second is distribution of the social product in such a way that without undermining the efficiency of production all would be guaranteed a worthy and dignified level of existence, and that would include economically, socially, and ecologically disadvantaged groups.

The solution to these two problems would create the preconditions for implementing all the basic elements of the socialist idea. And of course it would create a reliable foundation for the free, democratic political and spiritual development of society. This kind of value-based approach would free us from the temptation to destroy the existing society "to its foundations" in order to build a society based on some intellectualized scheme starting from a clean slate. In adopting such an approach, our task would be different: It would be to investigate trends and possibilities that have already made themselves evident, possibilities for realizing the values of socialism at the present time and in the real social world. We would attempt to bring together those forces that are capable of receiving and accepting these values, to promote or contribute to their education and organization, and to select adequate means and conditions for action. In other words, there would be no maximalistic utopias but rather a consistent and purposeful realism.

Here of course another question arises: How should we act, what should we do, since neoliberal values are the ones that prevail in society today?

Liberalism has denied and still denies socialist values. But what has it gained from this? Socialists and Communists deny and have denied liberal values, but what have they achieved in doing so? Such mutual negation is capable only of producing a dichotomy, a division of society and the world into two hostile camps. I do not think that is the road we want.

Historically both socialism and liberalism had a common source: the humanist ideas of the Enlightenment. *The difference is that liberalism bases its values on the individual principle, while the socialist idea places the freedom of the individual and his or her development within the framework of a system of collectivist relations.* There are grounds for each of these approaches. But are they really so irreconcilable?

The contradictions of early capitalism revealed the limited character of the political equality toward which liberalism oriented. Socialist theory linked progress with the establishment of social equality. This had a fundamental effect on the development of capitalist society. There occurred a steady process in which the intensity of exploitation was reduced and the participation of working people in the management of the economy, in political life, and so on, expanded (although this occurred both through sharp clashes, class struggle, and other forms of social confrontation and through compromises, agreements, and improved legislation).

When the limited nature of authoritarian collectivism, with its complete subordination of the personal to the public, of the individual to the collective, and in fact to government structures and other institutions, became obvious, the success of liberalism in practice in creating conditions for individual freedom and political rights became a challenge to the Soviet experience. It became clear that neither egoistic individualism nor authoritarian collectivism could produce optimal results.

Thus a historic interaction occurred between what seemed to be two opposing lines, approaches, or principles. I think that this interaction, and in a certain sense the competition between these two trends of historical action, can enrich each of them and help overcome one-sidedness in the social process.

What lies ahead for us? Time is introducing and bringing into circulation new value-based orientations. In our times these are becoming increasingly identified with the interests of humanity as a whole.

On the one hand, we are talking about the very survival of humanity. In the light of the existing dangers it is becoming more and more evident that *all the traditional ideologies are vulnerable.* Also evident is the one-sidedness of any politics that pursues only some private interest—whether class, national, or other. Today the starting point for any rational policy must be the interests of all humanity, regardless of religious alignment or national, ethnic, and social status.

On the other hand, we are talking about the criteria and goals of progress. Its historically conditioned characteristic progress was that the necessary material conditions were lacking for putting in practical terms the following problem: Human beings must be the goal and meaning of progress, not merely instruments for achieving that progress.

Posing such a task, on the level of civilization as a whole, as a global phenomenon, requires a new value-based orientation.

Briefly, we are all in need of some new conceptual vision of the future. It can be defined as *global humanism.* I am not the first to use this term, but it seems to me a good definition of the "meta-ideology," if you will, that will help us find a common language for the largest possible number of socially conscious people.

No one person and no one party or political tendency has a monopoly on solving the problems that face the human race today. These problems can hardly be solved in a definitive way, once and for all. The highest wisdom in politics is to move steadily in the desired direction, constantly searching for answers. And in this search there is room for all currents of modern democratic social thought.

The imperious necessity for such joint searching has been predetermined by the fact that civilization now finds itself at an impasse. It has exhausted its potential for positive development, or it is in the process of exhausting that potential. The external manifestations of this impasse are commonly known. There are the ecological spasms we all observe and the other global problems associated with them. There is the crisis in the contemporary forms of social existence, the accumulation of contradictions between the individual and society, between government and the individual.

And there is the obviously unhealthy state of international relations: Having emerged from the Cold War era, the international community to this day has not found the way to a new, genuinely peaceful world order. There is also the increasing complexity in the functioning of the world economy. And there is both a moral and an ideological crisis: None of the generally recognized schools of thought has been able to explain what is happening or to point the way toward overcoming the present dilemma.

But now I would like to pose the question in a somewhat different manner. The crisis is obvious, but what are its deepest roots?

I believe we have sufficient grounds for answering this question today. The roots of the present critical condition of civilization lie in a mistaken understanding of the relation between the human race and the rest of nature, a misunderstanding coming down to us from the time of the Renaissance. A basic postulate of the Renaissance has proven to be profoundly in error: the notion that "man is the king of creation," a notion we followed for too long. Fixation on technologically centered factors of growth has brought us to a global ecological crisis.

Unfortunately today, on the eve of a new century, prognoses are being made that to one degree or another link the future with further perfection or improvement of the technocentric model of development. The need to renounce technologically centered models of progress and make the transition to a new anthropocentric, humanist model is being ignored. This means we are risking not only the danger of not solving our current problems, which are already extreme, but we risk intensifying and multiplying those problems.

The deepest roots of civilization's present crisis, on the other hand, are social in nature. From time immemorial the fruits of economic development have been used, and are still being used, in such a way as to preserve and in many cases intensify social differentiation.

Existing social relations are characterized not by a search for a balance among the interests of differing social and national groups, but in most cases in hostile confrontation or opposition of these groups to one another. Unfortunately, among the prognoses being made for the future that are so widespread today, these same models of social structure prevail, even though they have essentially exhausted themselves. These models can only give rise to sharpening contradictions and dangerous conflicts, not only nationally but globally as well.

Obviously a different approach is needed, another paradigm, one that would be based not on the perpetuation of social antagonisms and national conflicts but on a consistent effort to avoid such clashes. Clearly we will never achieve complete social harmony. But what is most desirable, our optimal goal, is to bring harmony into social development as much as possible and free it from the vicious circle of the struggle of each against all.

The present crisis of civilization, in my opinion, is also deeply rooted in the sphere of international relations. In the twentieth century, international relations were imbued with the same confrontational approaches as permeated social relations. This resulted in the division of humanity into warring camps, each side claiming to represent absolute truth in its social orientations and seeking to defeat, if not physically exterminate, the other.

As a result of intense efforts based on new approaches, we have succeeded in bringing a halt to international confrontation. But what do we see happening today? Politicians and ideologists, in thinking about the international relations they envisage for the twenty-first century, too often return to the old models, to seeking geopolitical gains, to the idea that the world must inevitably be redivided into spheres of influence or that a single power, the United States, can maintain global hegemony. But what can such an approach achieve? Nothing can be gained but a repetition of the tragedies of earlier and recent times.

To generalize on what has been presented thus far, although of course the subject has by no means been exhausted, it is not difficult to draw the following conclusion: *The roots of the crisis of contemporary civilization lie in a profound separation from the genuine interests of humanity*. The motivating factor in contemporary civilization so far has not been the humanist approach but instead the instinct of self-preservation, of gaining advantages at the expense of others. If by force of inertia this situation continues, it can lead to new negative consequences.

Hence my conclusion: New approaches are needed, new orientations in both thought and action. We must make the transition to a new civilization. It is sometimes said that the time is not yet ripe for a new civilization. But the question cannot be posed as though a new civilization could start tomorrow, the way one might introduce new prices for energy sources.

We are talking of a *transition* toward a new civilization. No one knows what it will be like. What is important is to orient in that direction. The human race today is spending enormous resources to provide the means of existence, even the most basic ones. The quantity of resources being expended is growing, because human needs are constantly expanding and are even being artificially cultivated. This is occurring at the expense of resources that are increasingly necessary to solve other vital tasks, tasks that are being posed with ever increasing urgency. This is an abnormal development. In principle, humanity today has already outgrown the framework of the struggle against nature and similar problems previously dictated by necessity.

The time has come for normal development, for what I call *humanist progress*. The very idea of progress, by the way, needs to "progress" in order for humanity to rise to the level at which it can realize the full meaning and purpose of its own history. This cannot take place any longer at the expense of irreparable injury to the human race itself and to the rest of nature, nor by humiliating and exploiting certain groups or entire nationalities with the irreversible moral and spiritual losses that entails. Progress is only possible under conditions of universal and equal cooperation stripped of any element of armed coercion, that is, under conditions of *co-development*, the simultaneous development of all.

On the broadest scale, this new civilization can be envisioned not as some kind of one-sided, totally unified entity but rather as a differentiated, pluralistic one. Only thus would it be able to adapt itself in the best possible way to the rapid tempo of change and the challenges of our times.

I am convinced that a new civilization will inevitably take on certain features that are characteristic of, or inherent in, the socialist ideal. However, over the course of centuries, in both politics and social consciousness, a great number of differing ideas have been churned out—conservative and radical, liberal and socialist, individualist and collectivist. This is the reality encountered everywhere. An attempt to *synthesize* these views, trends, and phenomena, an attempt to achieve an optimal interaction among them based on strictly humanist criteria—that is what will ensure movement toward a new civilization.

I will not go into further detail. The effort to construct speculative blueprints for the future is not a productive task. The future grows out of the present, out of the challenges of tomorrow that we must answer today, out of the objectively determined developmental tendencies of the social organism.

The Gorbachev Foundation does not stand alone but works together with others in the world community who are ready to participate in the search for a way to a better future. Today the Foundation has undertaken the task of studying the problems created by *globalization*, problems affecting the entire world. Research on global problems is of course a fundamental task, and our work is only just beginning.

Preliminary conclusions have been reached, but they require further investigation. The first conclusions are as follows:

- The processes of globalization are not slowing down but are accelerating world development and making all its contradictions and problems more evident and more acute;

- Consequently, the crisis of the present-day civilization will not be easing; the tendency toward its intensification is becoming increasingly evident;

- Hence there is a quickly growing need to find new approaches and solutions aimed at overcoming the crisis, a need, at least as a start, to stop the crisis from deepening while taking into account the new conditions created by globalization;

- Obviously just as the future of civilization itself will prove to be global, so too will the path toward its formation and the solutions to its problems;

- Finally, all these factors, taken together, mean that the research on the problems that have accumulated, the efforts to work out proposals for solving them, and of course the implementation of these proposals—all must be the result of a joint effort on the part of both science and politics by the world community as a whole. Unifying these efforts, while taking into account the current world situation, is by no means easy; the world community is not yet prepared for this.

In light of all this, a question arises: Is a movement toward a new civilization realistic? I think the lessons of history—above all, the history of the perestroika era, which was, if I may say so, a practical test of humanist approaches to the transformation of society—allow us to give a positive answer to this question.

What do these lessons of history embody?

First, as perestroika demonstrated, the assertion of the ideas of humanism and democracy, even in a society burdened with the heritage of totalitarianism, is fully realistic. In the Soviet Union, in just over five years, enormous changes took place, as I have discussed above. How much more easily such changes could be made in countries where democratic traditions have long been established, however they may have been distorted in everyday practice.

Second, policy-making must play a decisive role in implementing change. But these must be policies that are linked with moral principles and serve the cause of humanism. Perestroika tells us that the elaboration of such policies and their implementation are possible even in a society bearing a painful legacy of the past. How much more possible they would be in countries without that heritage.

Third, these lessons confirm that genuinely progressive, democratic change is possible only if it does not remain the province of a small political group in the top echelons of society, only if it becomes a genuine concern of the people as a whole and of public opinion in the broadest sense.

Taking heed of the lessons of the eighty years since October, as well as those of the recent past, and inspired by the ideas of humanism and universal human values, I believe we can look to the future with optimism.

CHAPTER 8

Summing Up

ALL THAT I HAVE written above does not of course constitute a history of the October revolution or of the post-October period. These were simply reflections on that history, and if someone is displeased because certain events were not mentioned, there is no cause for complaint. This is especially true since much has been written elsewhere about the history of October and the years that followed. The key to the thoughts presented here, and my starting point, was to reflect on a many-faceted and contradictory past. Without giving way to the stereotyped thinking that has become ingrained in society and keeping my emotions in check (although that is difficult; after all a substantial part of post-October history took place before my eyes, and I played a direct role in it during the last few decades), I have tried to examine objectively the results of the path that has been taken.

I have shared my thoughts with readers. To summarize briefly, I believe that the October revolution undoubtedly left an ineradicable mark on the entire history of the twentieth century. This is simply a fact. In essence, the entire course of events since 1917 has absorbed all aspects—both positive and negative—of our great revolution and the decades that followed.

The revolution—despite the price that was paid—brought historical renewal to Russia, freed it from the heritage of the feudal and absolutist past, and allowed the modernization of our country to begin. And that was accomplished through the mental and physical labor of our people—a truly heroic achievement. To forget this, to portray the decades of Soviet rule simply as a lost era, would be dishonest. It would be especially dishonest to the people, the individuals, the entire populations that lived and labored during those times. True, an excessively high price was paid—above all, because of the totalitarian system, the product and consequence of Stalinism. One of the most important lessons of those years is the need to reject and condemn unconditionally the totalitarian system, a system that tramples on all that is human in human beings, that turns people into slaves.

Another aspect of this whole question is that Soviet history has shown once again that totalitarianism, which on the surface seems so solidly entrenched, so powerful, ultimately condemns a country to impotence. Alienating the people from government, property, politics, and culture and seeking to suppress the slightest manifestation of diversity, totalitarianism deprives society of any incentive toward self-development and thereby dooms itself. And conversely, one final conclusion may be drawn, a conclusion based on what we experienced: Only democracy can serve as the basis for society's healthy and dynamic growth, for drawing out and utilizing all its possibilities.

All these assessments are not just lessons from the past. They are reminders for all of us today. The tendency toward authoritarianism, if not totalitarianism, has by no means disappeared in the world. By no means has democracy triumphed everywhere, and where it has triumphed, fundamental improvements are still needed if democracy is to adapt to new global challenges and to the needs of individual citizens.

All this is critical for today's Russia. Entangled in a situation created by extreme radicalism [the extreme radicalism of a neoliberal school of thought], Russia has not yet found a reliable, democratic, and truly free road of development; it is still burdened with authoritarianism. It has not yet found a road that would enrich its citizens, not ruin them, a road that would ensure their political and social rights, rather than restrict or limit them.

I remain an optimist, not only because I wish my people well. I also believe in them. To be sure, much depends on what occurs in the current situation. Even two or three months can bring about great change. Perhaps an intention to change Russia's present course will arise. To democratize the process of reform and strengthen its social orientation. Perhaps an entirely different course will be taken. As of the summer of 1998, I see no fundamental changes occurring, but I am hopeful. If we are to examine the root of our problems, however, we will see that it is a question of democracy. Only with democracy will everything proceed more smoothly and naturally.

Once when I was in Japan (I was still president of the USSR), a young woman, a student, asked me: "You are for democracy and free elections. But you yourself might not be chosen in an upcoming election; what would happen then?" In reply I said that I would still believe I had won. I wanted people to have freedom of choice, and that is what I achieved.

One might ask: But what about the October revolution? It remains one of the most important and unforgettable turning points in world history. It is my hope that its lessons, and those of the entire subsequent development of Russia, will serve the further cause of human progress. The lessons of October are highly instructive and should be absorbed and reflected upon for their genuine significance, not simply used to make a particular point. All who strive for the general good and wish peace and happiness for all humanity should reflect on those lessons and take them to heart.

Part Two

THE UNION COULD HAVE BEEN PRESERVED

In the first part of this book I have written about what perestroika brought to the citizens of the USSR.

Perestroika was unable to give all it might have because of the difficulties encountered in the course of the reforms themselves. And of course, by December 1991, perestroika was scuttled and the Soviet Union was dissolved.

How was all this possible? How did it come about? In this part of the book I will try to answer these questions, which are of interest to many people.

CHAPTER 9

A Tragic Turn of Events

OUTSIDE THE SOVIET UNION, as both researchers and political leaders now acknowledge, no one foresaw the dissolution of the Soviet Union. And judging by all the evidence, no one other than rabid anti-Communists favored such an outcome. This dire turn of events shook the whole world.

How do I evaluate these events today? The same way I did six or seven years ago. It truly was a tragedy—a tragedy for the majority of Soviet citizens and for the republics that were part of the Soviet Union. Back then, I could not agree with the dismemberment of our country, the breaking apart of the Soviet state, and today I still consider this to have been a most flagrant error. The Union could have been preserved. A considerable number, and in some respects the overwhelming majority, of difficulties encountered by the peoples of the former Soviet Union, including the Russian people, are the result of the disintegration of the state we had in common, the destruction of a single economic, political, legal, scientific, informational, and military-strategic space that had been formed over centuries.

The dissolution of the Union radically changed the situation in Europe and the world, disrupted the geopolitical balance, and undermined the possibility of carrying further many positive processes that were under way in world politics by the end of 1991. I am convinced that the world today would be living more peacefully if the Soviet Union—of course in a renewed and reformed version—had continued to exist.

What was it that led to this deplorable finale? After all, the Soviet Union seemed to be such a giant block of stone, such a vast and powerful state, uniting people of more than a hundred different nationalities. Or did it perhaps only seem that way?

No, it was not just a false appearance. The Soviet Union really was a strong and solid multinational state. Its dissolution was by no means inevitable. At times the USSR has been called—and some still call it—an empire. But it was not an empire in the generally accepted meaning of the term.

The Soviet Union was a country that was formed historically over many centuries. In the course of its formation all sorts of events took place; for example, there were cases in which one or another territory or people voluntarily unified with Russia, and times when the tsarist government fought wars of conquest. There was collaboration among different nationalities in pursuit of mutual advantage, and there were injustices and the use of force. History is like that. The result of all this was a state that was an organic whole—of course with a tremendous range of unique qualities among its various components. It traveled a long road—and naturally there were serious difficulties, stormy turns of events, even tragedies. Yet this state withstood the test of the Great Patriotic War. Even in that tragic hour it did not fall apart, but stood its ground.

Were there problems in the Soviet Union, including ethnic problems? Yes, there were political, economic, and social problems—and problems between nationalities. *These were not, however, problems of our country as a whole but of the system that had been established.* This administrative-bureaucratic system, this totalitarian system, could not respond adequately to the problems that had built up. Not only did it fail to contribute to their solution; it deepened and intensified them. As a result, by the 1980s our country had entered a stage of severe crisis. It was in order to overcome this crisis that perestroika was begun.

Among the problems that existed in our country were those involving the various nationalities. I know this quite well from my own experience, because for many years I was in charge of one of the largest regions of the Soviet Union, the Stavropol region. I understood that relations among people of different nationalities and their common existence was an inseparable part of the real life of our society. I was aware of how important it was to adopt a cautious and sensitive attitude toward this delicate matter.

In the beginning, after the 1917 revolution, Lenin insisted on recognition of the principle that nations have the right of self-determination, up to and including secession, and he asserted the need to construct a federation of equal republics as a means of maintaining the integrity of the multinational state. It was on this basis that the USSR was founded in 1922, although events did not proceed without a certain use of force.

Stalin, during the years of his rule, drastically departed from this course. The Soviet Union was turned into a supercentralized unitary state. Within this framework, the central government, the so-called Center—that is, essentially, the party—did as it pleased. Borders were carved out arbitrarily, the rights of one or another nationality were flagrantly violated, and during and immediately after World War II many nationalities were subjected to wholesale repression. They were deported from their ancient homelands and resettled in remote parts of the country. Tens of thousands of these people perished in the process. Even under these conditions, however, closer ties and joint efforts among the various nationalities in the Soviet Union allowed all of them to accelerate their development sharply. National cultures flourished in all the republics, and each nationality developed its own working class and intelligentsia. The different nations and nationalities grew stronger, and each acquired an increasingly profound sense of its own identity.

In other words, contradictory processes were at work. These developments required attention and appropriate responses on the part of the Center. But that did not happen. Severe problems accumulated and were not resolved. Why did this happen? The official conception was that relations among the nationalities in our country were in sufficiently good shape, that in general there were no serious problems. The mistakes made in the realm of relations among nationalities remained in the shadows, and discussion of them was unacceptable.

When perestroika began we could not avoid paying attention to this extremely important area in the life of our society. That is why, at the Twenty-eighth Party Congress, which formulated a platform for the period ahead, one point was especially emphasized: "Our achievements should not give the impression that there is no problem regarding national processes. Contradictions are inherent in all processes of development, and they are inevitable in this sphere as well. What is important is to see all facets of these contradictions, which are constantly emerging, to search for reliable answers to life's continuing questions, and to provide those answers in a timely way."

The approach taken by this congress was correct and timely. Still, we suffered many setbacks in trying to resolve the national question. For one thing, we were late in dealing with this question; for another, we made some wrong decisions. No wonder. We were moving away from traditional attitudes and heading toward a policy aimed at transforming the bureaucratic, unitary Soviet Union into a democratic federation of independent states.

Meanwhile, the course of events, life itself, made it clear that nationality problems had to be resolved. The first wake-up call came with clashes that occurred as early as March-April 1986 between groups of Russian youths and Yakut students at the state university in Yakutia. Then in December 1986 there were mass disturbances on the streets of Alma-Ata, related to a change of leadership in Kazakhstan, whose capital is Alma-Ata. A conflict had broken out among local clans. The tense situation had to be defused. And this could be done only by someone who was not linked with any of the local clans. So the proposal was made to replace D. Kunaev, the former first secretary of the Central Committee of Kazakhstan and an ethnic Kazakh, with G. V. Kolbin, an ethnic Russian (who, incidentally, was nominated by Kunaev himself). Kolbin had experience working in the non-Russian republic of Georgia. It was thought that this would take the heat out of the conflict, especially since there were many Russians, Ukrainians, Germans, and representatives of other nationalities living in Kazakhstan. It was a blunder. The appointment of Kolbin was taken as a sign of disrespect and distrust of the Kazakh people. Crowds protested on the streets of the capital and other cities of Kazakhstan.

How did we react to this significant sign that all was not well in relations among the nationalities? I must confess that we reacted in the same old way, and if anyone reproaches me for lack of decisiveness, he should know that I regret the decisiveness that I showed during the Kazakh events of 1986. [We resolutely insisted on Kolbin replacing Kunaev.] Unfortunately this was not the only case. Only later did I understand that this was not the way to proceed, that we could not live by a double standard—[calling for democracy, while imposing solutions "decisively."]

The resolution the Politburo adopted at that time was aimed not so much at discovering the cause of what had happened or drawing lessons from the events as to teach a lesson to Kazakhstan as well as to others. We were guided by conceptions formed much earlier, the notion that everything was flowing smoothly in the channel of unity and friendship and that outbreaks of nationalism represented the only danger.

Later, much later in fact, both the decision of our Central Committee's Secretariat regarding Yakutia and the Politburo resolution on Kazakhstan were withdrawn. But what had happened made me think seriously about the nationalities questions. At the January 1987 Plenum of our Central Committee I spoke about the conclusions I had reached as a result of my first reflections on the problem:

We are obliged to acknowledge the real situation and the real prospects for development in national relations. Today, when democracy and self-government are expanding, when there is a rapid growth in national self-consciousness among all nations and nationalities, when processes of internationalization are being intensified, the timely and just resolution of conflicts that arise acquires great importance—and there is only one possible basis for resolving these conflicts: The interests of each nation and nationality must be able to flourish, as must the interests of our society as a whole. . . . The events in Alma-Ata, and all that preceded those events, require serious analysis and assessment on the basis of principle.

In mid-February 1987 I traveled to Latvia and Estonia. Once again I felt the great intensity of the national question. In the middle of that same year we encountered the problem of the Crimean Tatars, one of the nationalities that had been forcibly removed at the end of World War II to settlements that were run like concentration camps in the Urals, Siberia, and Central Asia. Ever since the 1960s the Crimean Tatars had been demanding justice and the right to return to their homeland in Crimea. With the coming of perestroika they sensed it was possible to have their national dignity fully restored, in deeds and not just in words. In July 1987 the Crimean Tatar protests became intense. For three days they demonstrated without interruption by the walls of the Kremlin, shouting the slogan "Homeland or Death." On July 9, 1987, the problem of the Crimean Tatars was discussed at a session of the Politburo. Rather than paraphrase the contents of the discussion, let me quote a section of the record:

GORBACHEV: Up to this time there has been a derogatory label circulating among us [referring to the Crimean Tatars]—traitors during the Great Patriotic War. But where were there not traitors? What about the Vlasovites [soldiers of Russian nationality who fought on Hitler's side]?

LUKYANOV: There was a Tatar division in the Wehrmacht.

GORBACHEV: Well, there was a Kalmyk division also. They operated in the Stavropol region. But we still restored the Kalmyk autonomous republic. Was there something exceptional in the behavior of the Tatars? It is true that some of them collaborated with the Germans, but others fought the Germans, just as the rest of us did. Over a period of forty-four years, 250 volumes of signatures and statements have accumulated calling for justice to be restored. Today, according to the census, there are 132,000 Crimean Tatars, but in fact there are 350,000. Can't better arrangements be made for them in Uzbekistan? What is your opinion?

The question is addressed to CHEBRIKOV *[head of state security].*

CHEBRIKOV: (states that they have had to confront this problem for twenty years, then continues): It seems likely that it will be necessary to organize an autonomous district in the Crimea. Otherwise we will keep coming back to this question again and again. But Shcherbitsky [head of the Ukrainian Republic, in which the Crimea is located] is opposed.

GORBACHEV: That is also democracy.

CHEBRIKOV: And how shall we deal with the question of the southern coast of the Crimea?* The Tatars will return and say, "This is my house, give it back." At the same time we have to solve the problem of the Germans. There are two million of them.** We can't get away from having to solve this problem no matter how long we postpone it. These problems have come to a head.

SOLOMENTSEV: Yes, although the problem is not simple, it must be solved. And it must be solved at the same time that we solve the problem of the Volga Germans. We have acknowledged that their deportation was unjustified. And we returned the Ingush, the Kalmyks, and the Karachai [other nationalities deported during or just after World War II]. . . . Almost all [deported nationalities] have been returned to their homelands. But not the Volga Germans and not the Crimean Tatars. I am not in favor of an autonomous district, however. The national composition of the population in the Crimea has changed greatly. Before the war Ukrainians comprised 15 percent; now they account for 26 percent. Russians comprised 49 percent; now they account for 68 percent. . . . An autonomous district would be a mongrel solution. Maybe I'm a maximalist, but we have a good decree signed by Lenin in his day. Since we are seeking to live according to Lenin, we could base our actions on his decree. It would be difficult for anyone to take offense against it. Neither Russians nor Ukrainians. The nationalities would learn to get used to living with one another.

---

*The Crimea's southern coast is a beach and resort area, a highly prized location.—Trans.

**These are descendants of German colonists invited to settle mainly in the Volga region in the eighteenth century. During World War II they were deported from the autonomous area created for them after the Soviet revolution.—Trans.

GORBACHEV: In other words, you think the Crimea should once again become part of the RSFSR (Russian Soviet Federated Socialist Republic), as in Lenin's decree? Don't you remember that Podgorny insisted that Krasnodar and the Kuban be given back to Ukraine? Because, in his opinion, the Cossacks were Ukrainians. Most likely from the historical point of view it would be correct to return the Crimea to Russia. But Ukraine would rise up against that.

VOROTNIKOV: This question should be postponed. There is a risk of creating one more enormous Ukrainian problem? I am in favor of an autonomous district, but for the time being it is necessary to create [better] conditions [for the Crimean Tatars] in Uzbekistan. I am against trying to solve the Volga German problem at the same time.

SHEVARDNADZE: I am in favor of creating [better] conditions in Uzbekistan and gradually allowing all who so desire, and are able, to move back to the Crimea.

YAKOVLEV: Set a fifteen to twenty year transitional period, for example, for returning to the Crimea. And for the time being, [have them remain] in Uzbekistan.

DOLGIKH: I support this position.

GROMYKO: Why are we being so hasty? No disaster has yet befallen us. So what if delegations are constantly traveling to visit the Presidium of the Supreme Soviet and other institutions? Let them travel. The decision to deport them was justified by wartime conditions. Transfer [of the Crimea from Russia] to Ukraine was of course arbitrary. But how can we take that back now? I am in favor of leaving the problem to the judgment of history. And don't create an autonomous district. Make arrangements for the Tatars in Uzbekistan. If this doesn't provide a complete solution, at least it will ease the pressure for a Crimean variant of the solution. Once again, I propose that we think about it and not make a final decision.

LUKYANOV speaks in favor of an autonomous district in the Crimea.

GORBACHEV: We cannot succeed in avoiding a decision. We must think everything through thoroughly. The idea of restoring a Crimean autonomous area, as in Lenin's decree, is unrealistic today. Over a period of forty-five years a great deal has changed in the Crimea. . . . It is no longer possible to give the Crimea to the Tatars. . . . Returning the Crimea to the RSFSR would create a fissure in a place where it would not at all suit our purposes now, that is, within the Slavic nucleus of the "socialist empire." Before the revolution, the strongest support for independence of the country was the Russian nation. Now it is all the others, too. It is necessary to create conditions for a full and satisfactory life for the Tatars in Uzbekistan and to be concerned and take care of them. Those who have already turned up in the Crimea, let them live there. They, too, must be given assistance. But steps must be taken to restrain resettlement to the Crimea. People should be urged to base their actions on reality.

A commission is created consisting of Gromyko, Shcherbitsky, Vorotnikov, Usmankhodzhaev, Demichev, Chebrikov, Lukyanov, Razumovsky, and Yakovlev.

GORBACHEV: For now we will not take up the Volga German problem. And if this commission shows its capabilities in resolving the Tatar question, we will assign it to the German question next. And let the commission go out to meet Tatar delegations and make statements for the press. In a word, we have to approach this process in a democratic spirit.

(Later, after the commission had worked for a while, a conclusion was reached jointly with the Ukrainian authorities: It was deemed possible to return some of the Tatars to their former places of residence. Thus a step was taken toward meeting the Tatars halfway, but the problem was not resolved. Later, in 1989, all the Crimean Tatars were given the right to return to the Crimea, but the commission reaffirmed the refusal to restore the Crimea to the status of an autonomous republic of the Crimean Tatars.)

I have cited the transcript of this Politburo discussion in order to show how we discussed such problems at that time. After mid-1987, the question of relations among the nationalities was practically always on the Politburo's agenda.

In August 1987 signs of intensifying national ferment in the Baltic republics became evident. Such ferment had always existed there, but earlier it had remained beneath the surface. The main cause was discontent over the Russification of the region. But there was no plan for dealing with this matter. Discussion of the question went nowhere. Besides, the local authorities themselves were seeking investments for industrial construction for which workers and specialists were needed. And since they did not exist locally, that meant more Russians would move to the area, and not only Russians. That's the way things were in real life.

Suppression of the real history of how the Baltic region was unified with the USSR played a considerable role in this whole problem. Demands that the truth be established and the actual history revealed began in 1987. At first it was only a question of restoring historical truth, but later demands were made that the situation existing before 1939 be restored. At the time we did not realize the full import of the processes that were taking place. We were late in responding adequately to what was happening.

In October 1987 there began a movement to reunify the Karabakh region with Armenia. A wave of public meetings and rallies swept across the region, and this provoked the emigration of Azerbaijanis from Karabakh. In response, a protest campaign developed in Azerbaijan with the slogan, "Karabakh is an inseparable part of Azerbaijan." In Karabakh, matters moved very quickly to the point of direct clashes between representatives of the two different national communities and a short while later to outright war between those communities and between the Armenian and Azerbaijan republics.

This forced the leadership of our country to view these national problems differently. At the February 1988 Central Committee Plenum the following statement was made: "We must examine the nationalities question at its present stage very thoroughly, both in theory and practice. This is a vital question of principle for our society."

On February 26, 1988, I appealed directly to the peoples of Azerbaijan and Armenia, urging the citizens of those republics to act only within a legal framework and within the boundaries of the democratic process, not to allow the question of their nations' fate to fall into the hands of blind passion and elemental emotions. But I did not succeed in stopping the mounting animosity. By the end of February, bloody conflict broke out, culminating in the massacre at Sumgait.

I remember well the intensity with which these events were discussed at the Politburo session of March 3. Summarizing the discussion, I urged everyone to remain calm and maintain a principled approach: "Don't make enemies out of people. . . . Function politically. Of course the government must be the government. Law must prevail." I also said that there could be no victors in this conflict, but that agreement must be reached. It was necessary at this time to affirm a carefully balanced, *political* approach to solving national problems.

Not only among ordinary citizens but in the Politburo as well, proposals were being made for the use of force. On July 4, 1987, Andrei Gromyko said: "Let the army appear in the streets, and immediately there will be order." We did not agree with this point of view. But it reemerged from time to time. Old ways of approaching things, attitudes that had been entrenched for decades, continued to make themselves felt.

Did we realize at the time that what was at issue was not so much resolving our most acute problems as changing our way of approaching them, working out policies that would be new in principle regarding the national question?

The answer is yes; by that time the idea that new policies were needed had matured in our thinking. At the February 1988 Central Committee Plenum I proposed that one of the next plenums be devoted entirely to problems of policy on the nationalities question.

Naturally the amount of attention we had to pay to national problems continued to mount. At the Nineteenth Party Conference I presented the Politburo's position: "Despite all the difficulties encountered along our way . . . the Soviet Union has withstood the test of time. It remains the decisive precondition for the further development of all the peoples of our country."

But matters were not limited to that statement. A program of practical measures was essentially formulated. We considered it of paramount importance to develop and implement measures on a large scale in order to strengthen our Union. We prepared proposals defining the jurisdiction of the Union and that of the Union republics, transferring a number of administrative functions to the republics, determining optimal variants for the possible transition of the republics and regions into self-financing entities, and developing direct ties among the republics so as to clearly specify how each might contribute in carrying out programs on the level of the Union as a whole.

Life confronted us with the need to make changes in the legislation concerning Union republics and autonomous republics, as well as autonomous regions and districts, and to expand legal guarantees to ensure that the national-cultural needs of the various national groups living outside their own territories would be met. A Unionwide law was urgently needed regarding the full development and equal use of the languages of all the peoples of the USSR. Thus we viewed the national question within the framework of the policies of perestroika as a whole. The orientation we adopted was, on the one hand, to respect the rights of the different nations and republics, ensuring them maximum satisfaction; on the other hand, we wished to strengthen the Union thoroughly and transform it into a genuine federation.

We had reached the next stage of political reform. And political methods for solving our persistent national problems had to be placed at the fore-front.

CHAPTER 10

Tbilisi . . . Baku . . . Vilnius

WERE WE SUCCESSFUL in keeping the course of events within this frame-work? After all, the events in Tbilisi and Baku, and then in Lithuania, did happen. I will go into each of those cases in some detail because a lot of non-sense has been stated and many false accusations made about these events.

First, Tbilisi. Beginning on April 4, 1989, several informal groups [groups not officially recognized] held unauthorized demonstrations for many days in front of the main government building with such slogans as "Independence for Georgia" and "Down with the Russian Empire." The local leaders, who considered political methods and direct discussion with the people to be manifestations of weakness (a typical attitude of many offi-cials of the old school), preferred to rely on force. On April 7 they proposed that a state of emergency be declared in Tbilisi. On that same day, a meet-ing at the Central Committee of the CPSU (involving Ligachev, Chebrikov, and others), decided that troops would be sent there. They were not sup-posed to be used; it was felt that, by itself, the appearance of soldiers would return the situation to normal.

On April 7 I was in London. Returning to Moscow late in the evening, I received information at the airport about what had happened. Taking into account all the facts that were known at the time, I immediately assigned Shevardnadze and Razumovsky, a secretary of the Central Committee, to go immediately to Georgia. On the morning of April 8 the Georgian lead-ership informed us that there was no need for representatives from Moscow to come immediately, that the situation had returned to normal. I think Dzhumber Patiashvili did not want Shevardnadze to come there, because his relations with Shevardnadze had been completely soured. On the night of April 9, troops were used to "clear" demonstrators from the central square. In the process sixteen people were killed and many were wounded.

But who gave the order to use force? This remains a mystery, which neither the Congress of People's Deputies nor numerous commissions investigating events in Tbilisi have been able to solve. I believe that the local military command in Georgia, entirely unsuspecting, was the victim of political intrigues. Apparently even at the time military operations were being influenced by those who later, in August 1991, set into motion the events that became known as the August coup. Recently General Rodionov [who was in charge of the troops that attacked the demonstrators in Tbilisi], in reply to a question from a journalist, said he was authorized to take action by Marshall Yazov, who was then the minister of defense. This confirms our suspicions. Rodionov assumed that Yazov's orders had the approval of the top leadership of the Soviet Union.

This was a cruel stab in the back. Speaking on radio and television immediately after the events, I stated:

What happened in Tbilisi undeniably is harmful to the interests of perestroika, democratization, and the renewal of our country. Decisions and actions by irresponsible persons have resulted in increased tensions in the Georgian republic. Anti-Soviet slogans are being heard, along with demands that socialist Georgia be broken away from the fraternal family of Soviet peoples. False orientations have led some people astray. Disturbances have broken out. People have been killed and innocent blood has been shed. The grief of the mothers and family members is immense, and the grief we feel is very deep.

A few days later, after Shevardnadze actually visited Georgia, a meeting of the Politburo sharply condemned the military action. By way of illustration, I will quote the words of Nikolai Ryzhkov, prime minister at the time, spoken at the Politburo meeting:

We were in Moscow during those days, so what did we know? I am the head of the government, but what did I know? I read in *Pravda* about the death of people in Tbilisi. The secretaries of the Central Committee knew, but we, the members of the Politburo and the Cabinet, knew nothing . . . We must have timely and accurate information. What's the good of all this? What is going on here? The commander of the military district takes action, but we in Moscow know nothing about it. He could arrest all the Politburo members [of the Communist Party] of Georgia, and we again would learn about it in the newspapers. Even Mikhail Sergeyevich Gorbachev did not know. So, then, what is going on among us? The army is used and the general secretary only finds out about it the next day. How are we going to appear to the Soviet public and in the eyes of world opinion? Everywhere you look in our country, actions are being taken without the Politburo's knowledge. That is even worse than the Politburo itself making a wrong decision.

Ryzhkov was right.

At this same Politburo meeting I was obliged, in rather sharp form, to raise the question of accuracy and truthfulness of information and to point out that the agencies providing information must approach the question with full responsibility. Of course I also raised the question of the army's role. I said to Defense Minister Yazov: From then on, the army was not to take part in such matters without the permission of the country's top leadership.

After the events in Tbilisi, the Politburo authorized army action only once—to avoid mass disturbances and bloodletting in Baku. This was related to a further worsening of relations between Armenians and Azerbaijanis in early 1990, resulting in pogroms against Armenians in Baku and to an "exodus" of Armenians from that city. The local authorities sought to restore order. But internal quarreling and divisions paralyzed their ability to act and to maintain control of the situation. Disturbances spread to a large part of the Azerbaijani republic, and destructive elements encouraged people to destroy the boundary lines [along the Azerbaijani border] over a distance of several hundred kilometers.

Representatives of the top Soviet leadership were sent to Baku—Yevgeny Primakov, a member of the President's Council, and A. Girenko, a secretary of the Central Committee of the CPSU. They reported that the situation was critical. On January 19 two documents were published simultaneously—an appeal to the peoples of Azerbaijan and Armenia from the CPSU Central Committee, the Presidium of the Supreme Soviet, and the USSR Council of Ministers; also published was a decree announcing a state of emergency in Baku, issued by the Presidium of the USSR Supreme Soviet. Late in the night of January 19 and the early hours of January 20 troops from the Ministry of the Interior and the Soviet Army entered Baku. All possible forms of provocation and obstacles were placed in their path as these troops moved forward. Gunmen of the Azerbaijani National Front opened fire on our military personnel, and our military units were obliged to respond in kind. As a result, on January 19-20, eighty-three people were killed in Baku, including fourteen military personnel and members of their families.

On January 20 I appeared on central television to give an assessment of the situation and to explain the actions of the leadership. I said that the leadership hoped that the measures taken would be understood and supported by all the nations and nationalities of our country.

But those events and the measures taken were interpreted in varying ways (and that is still true today). Some said that once again we were late in taking action and that a state of emergency should have been imposed sooner. However, the authorities of the Soviet Union could not, according to the Constitution of the USSR, take action over the heads of the leaders of the Azerbaijani republic. The central government intervened directly only when it became clear that the authorities on the republic level were paralyzed and unable to act.

Others have simply reproached or denounced us for imposing a state of emergency. There is only one answer to such accusations: If measures had not been taken, events might have followed a totally unpredictable course. I regret that blood was spilled, but the purpose was to stop further bloodshed at all costs.

I have long reflected on what happened. The lesson I have drawn from this whole tragic history is that the authorities cannot get by without using force in extreme situations. But such actions must be justified by absolute necessity and must be kept within very carefully weighed limits. Only political measures can provide a genuine solution to such problems.

Finally there was Vilnius, in Lithuania. This time it was 1991, and again it was January. I have said that the situation in the Baltic region, above all, in Lithuania, began to worsen from mid-1987 on. But in mid-1989 matters began to deteriorate with particular speed after the Sajudis organization in fact came to power in the Lithuanian republic. Let me remind readers that at first Sajudis was an organization that supported perestroika and defended it against conservative elements. Later it gradually became a stronghold for those forces that favored secession from the USSR. I personally, and many of my colleagues, put a great deal of effort into trying to defuse the sentiment in favor of separation, but our efforts were unsuccessful.

What arguments did the advocates of secession advance? On the one hand, they sounded the alarm about alleged domination by the Russian part of the population. This was an obvious exaggeration. The Russians accounted for only one-fifth of the population in Lithuania. But warnings that Lithuanians could ultimately become a minority within their own republic had an effect on many people.

Another argument was more practical in nature. Those favoring separation claimed that Lithuania, because of its excellent agricultural production, was supplying much of the food for Moscow and Leningrad. Yet the Lithuanian republic itself was suffering shortages of meat. This was true—or, more exactly, partly true. Nothing was said about the enormous quantity of goods supplied to Lithuania from other Soviet republics, primarily Russia, including grain, oil, metals, industrial goods, and consumer goods—or else the significance of those supplies was minimized. Nothing was said about the preferential treatment of Lithuania and all the Baltic republics out of political considerations. Owing to this preferential treatment (and of course to the higher productivity of labor there) the standard of living in Lithuania was higher than the average standard in the Soviet Union, but no one seemed to think about that. These half-truths had their effect: Not only Lithuanians but people of other nationalities began to think, "If we separate from Moscow, our lives will become better."

In any case, the situation gradually became hotter and hotter. On May 11, 1989, the Politburo discussed the situation in the three Baltic republics. The leaders of the Communist parties of those three republics took part in the meeting. During the discussion, especially after the secretaries of the Baltic Communist parties had left, different views were heard concerning what should be done. It was obvious that some participants at the meeting were not averse to applying pressure. In my concluding remarks, I said:

> Let us take as our starting point the idea that all is not lost. We also must be cautious in our assessments so as not to reach a point of desperation or of breaking off relations. . . . We cannot dismiss as extremists the various national fronts, which have the support of 90 percent of the people in those republics. We must be able to talk with them. . . . We must have confidence in the people's good sense. . . . We must not be afraid of experiments allowing republics to become fully self-financing entities. . . . We must not be afraid of differentiation among republics in terms of the level at which they exercise their sovereignty. . . . In general, we must think, and think hard, about how in fact to transform our federation. Otherwise everything will indeed fall apart. . . . The use of force is excluded. It has been ruled out in foreign policy and is absolutely inadmissible against our own people. . . . Let us take our analysis of what is going on to a higher level. . . . And we must

be more cautious than ever with any final qualifications or use of labels. After all, this is *the national question*.

At the First Congress of People's Deputies (May 25-June 9, 1989) the full range of national problems in the Soviet Union was posed for discussion and consideration in the broadest sense. The report I presented to the congress defined key aspects of nationalities policy under perestroika:

In a federated state, that which falls within the competence of the Union as a whole and that which is the sovereign right of the republic or autonomous entity should be clearly defined. Legal mechanisms need to be worked out for resolving conflicts that may arise in the relations between the Union and its component parts.

In the economic field, relations between the Union and the republics must be harmonized on the basis of an organic combination of economic independence and active participation in the Unionwide division of labor. From this standpoint, it follows that we need a restructuring of the way the unified economic complex of the country is regulated, by allowing republics, regions, and provinces to make the transition to a self-governing and self-financing basis as an organic part of the overall process of renewing the Soviet economy.

. . . *In the spiritual realm*, we take as our starting point a recognition of the multiplicity and diversity of national cultures as a great social and historical value and a unique advantage belonging to our Union as a whole. We do not have the right to underestimate, still less to entirely lose, any one of these cultures, because each is irreplaceable.

We are in favor of the full and rounded development of each nationality, national language, and culture and for equal rights and friendly relations among all nations, nationalities, and national groups.

The congress supported what I proposed as a basis for action. During 1989 and 1990 a great deal was done to put into practice the policy line I had projected. Several laws were adopted, for example, one on general principles of local self-government and the local economy in the USSR, which expanded the rights and powers of union republics and autonomous republics; a second on the languages of the peoples of the USSR, which set forth guarantees for their development and utilization; a third demarcating the respective powers of the Union of Soviet Socialist Republics and the component parts of the federation; as well as others.

As for the Baltic republics, they were granted broad rights in the economic realm by a special law passed by the second session of the Supreme Soviet of the USSR, rights that were extended to Byelorussia and Sverdlovsk Province as well.

In September 1989 a plenum of the Central Committee adopted, as the official position of the CPSU, a document entitled "The Nationalities Policy of the Party in Present-Day Conditions." This document formulated the main tasks we faced, and these are summarized as follows:

- transforming the Soviet federation into a genuine political and economic entity;
- enlarging the rights and powers of autonomous national entities of all forms and types;
- ensuring equal rights to every nationality;
- creating conditions for free development of national cultures and languages;
- strengthening guarantees that would rule out any restriction on the rights of citizens for reasons of nationality.

Thus, although belatedly, we formulated a principled political platform on the national question. This platform made it possible to resolve the accumulated problems. In the Baltic region, however, those who had made up their mind in favor of secession from the Soviet Union intensified their activity. Members of our party's leadership, including myself, met many times with representatives of the three republics, separately and together. I emphasized that the right to self-determination, up to and including separation, is an inseparable sovereign right embodied in the then operative Soviet Constitution. But I tried to convince people that secession would contradict the real needs of the nationalities of our Union. Decentralization, autonomy, a redistribution of powers—yes—but with the maintenance of cooperation and coordination. It made no sense to criticize the idea of a federation. We had never had such a system. We had lived in a unitary state. Let us first try living under a genuinely federated arrangement, I argued, and then decide what to do. The positive experience of federated states in other parts of the world was there for us to see.

On January 29, 1990, the Politburo considered several draft laws and amendments to the Soviet Constitution having to do with the national question.

On April 3, 1990, a law on secession from the Union was adopted. However, on the eve of its adoption the new leadership in Lithuania demonstratively declared that republic's independence. On March 22, during a discussion in the Politburo about the situation that had thus arisen, General Varennikov proposed that a state of emergency be proclaimed, that presidential rule be imposed, that troops be sent in, that the leaders of the Lithuanian republic be "isolated," and that all this be carried out under the pretext of an appeal from "patriotic forces." Naturally the Politburo refused to consider this "proposal." But the very fact that he made it was symptomatic of the mood in certain Soviet military circles, and not only in the military.

I presented my position publicly in a discussion with delegates to the Twenty-first Congress of the Young Communist League (the Komsomol):

> To be sure there is the constitutional right to self-determination. A law has now been adopted on the procedure for solving problems associated with the secession of a republic from the USSR, so let us begin the 'process of divorce,' but for them, that is, the Lithuanians, to adopt a decision overnight without consulting the people, without any referendum—that is an adventure.
>
> As the saying goes, you can't force someone to like you. Granted there is a desire to leave—but we must first tell the Lithuanian people what the consequences will be—these will be territorial, economic, defense-related, and will impact the arrangements for those who do not wish to remain in a separate state. That is one option. Here is another: If the republic remains in the Soviet Union, [we need to specify] what rights and powers it will have—political, economic, cultural-technical, and so forth, and what freedom and autonomy it will enjoy. In that case, the Lithuanian people, who are a wise people, will figure out for themselves that what Lithuania needs is autonomy within the framework of ongoing vital links with all the other republics.

I wish to remind readers that all these events were unfolding at a time when political reform was deepening in our country. The Congress of People's Deputies had been operating for a year by then, as had the Supreme Soviet elected by that congress. Free elections had also been held for government bodies in the Union republics and bodies of local self-government. A political struggle was mounting—a so-called radical wing had taken shape among the democrats and, in opposition to it, a no less radical wing of so-called patriots had been formed. Events in the Baltic region provoked strong reactions on both sides. The entire country was seized by a sense of alarm.

When I was in the city of Sverdlovsk at that time, I had occasion to answer numerous questions on this matter. The following is just one of my replies:

> We are encountering increasing strain in relations among nationalities, greater conflicts. Some say, Let this "empire" fall apart; others say, What are Gorbachev and the other leaders thinking about? They should have restored order and put everyone back in their place long ago. Neither of these two approaches is consistent with serious politics. As a Russian, as a Soviet citizen, and as a political leader, I cannot accept such extreme ways of approaching these questions. . . . Let us reorganize our federation and think about renewing the Union of Soviet Socialist Republics. Everything that contributes to carrying out the idea of renewal corresponds to the interests of Russians and of all other nationalities in our country. That we must take as our starting point.

In late April 1990 signals began to come from the Lithuanian leadership indicating a willingness to enter into a dialogue with representatives of the central government, suggesting that the decisions made by the Supreme Soviet of Lithuania could be considered a subject for discussion. Lithuania would not object to an interpretation of its declaration of independence as a document in which the status of the republic could be considered as "an associated member of a renewed, reorganized Soviet Union." The implementation of this kind of approach would have to be the result of a step-by-step process involving consultation and coordination with the central government of the Union. This was a basis on which to search for a practical solution.

This little-known fact tells us that at the time there was indeed a possibility for a political solution that would not have undermined the idea of renewing the Soviet Union. What prevented us, then, from reaching an accord? A new situation arose that radically changed the entire atmosphere—above all, in matters having to do with nationalities.

On June 12, 1990, the Supreme Soviet of Russia adopted a declaration on the state sovereignty of the RFSFR. In the wake of that action similar declarations were adopted by other republics, not only Union republics but also autonomous republics. The "parade of sovereignties" began. The search for ways of coming to an agreement with Lithuania was consequently frustrated and made impossible.

The declaration of sovereignty by Russia, as is well known, had even more far-reaching consequences. Not only was agreement with Lithuania undermined. Essentially the events of the summer of 1990, with the Russian declaration of sovereignty as the fuse, ignited a process that eventually led to the dissolution of the Soviet Union. That, if you will, was the prime cause of its dissolution. I will return to this point below.

At the end of 1990 the authorities in Vilnius continued to function according to the letter and spirit of their declaration of independence, and this led to a significant internal struggle within that republic. Those opposed to secession from the Soviet Union created their own organizations. The Communist Party of Lithuania broke apart at that time, and its fragments scattered in different directions. One element supported independence; another opposed it and acted, moreover, in an extremely radical way, sometimes in violation of the law. This segment of the former Communist Party of Lithuania began systematically to request that the central government impose a state of emergency, place Lithuania under rule by presidential decree, and so on. These demands, in fact, were met with sympathy and support on the part of certain forces in Moscow, forces exerting similar pressures (for example, as mentioned above, General Varennikov's statement in the Politburo meeting). In December 1990 and January 1991 these forces in Vilnius and Moscow were in fact coordinating their actions.

Even so, I felt, as before, that I did not have the right to take extreme measures. On January 10, 1991, I appealed to the Supreme Soviet of the Lithuanian republic and called for full and immediate restoration of the Soviet Constitution since the situation was becoming explosive. The Lithuanian authorities did not respond. As a result, those who demanded that Lithuania remain within the framework of the USSR sharply increased their activities and created a Committee for National Salvation. Anticonstitutional activities by some had called forth anticonstitutional activities by others. The struggle had passed from the channel of constitutional procedures and was flowing into the path of direct confrontation.

Yazov, Kryuchkov, and Pugo [ministers of defense, state security, and the interior, respectively] reported to me that they had taken measures in case the situation grew out of control and direct clashes began between supporters of Sajudis and the Communists, necessitating rule by presidential decree. That was the only factor considered, nothing else—just the need to act in the event of bloodshed. After arriving in Vilnius, General Varennikov reported that the situation was dangerous, and he again proposed imposing rule by presidential decree.

Under these conditions, one more attempt was made at a political solution. On January 12 the Council of the Federation discussed the situation in Lithuania. I stated that we were one step away from bloodshed and proposed that representatives of the Council of the Federation be sent to Vilnius immediately to investigate on the spot and suggest possible action. But before the delegation even arrived in Vilnius, the tragedy occurred. I demanded explanations from Kryuchkov, Pugo, and Yazov: How could this have happened, and who gave the order for the use of troops? All three denied any involvement in these events.

To this day all the details of what happened in Vilnius (and then in Riga) are not known, but as time passes, more and more facts are being disclosed. After I had ceased to function as president of the USSR I received information lifting the curtain a bit on the events of January 13, 1990, in the capital of Lithuania. Ultimately, without question, we will know exactly who gave the order for the troops to act, who led the entire "operation," and how they went about it.

In a speech on January 22, 1990, I said the following: "The events that occurred in Vilnius are in no way an expression of the policy line of the president; it was not for this that presidential power was established. I therefore emphatically reject all speculation, all suspicions, and all insinuations in this regard." The declaration stated firmly that any social organizations, committees, and fronts can aspire to come to power only by constitutional means and without the use of force. All attempts to resort to armed force in political struggle are unacceptable. Arbitrary actions on the part of the armed forces are equally unacceptable.

It is evident from the above discussion that these three crises—in Tbilisi, Baku, and Vilnius—were quite different in character. Only in Baku was the use of troops the result of a decision by the central government. The actions in the other two cases were totally opposed to the policy line of our country's leadership, which was oriented toward a peaceful, political resolution of the situations that had developed.

Toward a New Union Treaty

THE QUESTION OF drafting and signing a new Union treaty arose in the course of preparations for a plenum of the CPSU Central Committee on the nationalities question, although the problem of the renewal of our federation, as I have said, had come up earlier. Indeed the time was ripe to begin work on establishing a legal basis for the reformation of the Union, that is, the drafting of a new Union treaty. For our part, having formulated this idea in September 1989, we had actually begun practical consultations on such a treaty much earlier.

The platform of the CPSU Central Committee, drafted for the Twenty-eighth Party Congress, entitled "Toward a Humane and Democratic Socialism," which was approved by the February 1990 Central Committee plenum, stated: "The CPSU considers further development of the treaty principle in restructuring the Soviet Union to be necessary. . . . The Union republics, while voluntarily transferring strictly defined functions to the competence of the Union [in a Union treaty], will reinforce their status as *sovereign states*, assuring them constitutional guarantees."

This general position had not yet been "fleshed out" with an appropriately detailed elaboration. Discussions continued on what the actual content of the Union treaty should be. The following is an excerpt from the transcript of the Politburo meeting of March 1, 1990:

GORBACHEV: We have to examine and truly understand the conception of a federation. We cannot limit ourselves to expressing condemnation and feeling offended. Some people even suggest expulsion from the USSR. Public opinion has shifted in attitude from emotional reactions to arguments like the following: Why do we need such a huge Union? Russia and Ukraine together already have 200 million people. Then add Kazakhstan, where half the people are Russian. Well, maybe tack on Uzbekistan, too. But as for the rest of them, let them leave the Soviet Union.

That is why we must keep the initiative in our own hands. I repeat, we need a clear conception. And that conception is the renewal of the Union on the basis of a treaty. From discussions with representatives from the Baltic region, from Georgia, and from other republics, I see that they are all thinking about a new conception of the Union in their republics. Yet we keep insisting on the old formula. We need to draft a Union treaty and publish it, and it must be thoroughly discussed, without haste, in the press and in society—everywhere. Particularly so that everyone will see what the various nations would risk if they withdraw from the Union. Of course we cannot fall into the old [tsarist] slogan "One and Indivisible." [The old slogan of tsarist Russia had been "Russia, One and Indivisible."] But the question must be posed in such a way as to neutralize the desire to leave the Union. It is possible to have a federation with the different republics having different status; consequently different relations will result between the republics and the Center. After all, even in the Russian empire the status of different parts of the empire varied. There was the Grand Duchy of Finland, the Kingdom of Poland, the Khanate of Bukhara, and so on.

RYZHKOV supports the idea of a discussion of a draft treaty with the aim of, and within the framework of, drafting a new constitution. LIGACHEV sharply asserts that internationalism is being forgotten.

GORBACHEV (continues): If we do not examine and come to understand the idea of a federation, turmoil will continue. All that we are doing will be affected. We can't just "keep them in check." We must act very carefully to establish a procedure; otherwise we could end up defending ourselves against our own most ardent supporters, those who are in favor of a federation 1,000 percent.

How can we build a bridge? The starting point is the idea of the federation. Despite what the variations or various steps may be, going in one or another direction, still the pivotal point is the idea of a federation.

Two weeks later, at the Third Congress of People's Deputies, I was elected president of the USSR. In my first speech in this new position I immediately placed the accent on the problem of a Union treaty:

The fate of perestroika to a large degree will be determined by how successful we are in carrying out the transformation to a new federation. As president, I reaffirm my commitment to maintaining our country's integrity. At the same time I proceed from the idea that it must be an object of special concern by the president's office to take measures to strengthen the sovereignty of the Union republics, their economic and political autonomy, and to raise the status of the autonomous republics and other national-territorial entities.

While I share the opinions stated here on these questions, I consider it vitally urgent that a new Union treaty be drafted, one that will correspond to the new realities and requirements in the development of our federation and of each Soviet nation. In this process we should provide for differentiation in the various forms of federative relationships, taking into account the unique conditions and potential of each republic.

In other words, a very definite course was publicly presented for consideration by our country's highest governing authority. In that same speech, taking into account the situation in the Caucasus (the continuing conflict between Armenia and Azerbaijan), as well that in the Baltic region, and the spread of separatism and anti-Soviet sentiments in other regions of various republics, I found it necessary to focus on certain specific problems. The drafting and signing of a new Union treaty would contribute to overcoming those difficulties.

And I continued my address:

Emergency measures are needed to resolve the especially painful problems arising from quarrels or feuding among nationalities, above all, the problem of refugees. In this regard, measures must be taken by the governments of the appropriate Union republics and, when necessary, by the Union government itself.

In general, we have the right today to propose the following: The Union republics, while strengthening their sovereignty and acquiring broad autonomy, must also take full responsibility for ensuring civil rights for people of all nationalities on their territory—in accordance with both Soviet and international norms. This is a political, legal, and material responsibility.

In recent times the danger of the spread of nationalist, chauvinist, and even racist slogans has arisen. We must fight relentlessly against this, using the full force of the constitution and the laws of the land.

On June 12, 1990, a session of the Council of the Federation was held. This was a new body established (along with the President's Council) at the same time that the office of the president of the USSR was initiated. The leaders of all the Union republics belonged to this Council of the Federation. The June 12 session was devoted to problems concerning the structures of national governments and the Union treaty. The agreement was that we should establish a working group consisting of representatives of all the republics. *The Council of the Federation expressed itself in favor of establishing a Union of sovereign states*, with the possible combination of elements of a federation, a confederation, and a commonwealth.

Explaining the motivation for this decision to the delegates at the Twenty-eighth CPSU Congress, I said the following:

> Everything we have lived through and become aware of in the recent past has led us to understand that the transformation of the Union cannot be limited simply to an expansion, however significant, of the rights of the republics and autonomous entities. *A genuine Union of sovereign states is necessary*. We are talking essentially about the establishment of a national-governmental structure for our country of a kind that would allow various knots of contradictions to be untied, for cooperation among Soviet nations and nationalities to be raised to a new level, and for the totality of our united political strength and economic and spiritual potential to be multiplied in the interests of all who have joined this great Union of states. By the same token, our country's security will be reliably ensured and its international prestige heightened.
>
> At the same time there remains the requirement to give priority to human rights over any interests of national sovereignty or autonomy. This condition should be firmly embodied in the constitutional structure of the Union and of each republic. We cannot retreat a single step from this principle, by which we are also guided on the international level.

I have made these references to the Congress of People's Deputies of the USSR, to the Council of the Federation, and to the Twenty-eighth Party Congress especially to show that in the leadership of the CPSU there had developed an understanding not only of the necessity for reforming the Union but also a conception of how to carry out this task.

After that, the practical work began. On June 20 there took place the first meeting of working groups of representatives of the Union republics and the working group of the USSR Supreme Soviet and USSR Council of Ministers. This meeting was devoted to a discussion of approaches in drafting a new Union treaty. Later, additional meetings of working groups of the republics and a working group of the USSR Supreme Soviet were held. There were twelve such meetings from August 3 to August 28, 1990, the first between the working groups of the Supreme Soviets of the USSR and those of the RFSFR.

There was a special reason for beginning conversations with Russia: Boris Yeltsin, who had been elected to the post of chairman of the RFSFR Supreme Soviet, in his very first speeches at the Congress of People's Deputies, had called for a declaration of Russia's sovereignty. His understanding of Russia's sovereignty was quite unique: "The most important primary sovereignty in Russia is man and the rights of man. Then comes the enterprise, the collective farm, the state farm, and any other organization—that is where the primary and most powerful sovereignty should be. And of course the sovereignty of the district Soviet, just as with any other Soviet."

At this same Congress of People's Deputies, while supporting the desire to strengthen the sovereignty of each republic within the framework of a renewed Union, I noted: "Boris Nikolaevich [Yeltsin] asserts that sovereignty belongs to the individual and to the enterprise and the district Soviet. But I must tell you: This thesis has not been worked out either theoretically or politically. It is a highly dubious thesis, and he is carrying the question of sovereignty to the point of absurdity." Even then I understood that all these actions of our new Russian government would encourage separatism within the Russian Federation itself and would cause the nationalities of that republic to clash.

But Yeltsin did not limit himself to what he said in Moscow. On a trip around the country he continued to "deepen" these ideas. In Tatarstan he said: "Whatever kind of autonomy Tataria chooses for itself—no matter what it is—we will welcome it." In Bashkiria he said: "Take whatever share of power you are able to swallow." Sure enough, later, when the Chechen republic demanded the sovereignty it had decided on and declared its independence, a war began.

But it was not just a matter of how sovereignty should be understood within Russia, although that was quite a dangerous question, as has now become quite clear. The problem was how Yeltsin understood the sovereignty of Russia within the Soviet Union. Immediately after his election as chairman of the RFSFR Supreme Soviet, he stated: "Based on the declaration of sovereignty that will be adopted and on the necessary laws, Russia will be autonomous in all things and its decisions must be higher than those of the Union." This statement was as irresponsible as it was illiterate. In practice it meant that Russia would pay no attention to the Union or to the Union government and was not about to carry out decisions made on the basis of the federation as a whole.

Russia's actions resulted in an avalanche of sovereignty declarations by all the Union republics and by many autonomous republics—the so-called parade of sovereignties—and prevented a constructive dialogue with Lithuania. In fact those actions laid the basis for the dissolution of the Soviet Union.

Thus all the arguments claiming that the national conflicts in the Baltic region, the Caucasus, and Central Asia triggered the dissolution of the Soviet Union are nothing but attempts to justify, after the fact, Yeltsin's irresponsible actions, and those of the organization Democratic Russia, in causing the disintegration of the USSR. Neither then nor now has anyone been able to make convincing arguments as to why Russia needed independence from the USSR. The question is a simple one: From whom was Russia supposed to become independent? From itself? This question completely disarms and stumps those who have tried both at the time and now to argue that the actions of the Russian government were necessary. I remember sitting with Yeltsin at one point after the law on Russia's sovereignty had been adopted, and saying to him: "Boris Nikolaevich, our country, the USSR, consists of two hoops: the Union and the Russian Federation. If one of them falls apart, then everything will dissolve."

Looking back now at everything that happened, it is evident to me that the main orientation of Yeltsin and his entourage was to pursue a course aimed at the dissolution of the Soviet Union, at taking control of Russia, so as to seize power for themselves. Of course at that time, and even afterward, right up until the coup attempt in 1991, he could not act openly. He would not have had support even from the majority of his own supporters at that time. But secretly that was what was going on.

There is one more point of no small importance. It is now quite obvious that the line taken by the Russian leadership, aimed at the disintegration of the Soviet Union, intersected with the struggle against the leadership of the USSR which was being conducted by the fundamentalist forces, the old school of the nomenklatura inside the CPSU. Their stronghold was the Communist Party of the RFSFR, which had been founded that same year, in 1990, and was headed by Ivan Polozkov and others, including Gennady

Zyuganov. Both camps, those around Yeltsin and the leaders of the Communist Party of the Russian Federation, despite their seemingly opposite ideological positions,were encouraging, provoking, and instigating each other toward removing Gorbachev and undermining and destroying the process of renewal and reform of the Union government. That process did not suit their purposes.

But let us return to the process then under way—the drafting of a Union treaty.

On August 30-31, 1990, after consultations with twelve Soviet republics (the three Baltic republics were not included, although meetings were also held with delegations from those republics), a joint session of the President's Council and the Council of the Federation took place. R. Nishanov, chairman of the Council of Nationalities of the USSR Supreme Soviet, acquainted the participants with the results of the consultations. He noted a complete coincidence of views on the need for a radical renewal of the Union but stressed at the same time that the most varied opinions had been expressed on the form the future unified state would take—ranging from a federation to a confederation. The decision was made to form a preparatory committee to draft a new Union treaty; it would consist of authorized delegations from the republics headed by those in the top government positions and with the participation of the president of the USSR, the chairman of the USSR Supreme Soviet, and the chairman of the USSR Council of Ministers. This committee was to begin work in mid-September 1990.

At the end of September, the USSR Supreme Soviet joined in the discussion on the question of the Union treaty. Keeping in mind that during the course of these preceding discussions and consultations, it was sometimes expressed that the renewed federation would not be a single country but a weakly linked and not very viable conglomerate of republics, it was necessary that I affirm once again the majority position: "I am for a Union of sovereign states, a renewed Union, in which everyone would feel comfortable, all the nationalities, and each and every nation would realize its intellectual potential and everything else lodged within that nation. Each nation and nationality is great and unique in its own way. And I regard the Union of sovereign states as a *united multinational state*."

After this session of the Supreme Soviet, work continued. In writing the new Union treaty, seven drafts were used. These had been prepared by Byelorussia, Kazakhstan, Uzbekistan, Azerbaijan, Kirgizia, Turkmenia, and Tadzhikistan. Also used were two drafts that originated at the Soviet Academy of Science's Institute of Government and Law, three drafts that had been awarded prizes by a jury of the Interregional Deputies' Group, and one draft presented by a group of political parties. Problems having to do with the renewal of the Soviet Union were discussed three times at the Council of the Federation and twice by the USSR Supreme Soviet. The interim result of all this activity was presented to the Fourth Congress of People's Deputies (held December 17-27, 1990). The discussion there was very intense and sometimes quite strained. Rather than attempt to paraphrase it, I will cite an excerpt from remarks by G. Tarazevich, representing Byelorussia, chairman of the commission of the Council of Nationalities on nationality policy and on relations among nationalities:

If we analyze the various political views on the principles for a renewal of our Union, two opposing patterns reveal themselves.

The first proposes to destroy the existing Union. (Sometimes this is stated openly, sometimes in a veiled fashion.) In other words, those supporting this proposal are talking about eliminating the government structures and governing bodies of the Soviet Union and making the Union constitution no longer operative. At the same time the republics (so it is suggested) would begin a process of making treaties with one another, and on this basis a new Union would be established.

The second plan is based not on destruction but on reform. This one proposes to stop the decomposition of existing internal links binding the Union together. By agreement with the republics, the administrative and government bodies of the Union would be radically reformed. The republics, jointly with the president and the leadership of the top Unionwide government bodies, would conduct a process to arrive at an agreement on a new Union.

A bitter struggle, a contest for power, has essentially broken out between proponents of these two plans. The first plan is actually not that difficult to implement, since a consistently negative attitude on the part of the public has been formed in relation to the former central government and the existing one. In many respects this attitude is justified. But the truth is that in criticizing the Center and heaping all the blame on it, we fail to recognize that many of our present troubles are connected with a rather unwise destruction of this much-reviled Center.

But let us return to the question of implementing the first plan. As we have said, public opinion is generally against the Center. It is sufficient now for the leaders of several republics, especially if Russia is included, to have their parliaments make such ideas official in order to pull the rug out, so to speak, from under the Union's governing bodies. In my opinion, this process has already begun. Isn't that why we have not yet been able to consider a plan and a budget for the Union as a whole for the coming year? With events developing in this way, some political forces and their leaders will of course win out, but will our society and the people of our Union gain from this? I am convinced they will not. On the contrary, the destruction of the Union will bring new disasters to the people of that Union. . . .

Destruction of the Soviet Union in the present historical circumstances will inevitably lead to catastrophic consequences for our society. The politicians who are influencing processes in this direction in one way or another should understand their responsibility to the people and to history. *As far as the idea of a renewal of the Soviet Union is concerned, in my opinion the conception of the president [Gorbachev] should be supported because it provides not for the destruction but for the reformation of the central government.*

On December 24, 1990, the congress passed a resolution entitled "On the General Conception of a New Union Treaty and the Procedure for Concluding Such a Treaty." Having expressed itself in favor of a transformation of the existing Union into a "voluntary, equal Union of sovereign republics—a democratic and federated state," the congress noted:

A renewed Union based on the expressed will of the various peoples and based on principles set forth in the declarations by the republics and autonomous entities on state sovereignty—such a renewed Union is called upon to ensure the following: the equality of all citizens of the country regardless of nationality or place of residence; equality of all nationalities, no matter the size of the population, and their inalienable right to self-determination and free democratic development, as well as the right of the components of the federation to territorial integrity; guarantees of the rights of all national minorities; and a strengthening of the authority of the Union as a guarantee of peace and international security.

It was prescribed that further work on the draft treaty and the development of procedures for the signing of this treaty should be organized and carried out by a preparatory committee consisting of the top officials of the federation's components—the republics and autonomous entities, the president of the USSR, the chairman of the USSR Supreme Soviet, and the chairman of the USSR Council of Nationalities of the Supreme Soviet. In preparing a draft of a Union treaty the committee was to base its work "on the general conception presented to the congress as well as the conceptions held by the component bodies of the federation, while taking into account the proposals and comments expressed by the People's Deputies of the USSR and by public opinion."

A special point in the congress's resolution stated the following:

> The congress emphasizes that the chief condition for arriving at an agreement is for all government bodies, up until the signing of a new Union treaty, to abide by the existing constitution of the USSR and Unionwide laws and not to permit the adoption of resolutions that would restrict the sovereign rights and legal interests of the component entities of the federation.

This clause was absolutely necessary because, by the beginning of 1991, cases of violations against the constitution of the USSR were multiplying rapidly. It was not just a question of the Baltic region but involved a number of other republics as well. In this respect, Russia also set a bad example more than once.

At the very beginning of 1991, work on the draft of the new Union treaty began to pick up speed. But it was proceeding in extremely complicated circumstances: Both the radical democrats and the conservative opponents of renewal of the federation intensified their activities, seeking to prevent the implementation of plans that had been outlined and approved by the Congress of People's Deputies.

The radical democrats proved to be the most energetic. They tried to take advantage of the events in Vilnius and Riga, portraying them as a "conspiracy by the conservatives in the Kremlin." They interpreted any action by the central government authorities in that spirit.

At that point Yeltsin made a trip to Latvia and Estonia. Speaking at a press conference after the trip, he declared: "It apparently would not be possible" to defend Russia's sovereignty without a Russian army. Thus a Russian army was supposed to defend the sovereignty of Russia against a Union army, which was 80 percent Russian. How absurd! What is more, this was a gross violation of the constitution of the USSR. I had occasion to say this directly from the speaker's platform at the USSR Supreme Soviet.

Yeltsin's statements at this same press conference, which I quote from the news report in *Izvestia*, were as follows:

Yeltsin spoke of the fact that the leaders of the four largest republics—Russia, Ukraine, Byelorussia, and Kazakhstan—had decided, without waiting for a Union treaty, to conclude a four-sided agreement among themselves on all questions and, for this purpose, to meet in the near future in the city of Minsk. No exact date had been set.

Yeltsin stated, "It seems to us that such an action will be a good stabilizing factor for all of society. Our agreement can be adhered to later, if they wish, by the other republics and the central government."

This idea was not carried out at that time. What was actually involved, however, was an open attempt not only to undermine the Union treaty but to call the existing government into question.

By no means was it accidental that during that period, in early 1991, Yeltsin began an intense campaign against me as president of the USSR. On February 19, in an interview for central television, he stated that he was differentiating himself from the policies of the president of the USSR and was demanding that the president resign. The USSR Supreme Soviet interpreted this statement by Yeltsin as contradicting the constitution and creating an extraordinary situation.

At the end of February I traveled to Byelorussia. In my speeches there I gave the following assessment of everything that was happening, without of course falling into the kind of tone and accents used by my opponents. I feel obliged to quote extensively from my speech at that meeting on February 26 with the scientific and creative intelligentsia of Byelorussia:

Today the peoples' right to self-determination and self-government is recognized by law. We have entered the phase of transforming the Soviet Union into a federation of sovereign republics. . . .

It is necessary to state, however, that, given our democracy's current fragile and unconsolidated condition, certain political groups have been attempting to carry out their plans not within the constitutional framework nor through existing laws but in direct opposition to them. All the drama of the present situation and the root source of the difficulties we are experiencing essentially stems from this. . . .

The "war of laws" [in which the Russian Federation was adopting laws that contradicted Unionwide laws], which has been waged in accordance with a certain ideology, has in many respects paralyzed the government, torn the market apart, and disorganized vital ties that had taken shape over decades. Attacks have intensified against the Congress of People's Deputies, the USSR Supreme Soviet, and the president. A paradoxical situation has arisen in which people are accusing the central government of supposedly putting an end to reform and preparing a dictatorship when they themselves are departing quite far from the line of perestroika and are seeking in fact to change its goals and orientation. In reality a struggle for power is under way, and it is destabilizing society and threatening to divert us from the path of reform to that of confrontation. Until we can eliminate this situation, which is intolerable from the point of view of our society's and our government's viability, the crisis will deepen, threatening to develop into a civil war and seriously weaken the country, if not set it back for decades. . . .

The general conclusion of authoritative scholars and scientists from many countries comes down to this: It is impossible to carry out a successful transition to the market under conditions of chaos and disorganization. We want to reach these new forms of life and ensure a different dynamic for the development of our country precisely by reforming property relations, moving toward a market economy, and transforming the Union. Without cohesiveness, without a united majority of the people, we will not be able to shoulder these tasks. That is the essence of this entire complicated and dramatic situation. . . .

The political groups that are demonstrating under the flag of democracy are a mixed bunch, but the positions of their leaders have been made fairly clear. Where do they want to lead us, to what end do they offer their services, these newfangled "friends of the people"? The first point in their program is defederalization, by which they mean the disintegration of our great multinational state. One of the ideologists among the democrats, the chairman of the Moscow Soviet, Gavriil Popov, speaks candidly, without emotion, about the possibility of separating the Soviet Union into forty or fifty new states, resettling entire populations, and carving new borders among various republics. This plan that is both anti-Union and anti-people is put forward as the central core of democracy, and political actions follow in the wake of these programmatic orientations. I have in mind the frenzied attacks on the central government, that is, the attempt to cast suspicion on our Union and on the referendum regarding the future of our multinational state. . . .

And not only to cast suspicion but to try to distort our goals. Look at what attacks the referendum has been subjected to at certain forums. It is no surprise that the so-called democrats entered into a political alliance with separatist nationalist groups. They have a common purpose: to weaken and, if possible, destroy the Union. And for the democrats it is not a problem that the reputation of the extremists from Sajudis or [the Ukrainian nationalist movement] Rukh is not above reproach. They are able to forgive these allies for such "sins" as the organization of moral terror, and, in some cases, armed terror, against people who think differently or who speak a different language, the destruction of monuments to Soviet soldiers, and the promotion of profascist views. . . .

The opposition does not find it to their advantage when the reforms are carried out by someone other than themselves. That is why they try not only to discredit the policies of the central government but, insofar as they are able, to torpedo measures taken by the central government. All this is having a major effect on the economy in spite of the feverish efforts we all have taken. The activity of many republic-level government bodies has been affected, as has the search for proper and good relations between the central government and the republics. We can see where the processes of disintegration are leading. And if we do not stop them and if we do not maintain the economic ties that to a considerable extent have already been disrupted, we will face a decline in production with all the consequences, above all, social consequences, that will flow from that. And from the social consequences, political consequences will follow, because the people will not tolerate this situation any longer. . . .

So then, questions must be resolved within the framework of continuing perestroika—otherwise the disintegration and decomposition of economic ties and the disruption of production will end up requiring that harsh measures be taken. We do not want to permit this: chaos can only give rise to dictatorial methods and forms of rule.

I considered it necessary at that time to call things by their real names, to point to the danger of the challenges being posed by the radical democrats, to the importunity they displayed. But attacks were also coming from the forces opposing reform, those who attempted at the Congress of People's Deputies of the USSR in December 1990 to remove the president from his post. And although the supporters of these two different radical extremist currents hated each other, their interests objectively converged around the common aim of undermining a reformist central government.

CHAPTER 12

Referendum on the Union

I UNDERSTOOD QUITE well that the political struggle would develop mainly over the fate of the Union—whether it would continue to exist at all and, if so, in what form. (The fate of the reforms—economic, political, and legal—also depended on the answer to this question.) Understanding all this, I held the view that all these questions affecting the fate of the people could not be decided without their participation. I was convinced that if a referendum were held, the overwhelming majority of the citizens of our country would express themselves in favor of preserving the Union in its reformed aspect.

I submitted this question to the Congress of People's Deputies. On December 24, 1990, the congress passed a resolution to hold a referendum on the fate of the Union of Soviet Socialist Republics. And on January 16 the USSR Supreme Soviet decreed that a referendum would be held throughout the territory of the Soviet Union on March 17, 1991. The question to be taken up in the referendum was formulated as follows: "Do you consider it necessary to preserve the Union of Soviet Socialist Republics as a renewed federation of equal, sovereign states—republics in which the rights and freedoms of persons of all nationalities will be fully guaranteed?"

The separatists in all the republics waged an intensive campaign calling on voters to answer this question in the negative. I will cite an example. At the end of January 1991 the founding conference of the so-called Democratic Congress Bloc was held in Kharkov. This bloc consisted of Democratic Russia and a number of other parties akin to it from various republics. The conference expressed itself in opposition to preserving the USSR, and the consultative council established by that congress called for mass actions under the slogans "No on the Union referendum question" and "Support Yeltsin, chairman of the RSFSR Supreme Soviet."

In this way the leader of Russia was counterposed to the idea of preserving the Union. Moreover, he did not conceal his views. I have already referred to his speech of February 19 in which he called for the resignation of the president of the USSR. Three weeks later he spoke even more fiercely, calling on his supporters to "declare war on the leadership of the country because it is leading us into a morass" and claiming that "Gorbachev is deceiving the people and democracy."

In early February the three Baltic republics, along with Armenia, Moldavia, and Georgia, announced that they would not participate in the March 17 referendum. But citizens in those republics who wished to take part were provided with the opportunity to do so.

On the eve of the referendum, opposition to it reached the highest intensity. On March 9 Yeltsin declared, "We do not need a central government like this—huge and bureaucratic . . . We must get rid of it." Here, as the saying goes, he was rushing through an open door. After all, the issue under discussion was to renew the union not in order to have a huge, bureaucratic central government but rather to create a genuinely democratic federation of sovereign states; that, however, was of no concern to Yeltsin.

It was quite obvious from the first draft of the Union treaty, which had been approved by the Council of the Federation on March 6 (with the participation of representatives of the RSFSR Supreme Soviet) and published on March 9, that Yeltsin knew what the real issue was. He did not want this draft to win approval. Trying to reinforce his point of view, he hastily declared that the signatures of the two representatives from the RSFSR Supreme Soviet on the draft of the treaty did not obligate him or the RSFSR in any way. On the eve of the referendum, speaking on Radio Rossiya, he added: "The referendum is being held in order to win support for the current policies of the leadership of the country. Its aim is to preserve the imperial unitary essence of the Union and the system."

I, too, spoke on television on the eve of the voting, and said:

We are on the threshold of a Unionwide referendum. This is the first time in our country's history that such an event is taking place. When we participate in the referendum, each of us must have the full realization that he or she is helping to decide the main question concerning the present and the future of our multinational state. At issue is the fate of our country, the fate of our homeland, our common home, the question of how we and our children and our grandchildren are to live with one another.

This is a question of such great dimension and significance that it stands above the interests of particular parties, social groups, or political and social movements. Only the people themselves have the right to resolve this question. I call on all of you, my dear fellow citizens, to take part in the Union-wide referendum and to answer yes on the question before you.

Our yes will preserve the integrity of the state which is a thousand years old and was created by the labor, the intelligence, and the countless sacrifices of many generations—a state in which the destinies of many peoples have been inseparably interwoven, the fates of millions of people, your fate and ours.

Our yes is an expression of respect for the governmental power that has more than once demonstrated its ability to defend the independence and security of the peoples united within it.

Our yes is a guarantee that the flames of war will never again sear our country, to whose lot many ordeals have befallen.

Our yes does not mean preservation of the old order with domination by the central government and a lack of rights for the republics. The positive results of the referendum will open the road to radical renewal of the Union government, its transformation into a federation of sovereign republics where the rights and freedoms of citizens of all nationalities will be reliably guaranteed.

Our yes in the referendum and the conclusion of a Union treaty will make it possible to put an end to the destructive processes going on in our society and to make a decisive return to restoring normal conditions of life and labor. . . .

It will be difficult, if not impossible, to resolve the questions facing us without harmony and cooperation in society. Therefore it is necessary, while it is not too late, to stop the growing intolerance and bitterness and in some instances hostility. We can also do this jointly, all together—as one village, as the saying goes. A positive result from the referendum would lay the basis for the consolidation of society.

It is my firm conviction that if a profound split occurs in society, there will be no victors. Everyone will lose. All of us, both you and I, will be the losers. It is hard even to imagine how many misfortunes the disintegration of the country would bring in its wake, with the various peoples and nationalities being set against one another. And it would be a misfortune not only for you and me. The collapse of a power that today is one of the bulwarks of peace in the world would be fraught with the danger of a general upheaval, one of unprecedented proportions. . . .

Each of us now faces a historic choice. . . .

I appeal to you all, my dear fellow countrymen and women—say yes to the referendum regarding our great state, our Union, preserve it for ourselves and for our descendants.

The number of citizens taking part in the March 17, 1991, referendum was 148,574,606, or 80 percent of registered voters. Of these, 113,512,812, or 76.4 percent, voted yes. Those voting no numbered 32,303,977, or 21.7 percent. The number of spoiled or invalid ballots was 2,757,857, or 1.9 percent. These results spoke for themselves: The majority of citizens (a very substantial majority!) was in favor of preserving the Union as a renewed federation.

I cannot leave unexamined the conservatives' position on the question of preserving the Union. To the inexperienced it might seem that they were ardent defenders of the Union. Outwardly they spoke in its defense, and their group in the parliament was even called Soyuz (Union). But what kind of Union did they advocate? They spoke in favor of preserving the old Union and did not wish to see it reformed in any way. They represented forces interested in preserving the old order from the days before perestroika.

I have already indicated that the radical democrats began their offensive against the president right after the New Year in 1991. The conservative forces also stepped up their activities at that time. The founding of the Movement for a Great and Unitary Russia was announced. The leading figures in this organization were the future conspirator [participant in the August 1991 coup] Vasily Starodubstev, the writer Aleksandr Prokhanov, and Ivan Polozkov, head of the Communist Party of the Russian Federation.

Shortly after the referendum, one of the leaders of the Union group in the parliament, V. Alksnis, gave an interview to the British weekly *New Statesman* in which he essentially made public the program of the conservative groupings. He rejected the idea of the Union treaty, favored the use of force to preserve the Union, and advocated the formation of a Committee of National Salvation, to which all the power in the country would be transferred.

On April 9 a regular session of the Council of the Federation was held. I took the floor and spoke about the existing situation:

Our position is such that we must recognize the great danger that hangs over our country. It is a danger to our state system, the Soviet federation, for whose preservation the majority of the population has spoken; a danger of economic disintegration, with all the consequences which that would have for the interests of the people and for the welfare of our country's defense capability; a danger of the destruction of our institutions of government, jurisprudence, and law. . . .

It is now necessary that we act—moreover, that we act without delay and not in isolation, but in unity with all the healthy forces of society, setting aside feuds and quarrels. We must act so as not to let our country slide into disaster.

At the same time I proposed specific measures that would incorporate in legislation the people's will, as expressed in the referendum, for the preservation of the Union, namely, to restore the vertical co-subordination of all government bodies, to halt decisively the escalation of conflicts among nationalities, and to conduct negotiations in search of mutually acceptable solutions.

The subsequent development of events confirmed that I had taken the correct approach on the question. The problem was that after the referendum, which had opened the door toward the signing of a new Union treaty, the conservative forces inside the CPSU greatly intensified their activity, undertaking a determined offensive. At a conference in Smolensk, a number of party leaders from Russia, Ukraine, and Byelorussia openly called for emergency measures. And at meetings of smaller groups, they urged that Gorbachev be confronted with tough demands, that an emergency congress of the CPSU be called, and that the leadership of the party be changed. Similar moves were made at plenums of the party organization in Moscow and at the Leningrad provincial party committee. The slogan was "Let the general secretary resign!" I recall that, at the very same time, Democratic Russia raised the slogan that the president should resign.

The situation was growing white hot. Events were building to a confrontation. Something had to be done to keep things under control. In early April, in the course of a discussion among a small group of the country's leaders regarding the current situation, it was proposed that the president of the USSR meet with the leaders of those republics that favored preservation of a renewed Union in order to work out a joint program of action. And of course the leadership of Russia would be included.

On April 23 a meeting was held between the president of the USSR and the leaders of the top government bodies of Russia, Ukraine, Byelorussia, Uzbekistan, Kazakhstan, Azerbaijan, Kirghizia, Turkmenia, and Tadzhikistan. The assemblage met near Moscow in the suburb of Novo-Ogarevo (hence the expression used later, the "Novo-Ogarevo process"). In opening the meeting, I characterized the existing situation as both dangerous and demanding, and said that effective action would be needed to resolve the dilemma, that such action could not be routine or ordinary, and that it would have to be agreed on by all the leaders present. Differences regarding secondary matters had to be set aside, especially personal sympathies and antipathies. The country's interests had to take priority over everything else. This was our duty and the burden of our responsibilities. It was essential now to draw up a brief document that the people could understand so that they would see that the leaders intended to act decisively and in a coordinated way. This would immediately have a calming effect on society and would defuse the threatening atmosphere.

After an exchange of opinions, all participants at the meeting supported the proposal. A joint document was drafted and adopted, entitled "Joint Declaration on Urgent Measures to Stabilize the Situation in the Country and Overcome the Crisis." This document declared that the chief means for stabilizing the country was the signing of a new Union treaty as soon as possible. The document also indicated that the states in the Union would offer one another most-favored-nation status and that relations with the other former Soviet republics would be established on the basis of generally recognized international practices. The intention to continue with reforms was reaffirmed. The president of the USSR and the heads of the republics called on workers to stop striking and for all political forces to function within the framework of the constitution.

All this happened on April 23. The next day a regular plenary session of the CPSU Central Committee began. It was known that the party's conservative forces had decided to turn this session into a kind of investigation into "the case of General Secretary Gorbachev." A draft resolution had even been prepared that would have declared a death sentence on the whole course of reform.

Knowing all this, I decided to make clear to my opponents that I was not about to surrender, that I would uncompromisingly defend the policy of reform. In opening the plenum I said:

Not only in words but in deeds, attempts are being made to divert our country from the road of reform either by pushing it into one more *ultrarevolutionary adventure* that would threaten to destroy our state system or *to return to the past*, to a slightly touched-up version of the totalitarian regime. I do not think it necessary to explain that I am referring to the plans of the left-wing and right-wing radicals. The tendencies of both are destructive. And the greatest danger at the present moment is that they could join forces, despite what seems to be their irreconcilable mutual hostility.

Even in such an eventuality I sought to keep myself and my supporters on firmly democratic grounds. What I said next attests to this:

Every party and movement has the right to try to attain its goals by making use . . . of democratic institutions and Soviet laws. This naturally includes contending for political leadership and power. All attempts to operate by the methods of Pugachovism [a reference to the elemental peasant rebellion in the eighteenth century led by Yemelyan Pugachov] or by means of extra-parliamentary blackmail, up to and including grinding the country's economy into dust and ashes—all this must be emphatically rejected.

I regard it as my paramount duty to stop the violations of the democratic process and by all legal measures to strengthen decisively the constitutional order in the country. It is quite evident that without this constitutional order even the most ideal programs for overcoming the economic crisis would remain mere good intentions. Of course restoration and strengthening of the constitutional order is a direct obligation for all government bodies and for every person in office. But it is also a task for our society as a whole and for all genuinely democratic groups, forces, and organizations.

Naturally I had paid special attention to the meeting held the previous day at Novo-Ogarevo. Here is the context in which I discussed what had been said there:

The situation requires that all political forces and movements which take a patriotic position—and not just in words—must renounce ambitions and set aside their mutual claims at least for the time being in order to help our country get itself together at a particularly difficult time. I must say that at yesterday's meeting an understanding of this need was displayed by the presidents, chairpersons of Supreme Soviets, and government leaders of nine Union republics. The statement adopted at that meeting has been published. If the measures proposed in that document are carried out consistently—and we will do everything possible to ensure that they are—this could be the beginning of a turnaround in the development of the present situation. . . . First and foremost, to overcome the crisis we must undertake the task of concluding a new Union treaty, keeping in mind the results of the voting in the recent Unionwide referendum.

There followed a stormy debate during which the conservative wing of the Central Committee persistently attempted to "remove" the general secretary and to bury the reforms. (One of those who spoke, Gurenko, a secretary of the Central Committee of the Communist Party of Ukraine, bluntly proposed that "the status of the CPSU as the ruling party should be embodied in law," that the previous system by which leading party cadres were assigned government positions should be restored, and that the party's control of the mass media should be reestablished.) Despite all this the plenum ended on a constructive note. The declaration by the nine leaders of the Soviet republics and the president of the USSR was supported, and the following assertion was made: "In order to overcome the imminent catastrophe it is vitally necessary that (1) a new Union treaty be signed on the basis of the results of the nationwide referendum on the preservation of the Union of Soviet Socialist Republics; and (2) constitutional order and legality be reestablished in the country."

Thus the desperate attempt to divert our country from the path of reform, including reform of the Union itself, failed. We had passed through a critical stage.

The struggle over our political course in general, and over the Union treaty in particular, did not end there. Attacks against the idea of the Union treaty continued. The pressure campaign against the president and his supporters did not stop. But all these activities took new forms. I should emphasize that the conservative forces were especially active then. It is clear from evidence that was partially known at the time and well known much later that the conservative forces at that very time were beginning to prepare for the coup that began on August 19. In June they attempted to carry out a "coup by legal means," so to speak, through the parliament, by limiting the president's powers and transferring a substantial share of those powers to the prime minister, Valentin Pavlov (who later became one of the leaders of the coup). This attempt was also thwarted.

As for the Union treaty, preparations for its signing proceeded at full speed. There was no time to delay. On May 24 a session was held of the preparatory committee that had been established in accordance with the decision of the Fourth Congress of People's Deputies of the USSR to work on a draft of the new Union treaty and the procedure for its adoption. At this session it was emphasized that, as a result of the March 17 referendum, our country's nations and nationalities had expressed themselves firmly in favor of preserving and renewing the Union government. A broad constructive exchange of opinions was held regarding comments by the republics after the draft treaty was published in the press.

The participants unanimously supported the principle of constructing the new Union as a federation of equal republics. There was wide-ranging discussion of the procedure for the signing of the treaty by representatives of the sovereign states constituting the Union and on the structure and powers of the Union bodies of government. Special attention was paid to ensuring the participation of all the republics in the formation and functioning of the government bodies of the new Union. The goal adopted by the preparatory committee was to submit an agreed-on draft of the treaty for approval by the Supreme Soviets of the republics as early as June.

On June 3 the preparatory committee met once again in Novo-Ogarevo. Some decisive progress had to be made. To illustrate the totality of problems we had to confront, I will quote from a portion of the transcript of that session's discussion:

M. S. [MIKHAIL SERGEEVICH GORBACHEV]: I think that extensive discussion on the general character of the treaty should have ended at the last meeting. How many months now have we been going around in circles? Let's proceed page by page, clause by clause. First, the name of the treaty.

LUKYANOV reports that the opinion of the Supreme Soviet of the USSR is to call it a "Union treaty," not a "treaty on a Union of sovereign states."

The basic principles of the proposed treaty are easily agreed on, if we discount the argument with Kravchuk, who has insisted on the term state sovereignty.

Discussion is then diverted to a side issue: LUKYANOV demands that the treaty be signed at a congress. Later on, basic principles are again discussed.

LUKYANOV: We need to abide by the will of the congress, which passed a resolution that the name Union of Soviet Socialist Republics should be preserved.

KARIMOV, and after him KRAVCHUK, object to Lukyanov's statement. ("If each of us begins talking about the will of his own Supreme Soviet . . .") LUKYANOV partially gives in, but he continues to argue about the order of words in the modified form of the name: whether it should be the Union of Soviet Sovereign Republics or the Union of Sovereign Soviet Republics.

M. S.: If this kind of divisiveness goes on, we will never stop arguing. If the processes of disintegration continue at this pace, all the peoples of our country will be placed in a desperate situation; we will create chaos. . . .

There is a break.

NAZARBAEV: The most urgent questions are these:

1. Who will be a subject [component entity] of the Union?
2. Will there be equality between Union republics and former autonomous republics?
3. The Council of the Federation.

Let us assign these questions to specialists and continue to go through the other articles and clauses.

YELTSIN: Let the experts go into session.

M. S.: Experts are no substitute for the will of the republics. We must submit these ideas to them.

There follows a long and intense argument over the first article, membership in the Union, and then over taxes. YELTSIN, whose election campaign is at its height, gets ready to leave. SHAIMIYEV, not allowing Yeltsin to leave, is in a hurry to bring up a sore point: "On our territory, 80 percent of the enterprises are subordinated to the Soviet Union. But Russia is not paying its assigned amounts to the Union and so these enterprises are not receiving any funds from the Union budget."

YELTSIN leaves. The discussion flows into another channel. NAZARBAEV proposes that Gorbachev "at least for once use force."

LUKYANOV: And would you, Nursultan Abishevich [Nazarbaev], would you endorse such powers for the president?

(Silence in reply.)

NAZARBAEV: What would Russia's position be after the June 12 elections [for president of the RSFSR]?

The discussion returns to the article on membership, then suddenly jumps over to the question of the composition of the Supreme Soviet.
A break follows.
We then go on to Article 2, citizenship. SHAIMIYEV returns again to Article 1. We finish the discussion of Article 2. Next comes Article 3, territory.

M. S.: We shall now find out who among us has territorial claims.

Outside it has grown dark, and the discussion proceeds more quickly. M. S. tells a story from Stavropol, "The best speech is the one that isn't made," after which there are fewer comments.
    Then follows a discussion of Article 5, distribution of powers between the Union and the republics. Arguments regarding the name of the article proceed for more than an hour. Then, for some reason, everyone quickly agrees on the article as a whole.
    A discussion then ensues about property, and there is an argument. LUKYANOV appeals to Article 10 of the USSR constitution. NAZARBAEV proposes a compromise, which is supported by KARIMOV.
    There is a break. The meeting opens again with a question: Shall we adjourn until tomorrow?

M. S.: No. Let's keep working to a victorious conclusion . . .

We then go through the article on taxes in only two minutes. We get stuck on the next article, the constitution. Who would adopt it? It's approaching midnight. Discussion of the remaining articles proceeds quickly. NAZARBAEV makes some objections.

M. S.: Why are you grumbling like an old man? We have accepted your proposals . . . (then to everyone:) Thank you, Comrades! I congratulate you. We have worked well together. The new treaty is nearly done.

The discussions on all the questions taken up at this session proceeded not only among the heads of the republics. The Supreme Soviet also participated, as did the country as a whole. Numerous explanations had to be given in view of the various points brought up. I took an active part in all of this.

Opinions were expressed to the effect that the new Union treaty would conflict with the referendum. But the treaty defined the future Union as a sovereign democratic federated state. That was what people had voted for. That it would be a new federation was expressed, above all, in the affirmation of sovereignty for the republics and the expansion of their rights, powers, and responsibilities. The republics would essentially be reborn as sovereign states. And if someone thought this was a new idea, invented only at that moment, of course that wasn't the case. These very same ideas were written into the treaty of 1922 under which the USSR was formed; the needs of our present times and the desires of the people were thus expressed.

Further on, there was the question of the distribution of functions and powers between the Union and the sovereign republics—this division was such that there would be both strong republics and a strong center. This is an important point: In international affairs the Union acts as a sovereign state, the legal heir of the Union of Soviet Socialist Republics.

The people who voted for the referendum voted for the kind of Union that would guarantee the rights, freedom, and security of citizens of all nationalities throughout the territory, wherever they chanced to reside. This idea was fixed in the form of principles and was expressed in particular sections of the new Union treaty.

There had been debates at the congress on whether to include the word *socialist* in the name of the new Union, and the congress had expressed itself in favor of that. But the debates continued in the Supreme Soviets of the republics. The proposal at first was for the name "Union of Sovereign Republics," because many had simply changed their names to republics—such as Moldova and Kyrgyzstan—and because everything having to do with nationality policy, the relations between nations and nationalities, everything to do with this whole delicate subject, required a respectful attitude. But it turned out that we reached an agreement to include the word *Soviet* in the name—that is, Union of Soviet Sovereign Republics. This would emphasize continuity. The name would be linked with the whole preceding period, which was the product, so to speak, of the creativity of the masses. After all, "soviet" structures were still in existence as such, despite the appearance of mayoralties and other structures of executive power.

On July 12 the USSR Supreme Soviet, after once again discussing the subject of the new Union treaty, passed a resolution entitled "On the Draft Treaty for a Union of Sovereign States." It said in part:

> To support in all fundamentals the Draft Treaty on the Union of Sovereign States presented on June 18, 1991, by the president of the USSR in the name of the preparatory committee established by the Fourth Congress of People's Deputies of the USSR. To recognize as possible the signing of the treaty after appropriate further work and agreement among the republics with the participation of an authorized delegation from the Union government.

Subsequent points in this resolution contained clauses about the composition of the delegation from the USSR Supreme Soviet for the signing of the treaty, and the tasks to be assigned to this delegation were formulated.

On July 23, at a regular session attended by leaders of delegations from the republics, work on the draft Union treaty was completed. I will cite a brief excerpt from the transcript of that session:

Novo-Ogarevo, July 23

(Also present were Lukyanov, Laptev, Nishanov, Pavlov, Yazov, Bessmertnykh, and Shcherbakov. The task of the day was to resolve five questions on which there had been significant commentary: membership in the Union; the Union budget and taxes; property; the Supreme Soviet; and the constitutional court.)

M. S. [GORBACHEV]: A certain tendency keeps showing up in our discussions. We seem to reach an agreement but then, when we adjourn, we start to erode everything we had agreed on. The time has come for full clarity.

Second. Adherence to the Union as a federation.

Third. The fate of Russia to a significant extent will determine the future of the Union.

I feel there are dangerous tendencies. We must complete the treaty more quickly.

Karimov objects to the text that had been worked out, as usual, by a group of experts at Volynskoe [a Moscow suburb like Novo-Ogarevo used as a work site by official groups]. These experts had taken into account all the commentaries or observations that had been made.

KARIMOV: Where did this text come from? We agreed on something different on June 17.

M. S.: What do you mean, where did it come from? You remember that I was asked, as always, to take suggestions into account . . .

(It was then necessary to return to the text of June 17, in which there were more imperfections and several commentaries or observations from the republics that had not been taken into account.

(A very long and difficult discussion ensued on how relations should be regulated between a former autonomous republic and the republic of which it had been a part. A discussion on taxes then followed.)

DEMENTEI: If I don't participate in the formation of the property of the Union as a whole, at least through my 2 percent, with my two kopecks, which is the share due me as a citizen, then when I arrive in Kazan I will feel as though I am a foreigner; or if I travel to the Crimea, I will feel like an outsider. If someone comes to visit me in Byelorussia, he will also feel like an outsider.

(There is a break.)

M. S.: You have been drinking and eating, but we have been working. The proposal is as follows: Anatoly Ivanovich [Lukyanov], Boris Nikolaevich [Yeltsin], and Ivan Stepanovich [Silaev, chairman of the RSFSR Council of Ministers] are to work on the tax formula, in which it will be clearly stated that this matter will be monitored and will remain open at all stages until the percentages have been set in all cases.

(Further discussion followed: on the war of laws [laws being adopted by republics that conflicted with Union laws]; and on the structure and composition of the Supreme Soviet. Regarding the latter, a distinct point was made by Tataria: "The Tatar Autonomous Soviet Socialist Republic, as a sovereign republic, which has adopted an official resolution to sign the Union treaty on its own, declares its right to have a full quota of deputies' seats in the Council of the Republics of the Supreme Soviet of the Union of Sovereign States." Shaimiyev responded: "Our position is unchanged." An argument then erupted among Shaimiyev, Gorbachev, Plyushch, Nazarbaev, and Revenko.)

M. S.: Revenko has in this instance revealed qualities that are typical of the great Ukrainian people. This whole problem should be addressed to Boris

Nikolaevich [Yeltsin] and to Comrade Shaimiyev. Whatever they agree to, that's the way it will be. All right?

Once again the argument returned to relations among the republics.

M. S.: Well, comrades, I know that there is no Solomon among us. My mission is to keep you from losing the attitude you have today. We are very close to the signing of the treaty; just one more step . . . At the end, the procedure for the signing was discussed."

This procedure was proposed by two working groups under the leadership of Georgy Kh. Shakhnazarov and Grigory I. Revenko. Everything was spelled out in detail—from the seating of the heads of the delegations to the kind of paper on which the text of the treaty would be printed, from the issuing of special postage stamps to souvenirs for the participants in the ceremony.

On August 2, 1991, I appeared on television and reported that on that day the leaders of the delegations authorized by the Supreme Soviets of the republics had been sent a letter with the proposal that the treaty be made available for signing on August 20. This letter was also sent to those republics that had not yet clarified their positions. The first to sign the treaty would be the delegations from the Russian Federation, Kazakhstan, and Uzbekistan.

In that speech I said the following:

We are entering the decisive stage in the transformation of our multinational state into a democratic federation of equal Soviet republics. What does the conclusion of a new Union treaty mean for the life of our country? Above all, it is the realization of the will of the people expressed in the March 17 referendum. The treaty proposes the transformation of the Union on the basis of both continuity and renewal.

The state system of our Union, in which the labor of many generations of people and of all the nations and nationalities of our fatherland are embodied, will be preserved. At the same time a new, truly voluntary unification of sovereign states will take place, and in this unification all the nationalities and nations will direct their own affairs separately and freely develop their own cultures, languages, and traditions . . .

Of course matters should not be oversimplified. The treaty provides for a significant reconstruction of the bodies of government and administration. A new constitution needs to be drafted and adopted, electoral laws need to be renewed, elections need to be held, and the judicial system needs to be reorganized. While this process is unfolding there must be the active functioning of the Congress of People's Deputies, the USSR Supreme Soviet, the various governments, and other Unionwide bodies . . .

We have taken the road of reforms that are needed by the whole country. And the new Union treaty will help us overcome the crisis more quickly and return life to a normal channel. Today this is—and I think you will agree with me—the highest priority.

The Coup: A Stab in the Back—
and the Intrigues of Yeltsin

ON AUGUST 4 I went on vacation. On August 15 the July 23 draft of the Union treaty was published. But on August 19-21 the adoption of the new Union treaty was rudely interrupted by the attempted coup. Let me remind readers of what happened.

After the opponents of reform failed in their attempt on August 18 to win the president of the USSR over to their side, the coup began. At 6:00 A.M. on August 19 a statement by Anatoly Lukyanov, chairman of the USSR Supreme Soviet, broadcast a statement on radio and television. It contained objections to the new Union treaty. In his opinion, reconsideration of the treaty first by the Supreme Soviet and later by the Congress of People's Deputies was required. This meant, in fact, that the signing of the treaty on August 20 would be impossible. Lukyanov's declaration was dated August 16 but, as the head of the Secretariat of the Supreme Soviet later reported, it was written on August 19 before dawn.

A decree by Gennady Yanaev, the vice president, was also broadcast. It stated that he was assuming the functions of the president "since it was impossible, for reasons of health" for Gorbachev to perform these functions. Also broadcast was an appeal by the "Soviet leadership" (signed by Yanaev, Pavlov, and Baklanov) announcing the formation of a State Committee for the State of Emergency (Russian initials, GKChP) "to administer the country and effectively to implement the state of emergency"; also broadcast was an "Appeal to the Soviet People" and Decree No. 1 of the GKChP "On the Imposition of the State of Emergency." All this was based on fraud and deception. The attempted coup, of course, lasted only three days. After the defeat of the coup, in the early hours of August 22, I arrived back in Moscow. A decree abrogating the "anticonstitutional actions of the organizers of the coup d'état" was immediately published.

In my televised speech that same day, August 22, I said the following:

What happened these past few days is, to say the least, a "great lesson for us all." It is a painful lesson, a terrifying kind of education. And all the necessary conclusions must be drawn not only in the realm of government structures but in relations among the republics, among various parties and social movements, and among nationalities and of course in economic policy and in the spiritual and moral realm. . . .

We must proceed more quickly and in a more unified way along the road of radical reform. Tomorrow I will meet with the leaders of nine republics. We will discuss and weigh everything and consider urgent measures that need to be taken as well as short-term perspectives. . . . And we will tell the country and the entire world about this. . . .

I have already spoken with the leaders of the republics about further plans for action, and it seems that in the near future a new date will be set for the signing of the Union treaty. After that will come the adoption of a new Union constitution, a new electoral law, and elections for a Unionwide parliament and president. This work must be carried out in the established time frame without delay, because delays during the transitional period, as we have seen, are dangerous for democratic change.

As you can see my intentions were quite clear—to hasten preparations for the signing of the treaty. But this turned out not to be a simple task, not by any means.

The August coup caused a breakdown in the process of formation of new Unionwide relations among the sovereign states, created complications, and spurred on the process of disintegration—no longer of the government alone but of the entire society. On August 22 Boris Yeltsin issued a decree "on ensuring the economic basis of the sovereignty of the RSFSR." It provided for all enterprises and organizations subordinated to the Soviet Union as a whole to be transferred to the jurisdiction of the RSFSR with the exception of those whose administration had been turned over to government bodies of the USSR on the basis of laws passed by Russia. On August 24 the Supreme Soviet of Ukraine declared itself an independent democratic state and announced that *from that moment on only the constitution, laws, and decrees of the government and other legislative acts of the Ukrainian republic would be valid on the territory of that republic.* The decree stated that this step had been taken because of "the mortal danger threatening Ukraine in connection with the coup d'état in the USSR of August 19, 1991." On August 25 Byelorussia declared its independence, followed by Moldova, Azerbaijan, Kyrgyzstan, and Uzbekistan. On August 28 the leadership of the Russian Federation announced that Russia would establish its control over the USSR State Bank and the USSR Foreign Trade Bank.

These events determined the position I took and all my actions during the emergency session of the USSR Supreme Soviet, which was convened immediately after the attempted coup and called for an extraordinary session of the Congress of People's Deputies of the USSR without delay. Speaking before the Supreme Soviet, I said that a real threat of the Soviet Union falling apart had arisen. If this were to happen, all talk of reform would be empty chatter. Amendments needed to be made in the Union treaty, but it should not be renounced altogether.

Understanding the full danger of the new situation to prospects for democratic change, I regarded the resumption of work on the Union treaty as the top priority.

At the Congress of People's Deputies of the USSR, whose proceedings began on September 2, a statement was read from the president of the USSR and the top leaders of the Union republics. (It was signed by ten republics, and the republic of Georgia had helped draft the statement.) It proposed a program of urgent actions to extricate the country from its acute political crisis. It took note of the pressing need for a treaty establishing a Union of Sovereign States to be drafted and signed by all republics wishing to do so. In this Union, each republic would itself decide the form of its participation.

From the point of view of democracy, not everything at the congress went entirely smoothly, but it would have been unrealistic to expect that. Certain basic positions were developed at that congress—that a Union treaty is necessary and an economic treaty indispensable. A position favoring unified armed forces and the coordination of a common foreign policy was adopted.

After a heated and turbulent discussion, the congress passed a group of resolutions defining the tasks of *a transitional period*, including a law concerning the government bodies of the Soviet Union during that period. To arrive at agreed-on solutions to problems of foreign and domestic policy affecting the interests of all the republics a State Council was formed, consisting of the president of the USSR and the republics' top officials. One of the first decisions of the State Council was to recognize the independence of the Baltic republics.

Immediately after the congress, work proceeded energetically along two lines: A working group began to draft a new Union treaty, and a committee for operational management of the Soviet economy began drafting a treaty of economic union. The main purpose of this union was to consolidate the efforts of the sovereign states to establish a common market and carry out a coordinated economic policy as an indispensable condition for overcoming the current crisis. The draft of this treaty provided that signing the treaty establishing the Union of Sovereign States was not a condition for joining the economic union.

As early as September 16 the State Council reviewed the draft treaty for economic union. On October 1, in Alma-Ata, there was a meeting of leaders of thirteen republics who discussed this treaty. On October 4 the treaty was initialed by the republics. On October 18 a treaty establishing an economic community of sovereign states was signed in the Kremlin by the president of the USSR and the leaders of eight republics. A few days later Ukraine added its name to this treaty. The treaty was then sent to the parliaments of the various republics for ratification.

At the same time new Unionwide government structures were established in keeping with the changing situation, new leaders were appointed, and reorganization was begun of the foreign ministry, the defense ministry, the ministry of the interior, and the state security committee (KGB). An inter-republican Economic Committee was also established.

On October 1 comments by Boris Yeltsin were sent out to supplement the draft Union treaty which had been distributed earlier to members of the Political Consultative Council (a body established by the president after the coup). The future Union was defined in the text as "the Union of Free Sovereign Republics—a united democratic state exercising government power within the limits of authority voluntarily assigned to it by the participants in the treaty." Thus, recovering from the shock inflicted by the August coup, the leaderships of the Union and the republics resumed their work of transforming the Union along both political and economic lines. There were grounds for believing that the Novo-Ogarevo process had been restored. But only with great difficulty, many interruptions, and periodic setbacks did these efforts proceed during the autumn months of 1991.

While work on the new version of a Union treaty was under way in Moscow, Boris Yeltsin, who was in Sochi, received a document entitled

"The Strategy of Russia During the Transitional Period." It bore the inscription "Strictly Confidential." Here are several passages from this document, which had been drafted by a "think tank" of the Democratic Russia organization.

> Before the August events the leadership of Russia, in opposition to the old totalitarian Center, was able to rely on the support of the leaders of the overwhelming majority of Union republics, who sought to strengthen their own political positions. The elimination of the old Center inevitably brings to the fore objective conflicts between the interests of Russia and those of the other republics. For the latter, the preservation of the existing flow of resources and financial-economic relations during the transition period signifies a unique opportunity to reconstruct their economies at Russia's expense. For the RSFSR, which is experiencing a serious crisis as it is, this is a significant additional burden on its economic structures and undermines the possibility of its own economic renewal. . . .
>
> Objectively Russia does not need an economic Center standing over it and engaged in the redistribution of its resources. But many other republics have an interest in such a Center. Having established control of the property on their territories, they seek to use the Unionwide government bodies to redistribute Russia's property and resources to their own advantage. Because this kind of Center can only exist with the support of the republics, objectively, regardless of the personnel in the Center, it will pursue policies contradictory to the interests of Russia.

The authors of this memorandum gave two possible formulas representing two forms of unification (economic union plus immediate political independence, or economic independence plus temporary political agreement), and they unreservedly recommended that the second formula be chosen. They asserted, accordingly, that "Russia must refrain from entering into any rigid, long-term, all-encompassing economic union," that it "has no interest in the creation of permanently functioning general bodies of economic administration standing over and above the republics," that it should "categorically refuse to make tax payments to the federal budget," that "it must have its own customs department," and so on.

This conception essentially meant that Russia must renounce its role as the "nucleus" of the Union. The motivation was that by preserving its own resources, Russia could quickly grow rich. It was evident that the authors of the memorandum perceived the disintegration of the Soviet Union (an event made possible as a result of the coup) not as a tragedy but as a kind of "victory."

Yeltsin and I had a serious conversation about the conception embodied in this memorandum. He agreed with my arguments against it, and at the time he seemed quite sincere. But that had happened before. You could talk with him and reach an agreement about something, but the next day he would do just the opposite. And that's what happened on this occasion. (Incidentally, that is the way he has continued to behave, as was confirmed more than once in the years from 1992 through 1998.)

On October 23, at the Congress of People's Deputies of the RSFSR, Yeltsin presented a range of measures that he proposed be taken. De facto these measures would undermine the treaty establishing an economic community that had just been signed, or at least they conflicted with it. Yeltsin said, "The inter-republican government bodies are called on to play only a consultative-coordinating role. Real power is now being exercised by the republics. And therefore the Russian Federation must pursue an independent policy and operate on the basis of national interest, not on the basis of some pattern imposed from the outside."

Immediately after Yeltsin's speech I was interviewed by the editor in chief of *Moscow News*, Len Karpinsky. The interview went as follows:

KARPINSKY: For some reason, in the new situation an old formula that is now false is being mechanically repeated. It is said that if there is going to be a Center, unavoidably it will be the kind we have had to deal with for decades, and even, alas, right up until recently, the kind that represents a constant danger to our country's freedom-loving nations and nationalities and to their national state systems. The false alternatives presented are that either the republics are independent and thus there can be no Center, or, if the Center is preserved, then say good-bye to independence. But why not imagine a kind of Center little known to us in the past, one that would be different in principle, a structure for expressing and coordinating the interests of the republics, a mechanism for arriving at consensus?

GORBACHEV: I completely agree with your line of argument. You have touched on the central problem. In many respects, what we may expect in the future depends on how we resolve this problem.

The alternative is not, on the one hand, whether the republics will become sovereign states (they already are) or, on the other, whether the

Unionwide Center will be preserved. The real question is whether we will find a way out of our common difficulty and move ahead together or whether we will rush helter-skelter in all directions. By no means is it only the corridors of power that link the republics with one another, not just the artificial limb, so to speak, of a bureaucratic party and government apparatus. The ties between the republics have grown up over the years and now permeate the entire fabric of life of all the republics. Thus our interaction will be either through conflict and dissension or through civilized cooperation. The totalitarian bureaucratic Center, which embodied a policy and ideology of great-power chauvinism and forced unification, has already fallen apart. That is good for everyone, but that fact should not be confused with allowing the other ties binding our Union to collapse. Consequently we are talking about a new kind of Center, one in a different mold, not a despot ordering the republics around but a coordinating body authorized to play an intermediary role and provided with the resources to do that by the republics themselves. . . .

Among certain groups of politicians in Russia, including those in Boris Yeltsin's circle, there are those who think that Russia should secede "just like everyone else." It should shake itself loose from the burden of having "special responsibility" for others and instead should rely on its own natural resources, its own economic and intellectual potential, and begin to live independently. This is just another academic utopia—and a very dangerous one. . . . Let me speak frankly: Russia cannot extricate itself alone, because it is also dependent on the other republics. The danger of this extreme separatist plan flows from the present situation itself. Perhaps a few years from now Russia could cope with its problems in isolation. But that could only occur after several years. For the other republics, including Ukraine, isolationism would be a catastrophe.

KARPINSKY: On the other hand, why can't Russia, acting as the "legal heir" of the USSR, assume all the worries and concerns bequeathed to us by the former Soviet Union? In the last analysis, does it really matter where the magnetic center for consolidation is located?

GORBACHEV: As soon as Russia tried, let's say, to give direct orders to the republics, all the sovereign republics would immediately flare up: What's this, trying to revive the empire? The majority of nations and nationalities are ready to accept Russia's leadership but only in the form of a new Union and through Unionwide institutions in which Russia would in fact play its part. Such Unionwide institutions are necessary—above all, for Russia it-self. So that its role and image would be perceived naturally as that of an equal partner.

KARPINSKY: From what you said, you obviously understood very well the sig-nificance of Russia's position and the danger it represented, the fact that this position de facto created serious obstacles to continued work on the Union treaty. Nonetheless you kept insisting that the treaty be signed as soon as possible. Wasn't that an illusion?

GORBACHEV: Yes, I understood all this. But I based my view, as before, on the fact that a Union is necessary for all the republics, including Russia. My con-viction was that it is necessary to persist in the work we began, work that has come very far.

During this time I made a short trip to Madrid in connection with the start of a conference on the Middle East. There, on October 29–30, I met with leaders of the United States and Spain (George Bush, Juan Carlos, and Felipe Gonzalez), and later, in the south of France, with Francois Mitterand. Those with whom I met expressed their conviction that the quickest possi-ble signing of a Union treaty was essential. They could not understand what was going on with us. When I evaluated these discussions, I realized that the most essential item discussed was the fact that it was in our best interests and those of the West for us to undergo reform and renewal but, without fail, to preserve the Union as one of the fundamental supporting structures for peace in today's world.

Considering all aspects of the matter, I tried to speed up this effort. On November 4, at the regular session of the State Council, I made a sharp pro-nouncement: to delay the signing of the treaty any further would be intol-erable.

The transcript of my speech at that time has been preserved. The fol-lowing is the essence of what I said:

We are in a serious situation, indeed a formidable one. I believe that given the potential we gained after the coup, as a result of the decisions made on the basis of the joint declaration of leaders of the republics, that we handled this question too light-mindedly and not in the responsible manner it deserves. We all hoped at the time that we could deal with the situation, that we could take it in hand and lead the country confidently down the road of reform and out of the crisis.

At the time we felt intensely that disintegration of our state was impermissible. We had looked over the edge, so to speak, and seen the abyss into which we could plunge if that were to happen.

The first few weeks of collaborative effort reinforced our certainty about that. The people and the country supported our approach. But after the first few weeks there were delays in our response, and political intrigue resumed. The economic treaty is experiencing a painful birth. Our country is gasping for breath, lacking any clarity on these most important questions. This is all very dangerous.

On the eve of the November 4 session of the State Council I had one more meeting with Boris Yeltsin. There was a sharpness to the conversation. I posed all questions bluntly, particularly the question of what line Russia would follow regarding the treaty for an economic commonwealth. Yeltsin gave assurances that Russia would operate within the framework of the economic treaty and that Russia would even play an initiatory role. At the State Council meeting itself Yeltsin on the whole adhered to that position, stressing that his orientation was in favor of a "new treaty—a Union of Sovereign States."

On November 14 the State Council considered the draft treaty for the Union of Sovereign States, which had been updated based on the comments or objections of the various republics. Here is the brief transcript of that session's proceedings:

State Council. Novo-Ogarevo. November 14. Decision is made to go through the text. The preamble is quickly agreed to. There is an argument over the name— Union of Sovereign Republics or Union of Sovereign States.

YELTSIN: Union of Sovereign States.

M. S.: So let it be Union of Sovereign States. We must still solve the main question: Will we create a Union that is a state entity (*gosudarstvo*) or not?*

---

* Translator's Note: In the present excerpt from a transcript of November 14, 1991, and in the next excerpt, from a transcript of November 25, 1991, Mikhail Gorbachev argues for a renewed form of Union that would retain some significant aspects of central governmental authority while ceasing to have the highly centralized character of the former Soviet state. It has been suggested that in this context the phrase "state entity" best conveys in English what Gorbachev was advocating. The Russian term he used is *gosudarstvo*, normally tranlsated as "government" or "state."

YELTSIN: The intention is to create a Union.

NAZARBAEV: What kind of Union do we want?

M. S.: What is your opinion?

NAZARBAEV: It's very complicated to talk about a federation. Perhaps a confederation?

M. S.: A Union state entity. I categorically insist. If we do not create a state entity, I predict disaster, I tell you . . .

YELTSIN: We will create a Union of states.

M. S.: If it is not a state entity, I will not participate in this process. I can leave you all right now. (M. S. rises and begins to gather his papers together.) This is my position in principle. If there is not to be a state entity, I consider my mission to have been exhausted. I cannot come out in favor of something amorphous.

SHUSHKEVICH [head of the Byelorussian republic] tries to persuade Gorbachev to stay.

M. S.: I want you to believe that I do not have any ambitions and I do not aspire to any new posts.

YELTSIN: Let's call it plainly a confederation.

M. S.: You decide. I cannot force you. You have no less responsibility than I; in fact you have more.

YELTSIN: It must be done in such a way that Ukraine doesn't leave.

SHUSHKEVICH: I think they will come into a confederation.

There is a break.

M. S.: Well then, it seems we have found a compromise: "a confederated democratic state exercising power . . ."

It was then agreed that the treaty would be initialed on November 25.

After the session a press conference was held. Here Yeltsin said: "It is hard to say what number of states will join the Union, but I have the firm conviction that a Union will exist." Shushkevich said: "In my opinion, the probability of the formation of a new Union has substantially increased. I think there will be a Union." The leaders of Kazakhstan, Kyrgyzstan, Turkmenistan, and Tadzhikistan also spoke in favor of a Union.

I took the floor last and said that a treaty for a Union of Sovereign States was simply indispensable as a basis for reforming our unitary multinational state. It was also indispensable in order to solve our most urgent problems. Without an agreement among the republics, the reforms would go no further. We had to have agreement and coordination because that was how our fates had taken shape and nothing could be done about that. For us to separate now, while trying to guess whether that would turn out well, was simply impossible. If we go our separate ways as nationally distinct states, then even within the framework of a commonwealth the process of coordination and cooperation would become extraordinarily complicated.

It seemed that we had taken a significant step forward. Of course there were moments that caused one to sit up and take notice. These had to do in particular with the position taken by the Ukrainian leader Kravchuk. He had not taken part in the State Council meeting of November 14. But on November 8, when he returned to Kiev from Moscow, he held a press conference where he stated the following:

- What is most important is the referendum on Ukraine's independence (scheduled for December 1).

- The economic crisis must be overcome.

- Ukraine needs to establish its own national army.

- Ukraine also needs its own separate currency.

- Independent foreign relations are necessary; there is no need for the existence of a Unionwide foreign ministry.

Regarding the Union treaty, Kravchuk took the following position:

Let's stop all the talk about the Novo-Ogarevo process. And let's make it clear, finally, exactly what a Union is. And exactly whom would the Supreme Soviet of the Union represent? Would it be fifteen republics, as before, or would it be a Union of seven, as it has now become? And exactly what would Gorbachev's position be? The Novo-Ogarevo process is now in the pluperfect [i.e., a thing of the past]. . . . We will oppose any attempt to create central government bodies. We will not ratify a treaty if central government bodies of any kind whatsoever are hidden behind it. Indeed no Center of any kind should exist other than coordinating bodies that would be established by the states participating in the treaty process.

Clearly Kravchuk did not want a real Union. He was only willing to support something amorphous and undefined. But at that time he was the only one taking that position, although—as was evident in the transcript of the State Council session quoted above—Yeltsin's comments and proposals were largely in harmony with Kravchuk's views.

The next session of the State Council was held, as agreed, on November 25. The following is a transcript of that meeting's proceedings:

M. S.: As we agreed at the previous session of the State Council, the question for consideration at today's session is the initialing of the Union treaty.

YELTSIN: Unfortunately some formulations have shown up that we have not come to agree on.

M. S.: Well, let's go through the text. On the preamble there are no objections. On the principles. First . . .

YELTSIN: We have to come back to this.

M. S.: But we already reached an agreement here. We debated for four hours.

YELTSIN: I understand. But we held exploratory discussions in several committees of the Supreme Soviet. The majority agree that there should be no Union after all, that is, not a confederated democratic state but a confederation of democratic states.

An argument breaks out.

YELTSIN: Since I still have objections, I will submit a statement for the minutes while initialing the treaty.

Once again, a harsh discussion erupts between YELTSIN and GORBACHEV.

NIYAZOV (the first to intervene): I think we have to consider Boris Nikolaevich's [Yeltsin's] proposal. It seems to me that the essence of the matter does not change.

M. S.: It does change. There is no state entity.

KARIMOV: Our parliament also expressed the sentiment that the draft treaty should not be initialed until it is discussed in committee.

YELTSIN: There is another important aspect. Signing the treaty without Ukraine is useless. There would be no Union. Let's wait for Ukraine. That would also show Ukraine our respect.

M. S.: As someone said, "Gorbachev has become obsolete." Apparently that is your opinion as well. Therefore reach an agreement among yourselves. I do not wish to link myself with the chaos that stands behind your vague and formless position. If the intention is not to establish a Union, say so.

The decision is made to send the text of the treaty to the Supreme Soviets of the republics by decision of the State Council. An argument follows about how to formulate the submission.

M. S.: We should say that we consider ourselves in agreement on the text of the treaty and that we are submitting it for the consideration of the Supreme Soviets.

YELTSIN: I think we should be more concise: "The present draft is being submitted for consideration . . ."

M. S.: What's the difference?

YELTSIN: The difference is the phrase "agreed on."

M. S.: But if it is not agreed on, it shouldn't be sent out.

Once again an argument breaks out.

M. S.: I hold that the leaders of the republics, at a moment requiring great responsibility, are engaging in unnecessary maneuvering.

SHUSHKEVICH: I will not accept that with regard to myself. My view is that we initial the treaty ten days from now, but not today.

M. S.: Listen, let's do this. You stay here and come to an agreement among yourselves, without any witnesses; we will leave you. I ask the rest of you to stay.

GORBACHEV leaves and goes downstairs. After twenty-five minutes YELTSIN and SHUSHKEVICH come downstairs also. Together they have worked out a formula. After a break they resume.

The proposed text is as follows: "Resolved by the State Council of the USSR to submit to the Supreme Soviets of the Sovereign States and to the Supreme Soviet of the USSR the draft treaty that has been worked out for a Union of Sovereign States and to request that the Supreme Soviets consider this draft, with the idea of preparing the draft to be signed during the current year."

M. S.: Also add: "The draft is to be published in the press."

Yeltsin's statement for the minutes is then gone through page by page. In the main his comments are accepted.

And so the draft treaty was not initialed. Why did Yeltsin, and those following him, not want to take this action? I think his advisers persuaded him that he needed a free hand to make further corrections "behind the scenes" while work on the treaty continued. I do not exclude the possibility, however, that the Russian president already knew at the time that the document would not go into effect, and therefore he did not want to endorse it.

Immediately after this session of the State Council another press conference was held. This time the representatives of the republics did not want to participate. I summarized for the journalists the exchange of opinions that had taken place. I emphasized that all the primary clauses in the draft treaty had remained unchanged. I concluded my remarks as follows:

> We returned once again to a discussion on the question of a confederation, whether that is a Union or a state entity? The formula that had been agreed on at the previous session of the State Council was left untouched, namely, that a Union of Sovereign States is a confederated democratic state. That conception was present in all parts of the draft treaty. Thus the very difficult, highly responsible work at this important stage, represented by the State Council's consideration of the treaty, has been completed. . . . The leaders of the republics to some extent have left themselves room for maneuver and are correct in stating that the process must still be completed by the Supreme Soviets of the republics.

On November 27 the new draft treaty was published.

The discussion at the State Council on November 25, and what happened at that meeting in general, left me with a sense of foreboding. It seemed no accident that Boris Yeltsin had dismissed what we had agreed on concerning the main points in the new treaty, and that he had suddenly made public, for all the world to see, certain theses from the past that completely overturned the points we had agreed on. Evidently, even then, he had a completely different plan in mind.

We now know that Yeltsin had indeed adopted a course aimed at dissolving the Union, that in fact he had done so long before November 25. Leonid Kravchuk, in his book *The Last Days of the Empire*, states that there had been secret agreements and coordinated actions among Yeltsin and the leaders of Ukraine and Byelorussia and that this collaboration had long been established, virtually from the moment when preparations for the Union treaty began. According to Kravchuk, the "threesome" tried "not to attract excessive attention," which "was assured by the very narrow circle involved." As I have said, this only became known later. At that time, on

November 25, I had doubts about Yeltsin's position, but that was all. I wondered whether he was playing a double game.

On December 1 the referendum for Ukraine's independence was held, resulting in 90.32 percent of voters favoring independence. Kravchuk was elected president of the republic. And on December 2 Yeltsin recognized Ukraine's independence.

CHAPTER 14

The Belovezh Accord: Dissolution of the USSR

ON DECEMBER 3 the USSR Supreme Soviet approved the draft treaty for a Union of Sovereign States. At that time I sent a letter to the parliamentarians of the Supreme Soviets of the various sovereign states. The document read as follows:

> I am impelled by my growing feeling of alarm over our homeland's very existence to address this message to you. Among our numerous crises, the most dangerous is the breakdown of the state system. It is also the most painful crisis as it interferes with the ability of government authorities at all levels to fulfill their duties to citizens. Further, it disrupts the economy, slows down and threatens to ruin the reform process, corrupts morals and customs, pits one nationality against another, and leads ultimately to the destruction of our culture.
>
> In each of your sovereign states, democratically elected legislative and executive bodies have arisen. They are invested with the responsibility for policies that ought to serve the interests of the people. But things are going from bad to worse. It should be obvious that a main reason for this is the current process of disintegration, which, in violation of the historical logic of the very existence of an enormous integrated country, has gone far beyond reasonable limits to the point of becoming destructive.
>
> The draft Union treaty has been submitted for your approval. Your decision will either bring society closer to new forms of existence or will condemn our peoples to a long and difficult road from which they will have to seek, probably in vain, to extricate themselves individually, in isolation. What specifically would lie ahead for us in that event—for each of us individually, for all of us together, for the entire outside world—it is impossible to predict. One thing, however, is certain: The consequences would be painful. . . .

Each of you has the right to renounce a Union. But this requires that those whom the people elected must consider all the consequences.

Further on in the document is a summary of the possible consequences of the Union's disintegration. In my conclusion I return to the question of the treaty:

Two fundamental sets of ideas are contained in the treaty's conception of confederation, which define the character of the new and unprecedented state system: that of *self-determination, national state sovereignty*, and *independence* and that of *Union status, cooperation, coordination, and mutual assistance.*

My position is unambiguous. I am for a new Union, a Union of Sovereign States, a confederated democratic state. On the threshold of your decision I want to be sure that my position is well known to you. It is impossible to delay further. Time lost may have catastrophic results.

Therefore I ask you, as authorized representatives of your nations, to discuss the draft treaty for a Union of Sovereign States in the coming days and to approve it.

I hoped that the Supreme Soviets would approve the treaty. I was told that the greatest difficulties might arise in the Russian parliament. But I knew that when the treaty was reviewed by several commissions of the Supreme Soviet of Russia it had won support. The simple fact is, however, that the deputies of the Supreme Soviets of the sovereign states were not given the opportunity even to consider the treaty.

As early as December 4, the Kiev newspaper *Rabochaya Gazeta* reported that Leonid Kravchuk, in a discussion with the U.S. president the previous day, informed him that on the coming Saturday he, Yeltsin, and Shushkevich, the head of the Byelorussian parliament, would be meeting in Minsk to discuss "domestic and foreign policy questions of the states they headed."

Before his trip to Minsk, Yeltsin met with me to say that the purpose of his visit to Byelorussia was for bilateral Russian-Byelorussian negotiations. Kravchuk had been invited in order to draw him into the treaty process. Yeltsin said that "a Union without Ukraine was unthinkable" and added: "Everything must be done to convince the Ukrainians to add their names to the Union treaty." He did make one qualification: "If that doesn't work out, we will have to think about other variants." I pressed Yeltsin on this point: Ukraine could be drawn into the treaty process, but the best way to do that would be for the Russian Federation to be the first to discuss and sign the treaty. Then Ukraine would seek a place for itself in this process. It would have nowhere else to go if the other eight republics signed. But if an agreement could not be reached, we could then continue the discussion in Moscow.

On December 8 the threesome met. They issued a declaration: "The Union of Soviet Socialist Republics as an entity under international law and a geopolitical reality has ceased to exist." They signed an agreement to establish a Commonwealth of Independent States (CIS).

In 1993, during a meeting with deputies belonging to the parliamentary group Smena, one of them told me the following. (This deputy had been an ardent supporter of Yeltsin in 1991.) After returning from Minsk, the president of Russia gathered together a group of deputies who were closely associated with him in order to enlist their support for ratification of the Minsk agreements. He was asked to what extent these agreements were valid from a legal standpoint. Unexpectedly he went into a forty-minute oration, relating in a rather inspired way how he had managed to "pull the wool over Gorbachev's eyes" before his trip to Minsk, convincing Gorbachev that he would be pursuing one goal there when in fact he was preparing to do the exact opposite. "Gorbachev must be kept out of the game," Yeltsin had added.

Commentary, as the saying goes, is superfluous. The president of Russia and his entourage in fact *sacrificed the Union* to his passionate desire to accede to the throne in the Kremlin.

On December 9 I made a declaration regarding the agreement signed by the three heads of state at Belovezh:

> For me, as president of the country, the chief criterion in assessing this document is to what extent it corresponds to the interests of our citizens' security and to the tasks of overcoming the present crisis and preserving the state system while continuing democratic change.
>
> This agreement has positive aspects.
>
> The Ukrainian leadership, which recently had not been active in the treaty process, did take part in this agreement.
>
> The document stresses the need to create a single economic space operating on agreed-on principles, with a single currency and a single financial and

banking system. Willingness to collaborate in the fields of science, education, culture, and other areas was expressed. A certain formula for military-strategic coordination was proposed.

However, this document is of such significance and so profoundly affects the interests of the peoples, the nations and nationalities of our country, and the entire international community that it requires a further, comprehensive political and legal evaluation.

In any case, the following is clear: The agreement bluntly declares an end to the existence of the USSR. Undeniably each republic has the right to secede from the Union, but the fate of the multinational state cannot be determined by the will of the leaders of three republics. This question should be decided only by constitutional means with the participation of all the sovereign states and taking into account the will of all their citizens.

The statement that Unionwide legal norms would cease to be in effect is also illegal and dangerous; it can only worsen the chaos and anarchy in society.

The hastiness with which the document appeared is also cause for concern. It was not discussed by the populations nor by the Supreme Soviets of the republics in whose name it was signed. Even worse, it appeared at the moment when the draft treaty for a Union of Sovereign States, drafted by the USSR State Council, was being discussed by the parliaments of the republics.

In the situation that has arisen, it is my profound conviction that all the Supreme Soviets of the republics and the USSR Supreme Soviet need to discuss both the draft treaty for the Union of Sovereign States and the accord concluded in Minsk. To the extent that a different form of state system is proposed in the accord—a matter that should come under the jurisdiction of the USSR Congress of People's Deputies—it is necessary to convene that congress. In addition, I would not rule out holding a nationwide referendum (a plebiscite) on this question.

On December 10 the Supreme Soviet of Belarus and the Supreme Soviet of Ukraine, bypassing the question of the Union of Sovereign States, ratified the agreement concerning the founding of the Commonwealth of Independent States. Two days later a similar decision was made by the RSFSR Supreme Soviet.

Among those voting in complete harmony for the Belovezh accord were deputies belonging to groups totally opposed to one another.

On December 13 the leaders of the Central Asian states and Kazakhstan met in Ashkhabad, capital of Turkmenistan. Basically they approved the initiative taken to establish the Commonwealth of Independent States, but they emphasized that equal participation by all the former republics of the Soviet Union should be guaranteed in the process of developing documents and deciding the character of the new formation. A conference of eleven republics was set for December 21. I sent a message to those participating in that conference.

The following considerations determined my viewpoint. If the other republics arrived at the commonly held position that they wished to form such a commonwealth, I, as an individual devoted to the principles of democracy and constitutional rule, proceeding from these convictions and in view of my role as president, should respect that choice. But I favored a gradual process that would not contribute to chaos and dislocation. In accordance with these ideas, I wrote the following message:

The ratification of an agreement to found a Commonwealth of Independent States by the Supreme Soviets of the RSFSR, Ukraine, and Belarus, and the willingness of Kazakhstan, Kyrgyzstan, Tadzhikistan, and Turkmenistan to join in as founders of this Commonwealth, has changed the situation radically. The life of the numerous nations and nationalities of a great country regarding the governmental form under which they live is beginning a new history. On this country's territory several independent states are being formed. In place of the long and difficult historical era of the formation of a single country there comes a process of disunification and dismemberment. That, too, will not be easy. There should be no illusions. Society obviously has not yet realized that this turn of events is of colossal proportions affecting the very foundations of our peoples' and citizens' lives.

From the very beginning of perestroika we proceeded step by step toward having all the republics acquire genuine independence. But all along I insisted that the country should not be allowed to fall apart. That was and is my understanding of the will of all the nations and nationalities as expressed in the referendum [of March 17, 1991]—their desire for independence while preserving the integrity of the historical Union. This idea and this concern lay at the basis of my formula for a Union of Sovereign States, which initially met with your support.

I am not writing in order to return the discussion to that topic. The idea of a Commonwealth of Independent States is now becoming a reality, and it is important, vitally important, that this very complex process not intensify destructive tendencies that can be observed in society. After all, it is obvious to everyone that the transition will take place in circumstances of profound economic, political, and interethnic crisis, with a significant decline in the living standard.

I take a completely serious attitude toward the contents of the documents adopted at Brest [i.e., the Belovezh accord] and at Ashkhabad, and in the decrees ratified by the Supreme Soviets of the three republics. In considering the points I wish to make, I have taken into account the reaction of society both within and outside our country and questions that still remain open.

The purpose of the considerations outlined here is to specify minimum conditions without which, it seems to me, the Commonwealth under present circumstances cannot be viable. Let me make an immediate qualification: Among these conditions are some that are obvious and that all of you acknowledge, but I cannot omit them from this message.

First, a clear-cut understanding should be recorded that the Commonwealth is a multinational formation with absolute equality not only of the states themselves but of all the nationalities, religions, traditions, and customs, regardless of their locations. Therefore a more appropriate name, it seems to me, would be Commonwealth of European and Asian States.

Second, it is not enough simply to give official recognition to the Declaration of Human Rights and to democratic freedoms. Given the unique situation of people who have settled across an enormous space, where over the course of centuries the fates of millions of families have intersected, where there have been tens of millions of mixed marriages, the problem of open borders and of citizenship must be worked out with special care.

I am sure that in everyone not contaminated with nationalism and separatism, and that means hundreds of millions of people, there will inevitably arise a sense of loss of a great country. And when the practical work begins of defining governmental and administrative processes and other demarcations, and the terms for citizenship, a great many will be affected most directly—in their everyday lives, in production, in human relations. Therefore, possibly for a prolonged period, it will be necessary to agree on a Commonwealth citizenship alongside citizenship in a particular country.

I fear that if all this is not thought out, resolved, and reliably guaranteed, the idea of a Commonwealth will be rejected on the national level.

Third, of decisive importance to ensure the stability of the Commonwealth is the creation of a socially oriented market economy and the defense of all forms of property. I share the opinion of those who consider it essential to confirm the resolute stand of the participants in the Commonwealth to abide by the economic community treaty and to complete work on a range of proposals providing for the necessary conditions to establish a common "Eurasian market." This would include coordinated measures on such important questions as the currency, the financial and banking systems, the methodology of price formation and taxation, customs collection, budgetary allocations for defense, and other common purposes.

I am convinced that appropriate structures for economic coordination within the framework of the Commonwealth will be required. I am also certain that all this will become possible and will contribute to the welfare of the people of all our nations and nationalities only under conditions of effective guarantees of economic rights and freedoms for the individual and their unconditional defense both in law and practice.

Fourth, I believe I can say, with full responsibility and knowledge of the matter regarding an integrated system of military-strategic security for our country, that the slightest attempts to disintegrate that system are fraught with the danger of international disaster.

From the perspective of establishing genuine sovereignty of the Commonwealth members, there is no need whatsoever to divide up this complex and extremely costly system. The parties to the agreement could, *on an urgent basis*, specify certain structures for unified control and command of the strategic forces, including all the basic military, technical, and scientific defense components. Monitoring of the status and composition of the armed forces can be collective, and so can the pursuit of a coordinated military policy. But the notion of collective command is an absurdity.

The problem of reforming and reducing the size of the army also requires joint decision making. This is a very big *social* problem at the present time. It is also a problem of political security for the entire country, which, for centuries, has had unified armed forces.

Fifth, the independent, sovereign activity of each member of the Commonwealth in the world arena is valid. But if there is a Commonwealth and it is a political formation, it should have political representation within the international community. This could follow the model, let us say, of the European Community, which has status as an *entity under international law*. Such a status for the Commonwealth cannot be renounced because it inherits from the USSR the status of a nuclear superpower. It is not so easy to escape such a legacy. Otherwise international confidence could be undermined, and the treaty on the nonproliferation of nuclear arms could be violated, a treaty that all the sovereign members of the Commonwealth seem obliged to reaffirm.

I cannot imagine how a strategic defense system could possibly be maintained in common without a minimum common policy. The most sensible solution would be to have a structure for foreign relations adapted to the needs and principles of the Commonwealth, including the question of membership in the United Nations Security Council.

The signature of the Soviet Union is affixed to some of the most important documents of our era, both declarations and treaties. Fifteen thousand foreign economic agreements are now in effect. Simply to erase all this would injure the international prestige of the Commonwealth and its genuine interests from the very start.

Just as all members of the Commonwealth have apparently confirmed their commitment to principles of contemporary democracy (free elections; separation of powers; political, ideological, and religious pluralism; a government based on law, civil society, and human rights), they should also adopt a foreign policy course based on the new thinking, which has been recognized throughout the civilized world.

Sixth, irreparable harm will be done to the spiritual development of all our nations and nationalities if the members of the Commonwealth do not reach an agreement on coordination (and agencies for coordination) in the fields of science, culture, a language for communication among the nationalities, preservation of monuments, sources for maintaining museums, world-class theaters, libraries, archives, major institutes, laboratories, observatories, and so forth.

Seventh, regarding procedures for legal continuity, a new era in our country's history should begin with dignity, with the observation of legitimate standards. Indeed one of the reasons for our nations' and our nationalities' historical misfortunes has precisely been crude ruptures, destructive upheavals, and predatory or aggressive methods in the course of social development.

Both the necessary prerequisites and experience exist for us to function in a democratic framework. I therefore propose that, after the document on the Commonwealth is ratified and the ratification documents exchanged, a final session of the USSR Supreme Soviet be held at which a decree would be adopted terminating the Soviet Union's existence and transferring all its legal rights and obligations to the Commonwealth of European and Asian States.

These are the most general considerations I wish to raise. They are dictated by a feeling of responsibility for the ultimate success of the great work begun in 1985.

The scheduled conference of the heads of the independent governments was held in Alma-Ata on December 21, 1991, and there a declaration supporting the Belovezh accord was signed. The declaration stated: "With the formation of the Commonwealth of Independent States, the Union of Soviet Socialist Republics ceases to exist." The considerations I had presented in my message to the participants at the conference remained without sequel. At Alma-Ata no one was concerned any longer with the fate of our country. They were all in a state of euphoria, busily dividing up the inheritance. Yesterday hardly anyone had heard of them, but tomorrow they would be heads of independent states. What did it matter what fate they were preparing for their nations? Of course this unhappy fate became clear later on. And then they began searching for scapegoats.

On December 25 at 7:00 P.M. I made a final declaration on television:

In view of the situation that has developed—the formation of the Commonwealth of Independent States—I hereby cease my activity in the post of president of the USSR. I make this decision based on considerations of principle.

I have been a firm advocate of independence for the nations and nationalities of our country and for the sovereignty of the republics. But at the same time I have favored preservation of a Union government and the integrity of the country.

Events have taken a different road. The line favoring dismemberment of the country and the dismantling of the state has won out, something I cannot agree with . . .

Nevertheless I will do everything within the realm of possibility so that the agreements . . . lead to genuine harmony in society and facilitate the reform process as well as our emergence from the crisis.

Thus the Soviet Union ceased to exist, and perestroika was interrupted. With the beginning of 1992 one could no longer speak of perestroika—a different policy had begun. Instead of preserving the Union in a new form and with new content, the breakup of the country was accelerated. Instead of deepening reform in a gradual, evolutionary way—"shock therapy" was the rule, along with the collapse of production and people's living standards. Instead of the consistent use of democratic measures, force came into play, including the shelling of the parliament in October 1993, and the use of force was elevated to a principle of government policy. All this taken together could no longer be called perestroika.

After all I have said, the question arises: Could the Union have been preserved? Yes, absolutely. The signing of the new Union treaty was disrupted by the so-called State Committee for the State of Emergency. Even after the attempted coup of August 1991, however, as I have indicated above, the process of reforming the Soviet state could have continued. After the August coup, the conspiracy at Belovezh dealt a final blow to the Soviet Union.

Today the assertion can often be heard that the Union treaty that was to be signed in August 1991 would have meant the destruction of the Union anyway. No! The signing of that treaty would have been a real alternative to the breakup of the Union. It would have meant preservation of Union-wide citizenship, which was recognized as a separate point in that document. The citizen of any state belonging to the Union was simultaneously a citizen of the Union. That was Article 2 of the treaty. The new Union treaty would have meant preservation and development of a unified Unionwide market. Armed forces under a single command (not "joint command") would have been preserved. The state security of the Union as a whole and a unified foreign policy would have been assured.

Preservation, renewal, and reform of the Union was my main political and, if you will, moral task in my position as president of the USSR. I consider it my greatest sorrow and misfortune that I did not succeed in preserving the country as a single whole. All my efforts were focused on trying to preserve that unity.

Incidentally, more and more statements are heard today, including some by participants in the Belovezh accord, that the "soft form of Union Gorbachev proposed" might have protected our nations and nationalities from painful experiences. But, as the saying goes, the train has already left the station.

A fundamental question remains unclear to this day: Why did the Supreme Soviets of the republics support the Belovezh accord? I have given this much thought. I believe that the Supreme Soviets, however paradoxical it may seem, were acting on the basis of a desire to preserve the country. But in fact they helped cause its dissolution. In a literal sense they miscalculated: They thought that only seven or eight republics would sign the treaty Gorbachev proposed, whereas eleven republics were immediately ready to sign the Belovezh accord. And therefore they voted in favor of the accord.

Other forces were also operating. In the Supreme Soviet of Russia the vote for the Belovezh accord was almost unanimous, with only six opposed. In the Supreme Soviet of Belarus only one deputy (Lukashenko, the current president of Belarus) spoke out against it. What was this all about? The party nomenklatura [or bureaucracy] which had supported the August coup in order to prevent the signing of the Union treaty—supposedly to preserve the Union—now voted for its dissolution.

There was another motivation. A Communist delegate named Sevastyanov, notorious for his fundamentalist positions, made the following argument in the debates on the Belovezh accord: I am voting for the Belovezh accord, and I urge everyone to do so—so that we can get rid of Gorbachev. And on this basis the extreme Right and the extreme Left came together.

I am often asked this question: Are you sure you used all your powers as president to preserve the Union after the Belovezh accord? Yes, absolutely. I used all political methods available. I have also been asked why I did not use force, why I did not arrest participants in the Belovezh accord? But that would have meant taking a road that could have become bloody. For me such a road was closed, but, I was mistaken in my expectations regarding the positions the Supreme Soviets of the republics would take.

Essentially the decisions of the Supreme Soviets and the deluded expectations of the citizens of the Soviet Union deprived me of the authority to take firm measures toward abrogating the Belovezh accord. It was both strange and surprising; it seemed that in December 1991 only the country's president wanted to preserve the Union. But today it turns out that most people regret the dissolution of the USSR. Apparently it has become clear to everyone that a terrible mistake was made. It was clear to me at the time, and I spoke out about it more than once to the citizens of the USSR.

Above all, the initiators of the breakup of the Union contended that everyone would live better by going separate ways. But subsequent years have refuted this argument. Everywhere in the "post-Soviet space" the economy and culture have declined, and a majority of the population has fallen into poverty. In practice it has been confirmed that no economic methods can be effective in conditions where integrated systems are falling apart—transport, power, communications and information, health care, science, education, and social security. Even Russia, which had the greatest economic potential and natural resources, could not save itself from a massive collapse of production unheard of in peacetime and a decline in literally all areas of activity.

Furthermore, at the time that the signing of a new Union treaty was proposed a foundation for democracy had been laid in the country. Civil society and a government based on the rule of law had begun to take shape. The dissolution of the Union not only interrupted this process but resulted in the emasculation of democratic institutions. These institutions are being increasingly used as a screen behind which bureaucratic-nomenklatura capital dominates. Russia, which had set the tone for the democratization of Soviet society, provided a bad example for the Commonwealth. The dismissal and shelling of the Supreme Soviet of Russia, the imposition of an antidemocratic constitution on the country by means of force in 1993, infringement on the legislative branch of government, on freedom of the press, on freedom of conscience, and bureaucratic domination—all these are ominous signs that the country is slipping back toward authoritarian rule.

The years since 1991 have destroyed the hope that Russia would become a worthy heir to the Soviet Union and would inherit its international authority. Weakened by economic uncertainty and political instability, Russia has lost many of the previous positions it held in the international arena. Fewer and fewer people take Russia's opinion into account. Nor can it be said that the other former Union republics have gained great advantage from their present sovereign existence. Some are threatened with the fate of becoming objects of geopolitical intrigue and neocolonial plunder.

The dissolution of the Union greatly complicated the process of forming a new international climate that could have taken hold after the Cold War. The USSR was the cement that held together an enormous Eurasian space. Russia cannot take this kind of mission upon itself. The "post-Soviet space" has more than once become the scene of armed conflicts and terrorist actions, with crime and the drug trade running amok.

Outwardly the Commonwealth of Independent States seems to function—top-level meetings take place on the ministerial level and sessions of a parliamentary assembly are held. (This assembly is probably the most active element in the Commonwealth.) Agreements on customs and tariffs as well as other matters have been signed. On the whole, within the framework of the Commonwealth, several hundred documents have been adopted. But in the overwhelming majority of cases these agreements have no effect; they have only a formal status. An infrastructure for the Commonwealth as a whole either does not exist at all or is ineffective. Thus far there is no locomotive powering the integration of the CIS.

Yet I wish to remind readers that some far-reaching goals were solemnly proclaimed in the Belovezh accord. It provided for preservation and support under united command of a unified military-strategic space. It spoke of the coordination of foreign policy and collaboration in establishing and developing a common economic space, a coordinated financial policy, development of transport and communications systems, environmental protection, and a migration policy. In a supplemental statement to the Belovezh accord, the governments of the three countries signing it (Russia, Ukraine, and Belarus) promised to coordinate economic policy, to pursue radical economic reform in a coordinated way, to conclude banking agreements among the members of the Commonwealth aimed at limiting the printing of paper currency, and so forth. What happened to these goals? They went no further than the paper they were written on.

CHAPTER 15

What Lies Ahead?

TODAY, WITH THE benefit of hindsight, I believe that those who signed the Belovezh accord had no intention, even from the outset, of carrying out the commitments they made. They deliberately deceived their own people because, after all, they clearly saw that they could win support only by appearing to be concerned about preserving the Union—granted in the form of a commonwealth. It had to appear that they were not retreating from the choice the citizens made in March 1991.

To deceive the public, to lead it astray in order to paralyze any possible resistance to the operation they had begun—that was their aim. It was as though they were saying: "Look, we are preserving everything that Gorbachev wants to preserve with his treaty, but in our version almost all the republics will unite except for the Baltic republics. Gorbachev's version will unite only six, seven, maybe eight republics, leaving out Ukraine."

In general—and I think this is obvious from everything I have said above—the Russian leaders, along with their two partners, intended to deceive the public from the very beginning. They proclaimed one thing to our country and to the international community, but they did another.

The commonwealth scheme lacked any real impulse toward cooperation. Today's problems all flow from this. Of course, also sharing the blame are the politicians in the CIS countries. (I would exempt from this charge Nazarbaev, president of Kazakhstan, who insisted quite stubbornly, and still insists today, on the development of processes of integration.) The "top brass" in the CIS countries are happy playing the "sovereignty flute": They do not wish to relinquish one iota of power. But unless they do, no kind of unification is possible. In short, the interests of the political elites were given priority over those of the citizenry.

Especially noteworthy is the responsibility of the Russian leadership in all this. By no means was it accidental that at a summit of the CIS, held in Kishinev in the fall of 1997, all the participants criticized Russia and its leadership for the Commonwealth's state of paralysis. President Yeltsin even acknowledged that the criticism was justified: After all, for years he had been chairman of the Council of Heads of State, but during that time nothing ever moved from dead center. It is not yet clear what conclusions he has drawn (or will draw) from the sharp criticism lodged against him or from his own self-criticism. I, for one, do not expect much. True, recently there seem to have been some steps toward greater cooperation among members of the Commonwealth. Once the euphoria over independence had passed and sobriety had been restored, public opinion shifted significantly—and even the views of some of the political elite.

Under these conditions new attitudes have developed regarding the relations between members of the CIS—above all, those between Russia and the other member states. Here disparate interests clash and many different cards are being played—by Russia, the new states on the territory of the former USSR, their neighbors, Western Europe, and the United States. All this deserves separate analysis. Here I will examine only what applies to the subject at hand.

At issue, above all, are the natural processes of integration that are gaining strength in many regions of the world and also on a world scale. For the "post-Soviet space" this problem is extremely acute. Everyone is aware of the wide-ranging consequences that resulted from the disruption of historically established, diverse ties. But if these consequences are understood, it would seem logical for people to seek new forms of cooperation and integration. Yet neither in Russia nor in the countries of the so-called "near abroad" [the non-Russian countries of the former Soviet Union] is there the necessary clarity on this question.

Proposals for closer cooperation with the countries of the "near abroad" are regarded with suspicion by many in Russia. The reasons are political, because the question arises as to who was responsible for the destruction of the former Union. And economic motives are also involved, related to the financial difficulties Russia is experiencing today.

Another factor exists which, although not discussed openly, can be deduced from the position the Russian authorities have taken. They regard the current state of affairs as more advantageous for Russia because, in the absence of multilateral treaty mechanisms of integration, Russia can more easily pursue a differentiated policy on a bilateral basis, to carry out its own maneuvers, pursue its own narrow interests at the expense of the interests of others, and impose its will. In my mind, operating in this way means seeing no farther than the end of one's nose. It indicates a failure to understand the advantages that a new form of integration can bring.

Attitudes among ordinary Russians present quite a different picture. The latest sociological research shows that, increasingly, the Russian people understand they were deceived. But so far they are unable, or unwilling, to force their leaders to take a serious approach toward questions of integration within the framework of the CIS. Further, the press and television in Russia try to convince people that what is needed today, above all, is to think about "how to live in Russia" and that the rest is unimportant. *But in fact the very question of "how to live in Russia" involves the question of what to do about integration, how to arrange relations with other member states of the CIS.* These are essentially two sides of the same coin—unless of course one is occupied with constructing scholastic schemes and playing mind games, lacking the courage to assess the situation soberly, to evaluate the people's attitudes and their desire for cooperation among the states of the former USSR.

The same situation prevails in the other former Soviet republics. In these past few years all the new independent states have traveled a considerable distance and have strengthened their sovereignty. But among the peoples of these states, interest in the historical community that existed, in economic, cultural, and scientific ties, in the fact that for centuries we were all in the same melting pot—that interest persists. *The state represented by the Soviet Union no longer exists, but for the time being that country is still alive.* It has been broken into pieces, but those pieces are trying, so to speak, to form a network of capillaries so that the flow of blood will not be stopped completely. And, I repeat, this interest in the community that once existed is being expressed by the people themselves, which is decisive.

Another aspect of the matter is the position maintained by the West. In Western capitals judgments are made with extreme prejudice against processes of integration in the post-Soviet space. Such processes are regarded there as nothing less than attempts to revive the Russian or Soviet empire. Not only do they make no effort to hide this attitude, they actively oppose rapprochement among the new independent states. The United States has reacted with great concern. It does everything it can, taking advantage of momentary difficulties, to prevent integration in general, especially among Russia, Ukraine, and Kazakhstan. But such a policy is, to say the least, shortsighted. It will result in the very opposite of what is intended by encouraging Russia toward actions in the spirit of imperial policy.

Contrary to this view, a process of integration, if carried out within a legal framework of definitive rules, adhering to principles of equality, operating only voluntarily, and providing for the creation of effective multilateral mechanisms that would erect barriers against any manifestation of imperial ambitions—that kind of integration (and that is the only kind we are talking about) would be in the best possible interests of Russia, the West, the entire international community—that is, their interests as properly understood. But for this to occur many things must change: the policies of Russia itself, the positions taken by the other CIS countries, and the orientations and approaches adopted by the West.

In my opinion, integration among the CIS countries is both necessary and possible. As I have already indicated, strategic, economic, and cultural factors speak for reintegration. Above all, there are human factors that operate in favor of reintegration. But to resolve this issue, certain questions must be answered.

First, is a movement for a new Union even possible? If you consider that most of the heads of state in the CIS countries are the same politicians who concluded the Belovezh and the Alma-Ata agreements, and in view of the way they have operated within the CIS until now, I frankly am not optimistic. I do not think that they will display the will and initiative necessary for this process.

In my view, the locomotive for a revival of the Union, the engine that would drive a process of reintegration, could be the parliaments, which have a mandate from the people.

Second, what lies ahead? A return to the USSR? Today that would be a reactionary idea. Of course we all feel a sense of loss and injury for the country in which we lived and for which we bore responsibility. But there are distinct realities and circumstances, and a particular context in which the discussion is proceeding. Today this context consists in the fact that, whether we like it or not, *independent states* do exist. That of course is primary and cannot be ignored.

Therefore I do not believe that a return to the USSR is possible. If such a demand were raised, and especially if a policy consistent with that demand were pursued, defeat would be inevitable. And it would be a defeat for all those who care about our country and about what is happening to us now that we are living in separate states.

My answer is that Russia's relations with the now independent republics must be improved. I believe that *the republics would recognize relations that were based on equality and that, by improving relations in this way, these states could reach a new stage of cooperation.*

There are also those in Russia who say that the Russia that existed before the October revolution, before the formation of the Soviet Union, must be restored. But what does that mean? Do they want to ignore the nearly seventy years of the Soviet Union's existence, when Union republics were indeed a reality? However difficult the conditions under which these republics developed, they did exist. Does anyone think that this has no importance for Ukraine today, for Kazakhstan, or for any of the other CIS countries? Does this mean we should begin an all-out campaign to reunify these countries? I think such an approach would drag the Russian people, and not only the Russian people, into bloodshed. How many times can people be put in that kind of situation? I was always mindful of precisely that problem, always guided by concern about it, and I remain absolutely convinced that such an approach is not the answer.

And so the question arises: *What kind of new Union?* A federation, a confederation, an economic union like the European Economic Community? What would its composition be? A Union of only the Slavic states [i.e., Russia, Belarus, and Ukraine] or a Slavic union plus Kazakhstan? And so the questions go, and all require answers if we are to have a serious discussion, if we are to arrive at a serious policy.

I believe that it is realistic today to promote the idea of a solid Union among four states: the three Slavic states plus Kazakhstan. Let the CIS live according to its rules and its laws. But we should state emphatically, right away: "Here is the possibility of a genuine Union, a modern form of close cooperation."

Any political speculation on this subject must be decisively opposed. If we remain within the framework of the old thinking, the old philosophy, we will not move one step forward in the search for a policy suitable to our times.

We should not become euphoric. I have traveled in many regions of Russia, and the mood of the political elites in these regions is not to act hastily on the question of a Union. "Things are so difficult," they say. "We don't know how to solve the problems we already have, especially our economic and social problems. All responsibility has devolved to the regions; it is all on our shoulders. Wouldn't a Union mean that once again we would have to share our finances and resources with other republics?"

The political scientists with whom I meet monthly—people of varied ideological persuasions—constantly emphasize this aspect of the problem. When people are asked whether they would agree to a certain lowering of their standard of living in order to become reunited once again and to provide aid to the other republics who are in an even worse situation, the answer is most often (by nearly two-thirds of those polled), "No, we wouldn't want that." Still, in polls that have been taken in the three Slavic republics and Kazakhstan over an extended period, 72–75 percent of those questioned speak in favor of the revival of a Union in some new form.

To repeat, we should not become euphoric. To do so would make a bad situation worse and would only discredit the idea of reintegration. It would make it more difficult to start this process, which is now emerging from below.

As a first step we need a political declaration that would establish one goal: to create a Union of the four states. On the way toward this goal, a great deal must be done. There are partial goals we must achieve: the formation of an economic union, coordination on defense problems, and cooperation in humanitarian fields. Such a declaration would immediately remove many problems in relations with Ukraine, and it would have a calming effect in Kazakhstan and in Russia as well. The process would begin to flow in a normal channel.

These, then, are my practical proposals and my general conception of what is needed. I wish to add one reminder: Without an overall plan, we will constantly be bumping our noses against the main question, which remains unresolved.

The question is not one of restoring a unitary state. The nations of the Commonwealth will not renounce their independence. Nor will the nations and nationalities of Russia gain anything from attempts to impose political domination. The problem is to establish a reasonable balance between the independence of the participants in the Union and the powers that are granted to its common institutions.

The Union could have been preserved. A new Union can be created.

Part Three

THE NEW THINKING:
YESTERDAY, TODAY, TOMORROW

The shifts in world politics during the past decade have in many ways been related to what we call the *new thinking*. It is true that the new thinking is rarely referred to now, especially in Russia, where it was born. Sometimes people even ask whether this new thinking really existed. And what is it anyway? Is it a conceptual structure, a set of political principles and moral values, the latest variant of some ideology, or perhaps simply propaganda serving government interests?

Many opinions have been voiced on this subject, all marked by outlooks that are intensely ideological. This is understandable. We are all finding it difficult to free ourselves from ideological fetters—both in Russia and in the West. People everywhere are finding it difficult to say goodbye to old, stereotyped ways of thinking.

In the process of constructing new international relations the going has been rough, and still is. Of course no one envisioned a smooth, straight road. But it is alarming today to see that the world, which had begun to move away from confrontation and toward unity, is once again being pushed onto a dangerous path. This tendency has already found expression in actual policies and has led to new divisions, with certain nations being placed in hostile opposition to others. This is simply the result of an absence of new policies adequate to the tasks facing the world at this crucial juncture. The responsibilities of those involved in international politics increase with every passing day. A new and higher quality of world politics is required. At the time when the new thinking originated, we regarded perestroika as a chance not only to overcome the crisis in our own country but also to contribute to eliminating the nuclear threat to our planet and advancing the worldwide search for adequate answers to the challenges of our times.

What, then, in light of all that has transpired, does the new thinking represent? Is it perhaps limited to one historical period? Has its allotted time expired? Was it perhaps suitable only to end global confrontation? Is it not applicable as a means of problem solving in our new situation? Or is now precisely the time when the need for the new thinking is more acute than ever? All these questions are worth investigating—which is the primary aim of this final part of this work.

CHAPTER 16

The Sources of the New Thinking

As I described earlier, by the mid-1980s the danger of nuclear war had become a reality. The world's nations were at an impasse, and no one could see a way out. It seemed that the confrontation between East and West would go on forever. Countries on both sides of the Iron Curtain were preparing themselves for such a future. No one wanted nuclear war, of course, but no one could guarantee that it would not occur—even if it was simply the result of some unfortunate accident.

The Soviet Union and the United States constantly had each other "in their sights," as did all the other Eastern and Western countries. The accumulation and continual refinement of nuclear and conventional weapons had become an accustomed and seemingly inseparable part of the modern world's existence. Europe had been transformed into an arena for the nuclear arms race. With each passing year, indeed each month, Europe was becoming more and more densely saturated with missiles of varying range and capacity. The world's oceans swarmed with missile-bearing vessels, both above and below the surface. Not only the air above us but outer space as well had become part of the standoff. And regional conflicts continued to rage—in Asia, Africa, Latin America.

By the mid-1980s Soviet relations with many countries of the world were quite strained. And completing the picture were (1) the war in Afghanistan; (2) complications in the Soviet Union's relations with its giant neighbor, China; and (3) the unceasing, decades-long rivalry between East and West in supplying arms to certain Asian and African countries (which had become peripheral proving grounds for the Cold War).

Our country's security had by no means become more reliably guaranteed—and that was despite the fact that an inordinately large portion of our resources was being spent on the production of weapons. The race for military supremacy relative to any possible opponent (and that was the orientation) resulted in military spending that in some years reached 25–30 percent of our gross national product—that is, five or six times greater than analogous military spending in the United States and the European NATO countries.

Obviously this course could not continue. The rush toward the abyss had to end. The need to pay serious attention to questions of foreign policy had become urgent.

The problem was not so much Soviet foreign policy itself or the actions of Soviet diplomats as it was the concepts on which they were based. These concepts rested on a dogmatic world outlook, not on reality, not on a sober analysis of the situation nor on meeting the real and vital interests of our country and our people. Rather, our foreign policy was oriented toward harsh confrontation with the entire outside world (not including, of course, those we regarded as allies, although they occupied a rather subordinate position in our overall political doctrine).

Such was the foreign policy legacy of totalitarianism. By its very nature, wherever it might arise and in whatever garments it might be vested, totalitarianism cannot exist without a harsh ideological and political system, a set of stereotypes that distort reality and have only one purpose—to serve the interests of the regime, to create conditions for its further entrenchment, and to establish a way of thinking among its "loyal subjects" that is purely to the regime's own advantage.

The first stimulus of the new thinking was a dispassionate, even remorseless analysis of our own foreign policy concepts and the practices they inspired.

What was needed was a new, unbiased appraisal of the Soviet Union's place in the world arena; a clear definition of our country's real national interests and the real parameters and imperatives for our security; a serious analysis of the present state of the international community and the main trends of its development; and, finally, the elaboration, on this basis, of a well-thought-out program of specific actions in the main areas of foreign policy practice.

Even before perestroika we had reflected on all these questions. Within the framework of studying all the important questions that had accumulated since the beginning of the 1980s, considerable attention had been paid to international affairs. With the beginning of perestroika this effort went on more energetically and was no longer kept secret from the public. Our scientific research centers provided a great deal of valuable material. (Foremost among these centers were the Institute of World Economy and International Relations, the U.S. and Canada Institute, and the Institute on the Economics of the World Socialist System, among others.) In addition, individual appraisals were offered by scientists and specialists.

This work of reexamining foreign policy concepts was not easy or simple largely because the notions of foreign policy in the Soviet period had, so to speak, been foreordained: They were taken as a "given" based on ideological postulates that had long been inculcated among us. Reexamining these concepts ultimately necessitated a revision of those political assumptions and of the deeply rooted foundations of the prevailing ideology.

The difficulty arose first for those who undertook to reexamine the established views. After all, they, too, were children of their times. From their earliest days, beginning in school, they had absorbed the fundamentals of the official ideology. Certainly they had all been deeply affected by Nikita Khrushchev's exposé of Stalinism at the Twentieth Party Congress. These were the youth of the 1960s, but they were in no way free of the ideological chains of the 1950s. A struggle took place within their very depths—such was the process of emancipating oneself from ideological fetters.

On the other hand, there were also external difficulties. Society as a whole, including a substantial number of active party members, found it hard to accept new ways of thinking. For many, it seemed to be an inadmissible form of "sedition," even a renunciation of one's own self. What about everything we had been fighting for? This was a question that many asked—people who did not think especially deeply about the meaning of the official ideology but who worked, thought, and lived in an honest way. For the citizens of our country to understand and accept the new ideas, they needed time as well as consistent and convincing explanations, and practical evidence of the advantages the new approaches would bring them. Some of our citizens never did understand or accept these new ideas, as can easily be observed today.

A second impetus for the new thinking was a reflective analysis of world politics and the best way to implement it. This involved overcoming our old way of thinking, thinking that had become typical for us as a result not only of Soviet history but of world history. An analysis of world politics concerned above all the role of force in history, that is, the use of troops as the customary means not only of defending the state but of realizing its political intentions.

From time immemorial war has been recognized as a valid political tool by international law. True, in the second half of the nineteenth century certain legal restrictions were instituted to reduce the harmful effects of war on the civilian population. Rules were also established for the proper treatment of prisoners of war. After World War I the use of chemical weapons was banned. Attempts were also made to limit the production of certain other types of weapons. But none of this changed the fact that war was regarded as a legitimate way to conduct policy.

The situation radically changed with the appearance of nuclear weapons. Human beings now had a weapon with which they could commit collective suicide, and thus people were forced to abandon previously accepted approaches—or so it seemed. As we all know, this did not happen. On the contrary, the entire period up to the end of the 1980s was an uninterrupted arms race, primarily involving nuclear weapons. Various scenarios providing for the use of nuclear weapons or the threat of their use essentially became the basis for the military doctrine of every nation-state possessing atomic or hydrogen bombs and for the military alliances to which these states belonged.

An ever-increasing segment of world opinion—especially in the scientific community—sounded the alarm and demanded that measures be taken to prevent a nuclear holocaust. Some steps toward limiting the nuclear arms race were taken in the 1960s. Thus a nuclear test ban (on tests above ground, in the air, and at sea) was signed, followed later by a treaty on nonproliferation of these weapons of mass destruction. At the same time agreements were reached limiting or banning other weapons of mass destruction (for example, chemical and biological weapons). But none of this stopped the race to produce and refine nuclear weapons, and, covertly, the production and accumulation of forbidden or restricted weapons of mass destruction continued.

Scientific research—above all, by Soviet and American scientists—in the 1970s and 1980s showed convincingly what human beings faced in the event of a nuclear catastrophe. Eloquent testimony to what might happen was expressed in descriptions of a possible "nuclear winter." Obviously a radical change in the fundamental positions of governments was required, a change in their practical approaches to policy and their means of pursuing policy. Governments had to renounce approaches involving the use of force, fraught with the danger of the destruction of millions of people, if not the entire human race.

Such a reversal clearly would not be simple or easy. Historical traditions, which had become outmoded under the new conditions, were deeply rooted both in people's consciousness and in policy making. Further, the general state of relations between East and West during the Cold War was that of mutual distrust, permeated with the idea that whoever did not share one's own point of view was an "enemy" and invariably a mortal threat. Finally, material and political interests were another consideration. Some became rich from the production of weapons of mass destruction or from the arms industry in general; others saw in these weapons a reliable lever for guaranteeing their own primacy, a dependable instrument for asserting policy aimed at achieving and maintaining hegemony.

Nevertheless a radical reversal of this volatile situation was imperative.

Finally, the third stimulus giving rise to the new thinking was our analysis of the major changes that had occurred in the most fundamental aspects of daily life worldwide during the years after World War II. The shifting technological basis of the world economy, the rapid progress in computer technology, the emergence of new, enhanced methods of exchanging information worldwide, and the emergence of new means of transportation—all these revolutionary changes were affecting relations between nation-states and national populations. A new world economy and worldwide information and cultural systems were in fact taking shape.

Under these conditions everything became interconnected; all problems—both national and international—were tied in a single knot that had to be unraveled. And this had to be done in the name of one's own national interests (which coincided with the interests of all countries) and for the survival of the human race.

The changes that had taken place were not reflected in international relations or government policy. Or if they were reflected, it was in a one-sided way. The great powers were using the emerging new possibilities to exploit the less powerful, less developed countries. Interdependence among nations became an instrument of power for those who sought to pursue a hegemonistic policy in world affairs.

The Soviet leadership sought to base its analysis of these new problems on research carried out by the scientific and cultural community worldwide. This was a new development, not at all customary for the Soviet Union. Indeed, until the 1980s, the Soviet regime had largely regarded such research as hostile, unacceptable, and false. Earlier, in the Stalin era, genetics, cybernetics, political science, geopolitics, and so forth, were denounced as "bourgeois pseudoscience" (which resulted in our lagging behind significantly in the fields of science and technology, as well as in other areas). Even after the Khrushchev "thaw," even after the era of détente in the 1970s, ideas voiced by "dissidents" (whether in science or, especially, in politics) were rejected out of hand.

Gradually, during perestroika, the extremely interesting ideas of certain scientists and political figures, and the works of major writers and poets, all of which had been consigned to oblivion, began to be restored in our country. A living link with world science, with international culture, with the enormous reservoir of worldwide thought was also reestablished. Thus our own ideas about the surrounding world, our own theoretical generalizations regarding the state of the modern world and prospects for the future, were enriched.

Among the precursors, and to no small degree the coauthors, of the new thinking were such major Russian scientists as Vladimir Vernadsky, Pyotr Kapitsa, and Andrei Sakharov, and such foreign thinkers as Albert Einstein, Bertrand Russel, and Giorgio La Pira. There were many others besides these.

A question is often asked of us: Do you mean that before perestroika no one in the Soviet Union recognized the need for change in the realm of foreign policy, both in theory and practice? Of course such ideas did occur. We still do not know all the details of the past, but judging from the information we have, even in the later years of the Stalin era, before Stalin's death, a certain uneasiness about the course of events and a vague desire to change things in the realm of foreign policy made its appearance within our ruling circles.

After Stalin's death came the first "thaw" in the Cold War. Relations were normalized with many countries, the first summit meetings were held, and the first treaties intending to moderate the generally tense climate in world affairs were signed. The Korean War had ended, as did the first phase of the war in Indochina. But this phase of improved relations did not last long. The Hungarian crisis and the war over the Suez Canal put a brake on this course of developments.

The attempts at change undertaken at that time were by no means consistent, and they occurred in the context of internal struggle. Georgy Malenkov received no support, and in fact was condemned, after a speech he made to voters in Moscow in which he stated that the Cold War policy was "a policy of preparing for a new world war, which, given today's weapons, would mean the destruction of world civilization." In January 1955, at a plenum of the CPSU Central Committee, Vyacheslav Molotov stated that no Communist should talk about the "destruction of world civilization" or of the human race but rather should speak of "preparing and mobilizing all forces for the destruction of the bourgeoisie."

Of course a short while later Nikita Khrushchev (influenced by the events of the time, especially the Cuban missile crisis) took a position similar to that voiced by Malenkov. At Khrushchev's insistence, official party and government documents were to state that *peaceful coexistence* was the general line for Soviet foreign policy. But as early as 1964, after Khrushchev was relieved of his duties as first secretary of the Central Committee of the CPSU, this formula was discarded, to be replaced by a return to the basic foreign policy coordinates of the early 1950s.

In 1971, at the Twenty-Fourth Party Congress, another attempt was made, not revolutionary but substantial, to introduce correctives in the practices and line of conduct of the foreign policy being pursued. I am referring to the Peace Program adopted at that congress. It contained a number of sensible proposals regarding, above all, the necessity of reducing the danger of nuclear war. True, this program was adopted to a considerable extent because of the desire to improve the Soviet Union's image in the eyes of the world, an image that had become rather negative as the result of such actions as the suppression of the Prague Spring and the deployment of new medium-range missiles in Europe.

But the Peace Program soon died on the vine. The Soviet intervention in Afghanistan buried the possibility of improving international relations for a long time. This action essentially resulted in a new and more dangerous edition of the Cold War.

Thus there had been earlier attempts to refine or modernize Soviet foreign policy, taking the world's realities into account. But these efforts were inconsistent and, most important, were not reinforced by appropriate changes in the very conception of the fundamental principles of state policy.

The need for a change in foreign policy was referred to, in a general way, during the visit to Great Britain by a Soviet parliamentary delegation that I headed in December 1984. I then stated that the nuclear age inevitably dictates *new political thinking*, that "now more than ever" there was a need for constructive dialogue, for a search for solutions to key international problems, an attempt to find areas of agreement that could lead to greater trust among different countries, the creation of an atmosphere in international relations that would be free of nuclear threats, suspicion, fear, and animosity; it was time for everyone to gradually learn to live together, based on the realities of a modern world that was constantly changing according to certain basic regularities inherent in it.

This was a clear statement, but obviously practical implementation of the ideas expressed in it was not possible until after I had been elected to the post of general secretary of the CPSU Central Committee in March 1985 and a new Soviet leadership had been formed, a leadership that would chart a course toward profound change.

CHAPTER 17

The Very First Steps

Does this mean that everything had been clearly thought out by the time of the March 1985 plenum of the Central Committee of the CPSU—which was the starting point for change in the policies of our party and country? Of course not!

Some of our thinking had matured by then, including considerations that were highly important in principle, but we were far from having resolved everything. In general, the principles of the new thinking, and the corresponding "moves" that were made, underwent constant evolution. They developed as part of a process—a process of thought, discussion, debate, and theoretical elaboration—that continued throughout the perestroika era.

For now I would like to devote special attention to the brief period from March to December 1985, a time that researchers have paid little attention to, as a rule. It was an extremely important period, marked by an intense search for new policy approaches leading to conclusions that became the core of the new thinking. These conclusions were not drawn until 1986-87, when they were developed further, but the search for new approaches began in 1985.

At first, as the general secretary of the CPSU Central Committee, I spoke of our country's unchanging foreign policy course, stating that there was no need to change it. This position was justified: Any renewal had to be combined with continuity. But continuity itself was understood (as was stated at the April 1985 Central Committee plenum) as a "steady movement forward, discovering and resolving new problems and removing everything that hinders progress."

Our activity in the realm of foreign policy began to unfold in this spirit, beginning literally with the first working day of the new leadership of the party and the country.

On March 11, 1985, the Central Committee plenum reaffirmed "A Course Toward Peace and Progress" outlining the basic direction of our country's foreign policy. I stated: "Never before has such a terrible danger hung over the heads of humanity as in our times. The only rational way out of the current situation is for the opposing forces to agree to immediately stop the arms race—above all, the nuclear arms race—on the earth's surface and not allow it into outer space. This agreement must stand on an honest and equal basis, without any attempts by one side to 'outmaneuver' the other or dictate conditions."

On March 13 I held a series of meetings with the heads of delegations from foreign countries that had arrived for Chernenko's* funeral. The transcripts of those discussions were not published, but they are undeniably of great interest. For it was precisely in those discussions that Western leaders at the highest level were told for the first time about the principles on which the new leadership's activities would be based in world affairs, principles that foreshadowed the ideas of the new thinking.

In a discussion with President François Mitterand of France, the following observation was made: "We have reached the point where a certain question arises: Where can we go from here? Is it not time to make decisions corresponding to the interests of all nations and all peoples, decisions that would not allow the world to slide into the abyss of nuclear catastrophe, the consequences of which it is difficult even to predict."

The need for a major reversal in world politics was subsequently repeated in discussions with other foreign leaders, including those of the United States, Great Britain, West Germany, Japan, India, and China.

Perhaps of special interest was the meeting with U.S. Vice President George Bush and Secretary of State George Schultz, where we presented our views on Soviet foreign policy. I will quote several passages from that meeting:

> The Soviet Union will pursue an active and constructive policy based on an understanding of its role and responsibility as a great power. On the global level we see our task as that of promoting, in all our relations with other governments, the aim of creating a healthier international situation and of generating conditions for the expansion of international ties, cultural exchanges, exchanges in the fields of science, technology, and so on.

* Konstantin Chernenko was Gorbachev's predecessor as general secretary of the CPSU Central Committee.

We attribute great importance to our relations with the United States. We have no desire to achieve military superiority over the United States, and we have no intention of infringing on the valid interests of the United States. In our opinion, there are great possibilities for fruitful cooperation between us.

We must learn to construct international relations in the real world. The formulation of policy and its practical implementation in all likelihood will depend on how those realities are understood. . . . Every country has certain constant or permanent interests. Accordingly, in carrying out our foreign policy we must take into account the interests of each state. We cannot proceed on the basis that might makes right. . . . We cannot understand the present policy of the United States. It simply does not fit in with the concept of normal international relations.

A short while later, on April 10, 1985, as general secretary of the CPSU Central Committee, I received a visit from Thomas ("Tip") O'Neill, speaker of the U.S. House of Representatives, and a meeting with him ensued. This meeting was along the same lines as the previous one, but with a greater degree of candor. In my effort to convey to the American congressman my views on the seriousness of the moment, the new possibilities emerging, and the terms and conditions that should be observed if these possibilities were to become a reality, I said the following:

The relations between our countries are presently in a kind of ice age. We favor restoring Soviet-American relations to normal channels. At bottom, our position includes the understanding that *a fatal conflict of interest between our countries is not inevitable.* Further, we have a common interest— in avoiding nuclear war, in guaranteeing the security of both our countries, of preserving life itself for our respective peoples. . . . We do not wish to remake the United States in our own image, regardless of what we like or dislike about that nation. However, the United States should also not undertake the quixotic task of remaking the Soviet Union to suit its own tastes. That would just lead to war. . . . Many problems exist in the world— political, economic, and social—but there is a way out, namely, peaceful coexistence, *the recognition that each nation has the right to live as it wishes. There is no other alternative.* . . . We must build a bridge toward cooperation. But to build such a bridge, as everyone knows, construction must proceed from both sides.

In these two discussions—first with George Bush and George Schultz and then with Tip O'Neill—in addition to the kind of ideas the Soviet government had previously formulated, new ones were presented that had not been part of Soviet policy in the past. I am referring to the principle of balancing interests (and, accordingly, the renunciation of "zero-sum" diplomacy), that is, the need to search for mutually acceptable compromises, to recognize freedom of choice for each nation, and to acknowledge that any system is valid if chosen by the people.

The same principles were posed in meetings with Margaret Thatcher and Helmut Kohl. Also touched on in these meetings were specific problems of bilateral and Europeanwide relations.

An important step in the conceptual development of our new views on foreign policy was taken at the April 1985 Central Committee plenum—the same plenum at which a presentation of forthcoming changes in our government's domestic policy were first set forth. To quote from the general secretary's report:

We are in favor of proper, correct, smoothly functioning, and, if you will, civilized relations between states based on genuine respect for international legal norms. But one thing must be clear: Only if imperialism renounces any attempt to resolve by military means the historic dispute between our two social systems will we be successful in bringing international relations back into the channel of normal cooperation.

This was the general framework defining what we saw at the time as the limits of what was possible.

Later in the report two other points were singled out: First, "disputed questions and conflict situations must be resolved by political means—that is our firm conviction"; and, second, "the CPSU, and the Soviet state, unalterably support the right of self-determination for all peoples, that is, the freedom to decide their own socioeconomic conditions and build their future without interference from the outside. To deny any nation this sovereign right is a hopeless task, doomed from the start."

This principle was universal in the renewed form of Soviet policy. It applied to all governments and states, including those belonging to the so-called socialist system. This was emphasized at two meetings that took place in 1985 with leaders of the Warsaw Pact countries, one on March 13, the other on April 26. The following summarizes what was said at those meetings:

The relationship between allied countries [i.e., between the Soviet Union and its allies] had to be reshaped. Relations were to develop based on principles of independence, equality, and noninterference in one another's internal affairs. Each country was to bear responsibility for the decisions it made. In other words, and this point was emphasized, we were ending the so-called Brezhnev doctrine; we were turning a new page, leaving behind the old one on which were recorded episodes of the USSR's intervention in its allies' internal affairs.

Not all the leaders attending the Warsaw Pact meetings may have fully appreciated the meaning of what was said. After all, similar words had been spoken in the past, which had by no means prevented our troops from being sent, for example, into Czechoslovakia. But soon everyone realized we were talking about a serious and firm orientation.

On May 8, at a meeting celebrating the fortieth anniversary of the victory over fascism, another proposition was put forward signifying an important step toward expanding the framework of the new foreign policy. The following statement was made: "The only sensible solution today is to establish active cooperation among all governments in the interest of a peaceful future for all; it is the creation, utilization, and development of international mechanisms and institutions of such cooperation that would make it possible to find optimal correlations between national interests and the interests of humanity as a whole." The advancement of this thesis indicated that the USSR's concept of foreign policy, in contrast to that of the past, was beginning to move away from narrow class positions to include the new realities in the new world.

This theme was developed further during my visit to France, in discussions with President Mitterand and at meetings with parliamentarians, as evinced by the following statement made at that time:

There is closer and closer interconnection and interdependence among countries and continents. This is an inevitable condition for the development of the world economy, for scientific and technical progress, for the accelerated exchange of information, and for the movement of people and goods on the earth's surface and even in outer space—in short, for the overall development of human civilization. Unfortunately the advances of civilization are by no means always used to promote the people's well-being. Scientific and technological achievements are too often used to create means of destruction, to produce and stockpile ever more terrifying weapons.

Under these conditions Hamlet's question—To be, or not to be?—no longer confronts just the individual but challenges the human race as well. Indeed it is becoming a global question. There can only be one answer: Humanity and civilization must survive. But this can be ensured only by learning to live together, to get along side by side on this small planet, by mastering the difficult art of considering one another's interests.

In the person of Mitterand I had found a partner who took these questions seriously.

During the meeting with Mitterand our side advanced one more proposition that further developed the theme under discussion: "We think that in current circumstances it is especially important not to carry ideological disagreements, in imitation of certain medieval fanatics, into the realm of relations among states."

Based on all these ideas, and as a means of renewing international relations, a meeting was held in November 1985 between the general secretary of the CPSU Central Committee and the president of the United States, Ronald Reagan. Summarizing the results of this meeting, which was marked, above all, by progress on these very questions regarding human survival and a mutual recognition of the inadmissibility of nuclear war or a policy course aimed at achieving military supremacy, I said the following:

Yes, I am convinced that at the present stage of international relations, which is characterized by greater interconnectedness among states, by their interdependence, a new policy is required. We believe that a new approach requires that the current policies of all states be nourished by the realities of today's world. This is an essential prerequisite for any state in constructing its foreign policy and will also contribute to improving the world situation.

I hope readers will take an understanding attitude toward my use of frequent quotations which I feel obliged to make in order to demonstrate persuasively the line of argument that took place in 1985. In just nine months of that year important steps were taken in forming and developing Moscow's new worldview and, accordingly, our country's new foreign policy conception. The basic features of this conception are discussed in the next chapter. For now it is important to stress the following: The development of theoretical views was immediately reinforced by appropriate practical measures. This of course was essential. Because of the prevailing mistrust between East and West, only specific measures could contribute to establishing trust. And without trust even the slightest improvement in world affairs would be impossible to achieve.

When the Soviet leadership declared its new approach to negotiations on nuclear and space-based weapons, it took an immediate and concrete step in that very direction. On April 8, in an interview in *Pravda*, I stated that from that day on the Soviet Union would place a moratorium on the deployment of medium-range missiles and would stop taking certain measures in Europe that had previously been the Soviet Union's response to specific U.S. actions. The moratorium would last until November 1985. The decision as to what would follow would depend on the response by the United States. In early October a declaration was made in Paris regarding cutbacks on certain types of Soviet medium-range weapons in Europe. At the same time we advanced the idea of building a "common European home"—developing all-round cooperation and genuinely peaceful, neighborly relations among all the European countries.

Seeking to end the nuclear arms race, on July 30 we declared a moratorium on nuclear testing, to begin on August 6, 1985 (and this was extended several times). We appealed to the government of the United States to follow our example.

At the same time a message was sent to President Reagan proposing a substantial reduction in strategic nuclear weapons, which would of course be linked with the renunciation of a nuclear arms race in space.

On September 17 we published Soviet proposals to the United Nations concerning the basic directions and principles of international cooperation in the peaceful utilization and nonmilitarization of outer space.

The above is an incomplete list of initiatives taken during 1985. But it shows well enough that the proposals we introduced were quite specific, and their implementation was easily verifiable. These were realistic measures aimed at stopping the expansion of the nuclear arms race.

It should be noted that the measures taken by the Soviet leadership were in some cases unilateral, whereas at other times proposals were addressed equally to both sides. What was involved, then, was the desire to give material content to the idea of a renewal of international relations, based on the principle of equal security for both sides and freeing them both from a confrontational approach.

The idea was precisely for all to have *equal* security. For example, when the Soviet Union stopped taking countermeasures in response to U.S. actions in Europe, the level of security increased for the entire continent; at the same time no harm was done to the interests of the USSR itself, for at the time the USSR had superiority in medium-range missiles in Europe. All the appropriate measures were carefully worked out, of course, with the active participation of both our political and military leadership.

Were the new Soviet ideas and the corresponding practical measures assessed fairly in the West? The answer is yes and no. Western observers at the time noted that something new was apparent in the Soviet proposals, but they often regarded this as merely a propaganda maneuver.

The appraisal of the specific actions taken by the USSR was basically positive, but by no means was a symmetrical response made all at once. (True, the United States, beginning in late 1985, did in fact slow down its deployment of medium-range missiles in Europe.) The cessation of nuclear testing on our part, which received a broad and positive response from most governments and world public opinion, was not reciprocated by the United States, which continued its testing.

Obviously hard work lay ahead and possibly for a long time. At a CPSU Central Committee plenum on October 15, 1985, taking into account the events that had transpired, we took note of increased "counteraction by the aggressive forces of imperialism in response to the positive changes in the world." These forces aspired to social revenge and, for that purpose, sought to maintain international tension.

In all meetings and discussions between the general secretary of the CPSU Central Committee and representatives of Western governments, constructive ideas were advanced but these were often accompanied by serious, specific, and sometimes quite sharp criticism of the foreign policy positions held by our negotiating partners—above all, the Americans. In all cases the observation was made that steps toward new world relations must be mutual; otherwise nothing would come of them.

At the Twenty-seventh CPSU Congress in February-March 1986 a balance sheet was drawn on the work that had been accomplished. It was at this plenum that we first formulated the basic, general conclusions that would become the decisive framework of the new thinking. Nothing can diminish the importance of these first steps—both theoretical and practical—that were taken during 1985 toward promoting world cooperation. All this was a substantial prologue to the active and assertive promotion of the new principles and methods in world affairs.

CHAPTER 18

The Conception (1985–1991)

AS SAID ABOVE, the ideas of the new thinking were not fixed for all time. They constantly evolved. Three main phases in their development can be identied.

The first phase was connected, above all, with the position put forward at the Twenty-seventh CPSU Congress and the deepening of that position in the subsequent period. It was characterized by a theoretical-political analysis of major changes in the world that had taken place since World War II and by the political requirements those changes raised. The practical task was to search for a realistic way to end the Cold War and find a way out of the vicious circle of mistrust, hostility, and confrontation.

The second phase found expression, above all, in the speech by the general secretary of the CPSU Central Committee at the UN General Assembly on December 7, 1988, at a time when the first changes for the better in international affairs were becoming evident. This phase was marked by the advancement of major ideas having to do with prospects for planetwide development. We were no longer talking about "the struggle between two camps" but about the global interests of humanity, the principles of a new world order, and the urgent need for a future based on the codevelopment of all members of the international community.

The third phase was reached in 1990–91. It embodied the idea that changes in the realm of international relations alone were insufficient, that the future of humanity could be reliably assured only along the lines of a new paradigm of civilization itself, in a process in which a new form of civilization was emerging.

What are the basic postulates of the new thinking? Its starting point is the recognition that despite their dissimilarities all the nations of the world are interdependent. We speak of recognition because this interdependence, which is a form of unity or oneness, had been taking shape for decades. This dynamic had been studied by scientists and scholars outside the Soviet Union and was taken into account by Western foreign policy. As early as 1975, for example, Henry Kissinger declared that global interdependence had become a central factor of U.S. diplomacy. In the Soviet Union, on the other hand, this viewpoint concerning interdependence was perceived as an "alien class" concept. Nonetheless interdependence was a tangible reality, impossible to disregard, and by the mid-1980s it had become the foremost tendency in world relations.

On the one hand, the internationalization of economic life, the mutual influence or reciprocal effect of political decisions taken by various nations, and the formation of an increasingly dense worldwide informational and cultural network—all this was creating an entirely new picture of the world. On the other hand, many complicated and acute global problems had accumulated—for example, problems of ecology, demography, raw materials, and energy sources—and were impossible to resolve within the framework of a single country or even region.

Along with these global problems, national and regional difficulties continued, which included social and class problems. In the last analysis, the resolution of these problems proved limited or entirely impossible unless the new global realities of a world that was becoming a single whole were taken into account.

A new configuration of the driving political interests was taking shape. Interests that were not national, local, or class-based but universal were coming to the fore. It was precisely the satisfaction of these needs that turned out to be the precondition for satisfying all others. The conclusion that in our day universal human interests and values take priority essentially became the core of the new thinking.

This proposition that universal human values must take priority largely contradicted the views that had become solidly established almost everywhere. The assimilation of these new realities in the Soviet Union proved especially difficult because the conception of world development that had become entrenched in our country after the 1917 revolution was based on the postulate of an inevitable, profound division in the world. Despite the major shifts that had taken place, the old views and the old approach to problems still remained in the arsenal of the Soviet government.

Let me return to the question of the wholeness and interdependence of the world. The recognition that interdependence was the real state of affairs in the world meant that the foremost trend of development was not one of ever deepening division but one of ever greater unity in the worldwide system. And the Soviet Union—as a part of this system—should search for and find its new place within this framework.

An international conference of political parties and movements held in Moscow in November 1987 formulated the conclusion that it was no longer possible to regard world development solely from the standpoint of the struggle between two opposing social systems. From this it followed that international relations had to be freed of ideologies. At the UN General Assembly in December 1988 I argued that it was necessary for cooperation to develop into "co-creation" and "co-development."

The second fundamental proposition of the new thinking was that we had to allow for diversity among nations as well as their interdependence and common interests. Thus a key force driving modern progress is the dialectic between wholeness and diversity, between unity and individuality, and between nations and regions. The world is not uniform but exhibits unity within diversity, the juxtaposition and harmonization of differences.

These propositions of course are not new. What new contribution did the new thinking make to the understanding of this reality? It carried the recognition of diversity to the necessary logical conclusion: recognition of the fact, above all, of the undeniable freedom of choice for all peoples, the freedom to choose their own path of development and way of life.

Every country and every nationality has its own rights, national interests, and aspirations. This is a most important reality of our times. But the assertion of these rights and freedoms has obviously outpaced the ability of some political leaders in the major Western countries to understand and grasp the significance of the irreversible changes that have taken place. Hence the relapses into attempts to impose hegemony, subordinate other countries to the interests of the major Western powers, and dictate to other countries by political, economic, or military means. Any attempts at interference in the internal affairs of another country must be ruled out. It is equally impermissible to attempt to destabilize legal governments from the outside. This kind of approach is the essential prerequisite for genuine democratization in world politics. Many people talk about democratization, but too often they forget: This is not just a verbal exercise; it must be carried out in political practice—above all, in the political practice of the strongest and largest states. The behavior of these states decisively determines the character and forms of development of international relations. Have the politicians assimilated this reality? On the level of rhetoric, yes. But there are still too many instances that prevent us from giving a positive answer to this question.

A big question is whether a contradiction exists between the increasing unity of the world and ensuring real freedom of choice. There is certainly a contradiction. As the world becomes more integrated and interdependent, it is, figuratively speaking, shrinking, but at the same time it is becoming increasingly multifaceted. In a sense it is expanding. We cannot ignore either of these tendencies as they are two sides of the same dialectically developing process.

"To oppose freedom of choice is to set oneself in opposition to the objective course of history." This is a statement from my report at the Nineteenth CPSU Party Conference in June 1988. I concluded that our concept of freedom of choice occupied a key place in the new thinking. Taking into account the new situation in the world, the problem of interests must be addressed in a new way. Instead of some countries imposing their interests on others, a genuine balancing of interests in international relations must be found.

To be sure, it is important that every nation properly identify its own interests. This is the politicians' responsibility in every country and a measure of the honesty of their intentions.

Finally, a third group of problems that was addressed by the new thinking involves the nature of modern weaponry and humanity's entry into the age of nuclear missiles.

Albert Einstein was one of the first to speak of the necessity for new thinking in the nuclear age. But no one listened to his warnings. (In general, scientific conclusions usually go unheeded even today.) Yet the very first atomic bomb explosions at Hiroshima and Nagasaki demonstrated that we had entered a new stage in human history. For the first time in its history, the human race had weapons that could extinguish all life on earth. The Day of Judgment, instead of being a biblical allegory, could become a reality, a tragedy made by human hands. This realization was what dictated my statement as CPSU general secretary on January 15, 1986. The main point of that statement was the proposal that we move toward a nonnuclear world in the twenty-first century.

Deep reflection on the situation, on the possible consequences if weapons of mass destruction were used, forced us to draw three theoretical-political conclusions of prime importance.

The first was that the nature of modern weaponry leaves no country any hope of defending itself by purely military and technical means, not even if, for example, it created the most powerful defense system possible. The problem of guaranteeing security appears more and more clearly as a political problem that can and must be solved, above all, by political means. And political means imply negotiations—and still more negotiations. Negotiations presuppose patience, tolerance, and a consistent search for mutually acceptable compromises.

Security could no longer be built on the fear of an inevitable retaliation, meaning that the doctrines of containment or mutually assured destruction were outdated. The only sure way to security was to eliminate nuclear weapons and to reduce and limit weapons production in general. Throughout history the justification for warfare, its "rational purpose," was the possibility of achieving certain political goals by military means. But nuclear war is irrational; it makes no sense. Worse yet, even warfare involving only conventional weapons could have consequences comparable to those of a nuclear war in view of the widespread existence of countless nuclear power stations, nuclear-fuel production plants, and nuclear storage facilities, as well as petrochemical and chemical plants in general—damage to any of which would itself cause enormous disasters. Thus a completely new situation has arisen: It is impossible to achieve political goals by using modern weapons, above all, nuclear arms. On the other hand, it is entirely possible to plunge all of humanity into the abyss of destruction.

A second conclusion—actually a corollary of the first—is that politics based on the use of force is doomed.

Of course there are attempts to show that this is not so, that wars—even small ones—can still serve as a continuation of politics by other means and can produce definite results. But the experience of the entire era since World War II shows that not a single armed conflict has given its participants or, above all, its initiators any serious political dividends.

A peace based on positions of strength is internally unstable, no matter how one may argue the case. By its very nature, such a peace is based on confrontation, secret or open, on the constant danger of eruptions of fighting, the constant temptation to attempt to achieve one's aims through the use of force. This kind of peace is advantageous (if under present-day criteria such a thing can be considered an advantage) only to the arms manufacturers.

It is already true today and will especially be true in the future that the authority or prestige of a government, and its place in the international community, will increasingly be defined not by the size of its armies but by its civilized conduct, by its commitment to universal human interests, by the freedom and prosperity of its citizens, by its ability to preserve and enrich its uniqueness not at the expense of others but through honest and mutually advantageous cooperation with others.

We must be realists. The road to such a world will be long and difficult. Renunciation of the use of force in politics, renunciation of the practice of measuring the security of a country by its armed strength—these aims will not be achieved all at once.

With minimal agreement among nations, the field of operation for the politics of force can be limited or narrowed. Unsanctioned use of force on an international level would immediately be subjected to rigorous collective counteraction.

A third conclusion, which is a logical continuation of the first two, is that security under contemporary conditions (especially if we speak of the major nuclear powers) can only be mutual. Taking world relations as a whole, security can only be universal.

These were the considerations that inspired Soviet policy, leading us to advance a program in 1986 for creating a universal system of international security that would encompass not only military but also political, economic, and humanitarian fields.

The theory and methodology of the new thinking were based on the desire to combine military policy with a moral approach to world affairs. This is a highly complicated task; much has been said and written about it in the past as well as at the present time, but no solutions have yet been found. We cannot say that a full solution was achieved even in the perestroika era. Nevertheless it cannot be denied that the basic international decisions made in that era did correspond to principles of morality. Reflections on the essential problems of the modern world, the ways in which the world has been developing, and the principles of relations among nations gradually led us to the following conclusion: It is impossible to provide for and guarantee new horizons in the future by limiting oneself to the improvement of international relations—that is, the existing ties among nations. The ultimate solutions lie in the very basic elements of human existence, the deep-running processes that determine the life of the human community.

"A new revolution in consciousness is needed," I stated in Rome on November 30, 1989, on the eve of a meeting with President Bush. "Only on this basis will a new culture and a new politics adequate to the challenge of the times be created. The key point of support in this experiment or attempt at solving this world-historical problem will be the eternal moral precepts, or, as Marx called them, the simple laws of morality and humaneness.

I devoted much attention to this topic in a speech I gave on May 31, 1990, at a meeting with intellectuals in the United States:

> It seems to me that in recent times a very general idea stands out ever more clearly, one that has taken hold of people's minds on the eve of the twenty-first century. This is the idea of universal unity. To embody this idea in practical terms is an epoch-making task. . . . For humanity to rise to a level at which it can realize the meaning of its own history, this must occur without irreparable harm to the environment, without exploitation of some by others and certainly not of entire nations, and without irreversible moral and spiritual losses.

These ideas were not fully fleshed out before the end of 1991. But they did serve as a kind of spiritual culmination of the explorations connected with the emergence of the new thinking.

Thus far we have spoken about the basic conclusions of the new thinking in the form in which they were stated and applied in the years from 1985 to 1991. These conclusions were subsequently developed further in theoretical aspects, but we will discuss that in a later chapter. For now, we must try to answer an important question: What were the practical results of applying the principles of the new thinking?

CHAPTER 19

Overcoming the Cold War

THE NEW THINKING created a new basis for practical action in the realm of Soviet foreign policy.

First, it removed the internal contradictions characteristic of previous foreign policy conceptions. After all, no matter how much you may talk about peaceful coexistence, when you proceed from the assumption that the twofold division of the world is inevitable, involving the victory of one side over the other, your policies will inevitably be confrontational.

The new thinking made possible the assertion of a genuine unity between our country's interests, as properly understood, and the interests of all humanity. Thus the opportunity for fruitful cooperation with all nations was created.

Finally, the methodology of a politics based on the new thinking, which presupposed reliance on the primacy of reason, not the irrational use of force; on mutual respect for one another's rights and interests, not on imposing one's position on others; on tolerance and a search for mutually acceptable solutions through negotiations—this methodology in fact opened the way for the peaceful resolution of any problem, even the most tangled and complicated one.

The first document in which the new concepts and practical ideas were comprehensively expressed was the January 15, 1986, declaration by the general secretary, described above. This declaration indicated the path toward a nuclear-free world.

In the West, and to some extent in the USSR as well, the proposals contained in this statement were at first considered utopian and unrealizable. At best the statement was thought to be a good propaganda exercise. At the same time Soviet diplomacy persistently sought to put these ideas into practice, formulating specific and realizable initiatives, step by step. In this process it became clear that working out such steps was simply impossible without consciously involving not only diplomats and scientists in this work but also those in the military, those engaged in economic management, representatives of the military-industrial complex, and representatives of educated society in general. Incidentally this approach to carrying out practical measures in foreign policy became standard practice and saved us from many mistakes, although some miscalculations did occur.

A real breakthrough occurred at the Reykjavik summit meeting with President Reagan. At that meeting we did not reach the point of a joint signing of documents, but we moved a considerable way toward one another on major questions of security. Later on, after the results of this meeting had been thought over, we began to work out specific steps toward nuclear disarmament.

As a result, in December 1987 a Soviet-American treaty for the elimination and destruction of medium- and short-range missiles was signed. This was the first time in history that a treaty on the destruction of an entire class of nuclear weapons was agreed to by both sides. It is difficult to overestimate the significance of this step.

In July 1991 a Soviet-American treaty on substantial reduction of strategic offensive weapons was concluded. A great deal of work was put in to arrive at this agreement. In addition, in 1992 agreement was reached in principle for further reduction in strategic nuclear arms. A treaty on the complete cessation of nuclear testing was agreed to in 1996 (implementing a pledge contained in the nuclear nonproliferation treaty, which had been extended indefinitely in 1995).

We can look back on all this now with great satisfaction —the proposals of January 15, 1986, were not utopian after all! And although the road to a nuclear-free world may turn out to be longer than one might wish, this noble and salutary goal is reachable, given the good will of all members of the international community, above all the nuclear powers, and, after them, those on the verge of becoming nuclear powers.

My statement of January 15, 1986, along with the proposal for moving ahead toward a nuclear-free world, also contained proposals for reducing conventional weapons in Europe. Negotiations on this question continued into 1990. At last, in November of that year, the treaty was signed in Paris. The reduction of conventional weapons in Europe has already become a reality—granted that it turned out to be a complicated process, not without conflicts, and granted that geopolitical changes in the 1990s forced new elements to be introduced.

The implementation of these treaties, both those concerned with nuclear weapons and those concerned with conventional weapons, has proceeded under strict international verification, including an "open skies" policy and on-site inspection. The decisions regarding monitoring (which were also arrived at through difficult negotiations) by themselves testified to the increasing trust between the two sides. At the same time these decisions stimulated broader contacts between the military leadership on both sides, which, in turn, could create the basis for further strengthening of mutual understanding.

During perestroika notable progress and concrete results were achieved in negotiations on banning chemical, bacteriological, and biological weapons. The production of chemical weapons was ended and agreement was reached on destruction of stockpiled chemical weapons.

If the new thinking had provided impetus for no other accomplishments besides those named above—stopping the nuclear arms race, reducing the production of nuclear and conventional weapons in Europe, and eliminating chemical arsenals—by themselves these would have constituted major historic achievements. The arms race, of course, was both a result of the Cold War and a cause as it constantly provided new stimuli for continued rivalry. The decisions to reduce arms production, in fact, became an important step on the road to ending confrontation and creating healthier relations between East and West.

Meanwhile, the Soviet Union continued to advance proposals for the creation of a comprehensive system of international security. The proposals were translated into specific diplomatic documents and démarches, including some that were sent to the United Nations for consideration. In the years up until 1991 this world organization received four documents embodying the Soviet leadership's conceptions, and the UN formulated specific proposals for implementing those proposals. Unfortunately not all were implemented; many were simply forgotten as a result of changes in the international scene following dissolution of the USSR.

In any case, the general idea of comprehensive security was made specific after 1986 in two proposals directed at specific regions. The first concerned the creation of what we called "our common European home." This idea, as we have said, was first proposed in Paris in 1985 and was presented in more fully developed form in a speech I gave at the Council of Europe in 1989. It was further supplemented and detailed in 1990. The central purpose behind this idea kept developing and expanding.

In 1989–90, treaties of major significance providing for wide-ranging cooperation were concluded between the Soviet Union and France, Italy, Spain, and West Germany. Relations were established between Moscow and the European Union (although they were not fully formalized at that time).

Once confrontation ended, the next stage had the altogether different goal of making a transition in Europe toward a fully developed system of stable, long-term peaceful cooperation.

These ideas were favorably received by the European countries, the United States, and Canada, and in November 1990 the ideas were embodied in the *Charter of Paris for a New Europe*. This document contained the fully worked-out principles and standards for international relations in Europe, including the requirements of the new era that had begun. Unfortunately, although some steps of an organized nature were taken after this, on the whole the tasks that had been outlined were not carried out. To a significant extent this was the result of the dissolution of the USSR.

A second proposal, concerned with Asia, aimed at concretizing the general idea of an all-embracing system of regional security. In 1986, and again in 1989, the Soviet leadership took the initiative of proposing a system of security and cooperation in the Asian-Pacific region. What we had in mind was by no means simply to transfer to the Asian continent what had been proposed for Europe. There was no talk of a "common Asian home" as political conditions there did not at all resemble those in Europe. However, the region obviously needed a series of collective endeavors, for dangerous hotbeds of conflict also existed in Asia.

The progress of these ideas in Asia was delayed at first. Even today there is a long way to go in creating an organic system of peaceful relations on an Asia-wide scale. Still, some positive changes did unfold there in later years. The ideas we expressed at Vladivostok and Krasnoyarsk began to have an effect, and discussions about them did begin. In Japan a roundtable was established for the regular discussion of proposals we had made at Vladivostok and Krasnoyarsk. At the same time cooperation among the countries of that region began to develop more energetically.

From this point of view, the normalization of relations between the USSR and China was highly significant. (Those relations had of course been quite strained since the late 1950s and early 1960s.) A number of quarrels were resolved, including border disputes. The revival of normal dialogue between the USSR and Japan in 1991 was also important, as was the establishment of normal relations between the USSR and South Korea. No such relations had previously existed.

As early as 1985 the Soviet side proposed initiation of coordinated actions by the USSR, the United States, and other countries in the international community for the resolution of regional conflicts by political methods. Many of these conflicts, if they were not a direct expression of the rivalry between the Soviet Union and the United States, were being used by each side to try to weaken the other's position.

It is quite clear that in this process the genuine interests of the populations of the countries involved were, to say the least, considered only to a very slight degree. Sometimes those interests were not taken into account at all. Policy based on the new thinking necessarily included determined efforts to restore peace wherever it had been disrupted, and to unconditionally respect the rights of the respective countries to choose their own path of development free of outside interference.

As early as 1985, during discussions in the Politburo, the question of ending the war in Afghanistan was raised. In February 1986, at the Twenty-seventh Party Congress, the political report from the party Central Committee publicly declared that the war must be ended. Soon after, some Soviet troops were withdrawn. Still later, all Soviet troops withdrew from Afghan territory. This process was completed on February 15, 1989. A shameful and unhappy page in history had been turned.

Today I am often asked why I failed to end the war promptly in 1985?

It was necessary first to arrive at a unified position within the Soviet leadership; to ensure coordination of our actions with the Afghan leadership (which proved to be the most difficult task); and, finally, to establish the necessary external conditions for the withdrawal of our troops, inasmuch as other countries had also been drawn into the Afghan conflict, chiefly Pakistan and Iran. Moreover, the United States had been supplying arms to the Afghan *mujaheddin* [Islamic fundamentalist] rebels and had been energetically supporting Pakistan. Rather prolonged diplomatic negotiations were required, and these culminated in acceptance of the necessary and appropriate agreements, but not until May 15, 1988. Immediately after that, withdrawal of Soviet troops began.

At the very first meeting between the Soviet and American leaders, in Geneva in November 1985, agreement was reached on the need to encourage an end to local conflicts. Somewhat later, joint actions by the two governments began, coordinated with other interested countries, aimed at resolving conflicts in Africa (Namibia, Angola, Mozambique), Asia (above all, in Cambodia), and Central America. These joint efforts produced quite satisfactory results in Namibia and Central America. Existing problems in other regions were not resolved until later. Still and all, the peace process was begun everywhere.

A special case was the regional conflict in Yugoslavia, which broke out at the end of the perestroika era. At that time I, as president of the USSR took a lively interest in the development of those events, even though it was a difficult time for me, after the August coup and not long before the dissolution of the Soviet Union.

The position of the Soviet president, as expressed to President Bush, Austria's Chancellor Vranicky, and later to Croatian and Serbian leaders who had been invited to Moscow, was as follows: Let the opposing sides sit down at a negotiating table and sort matters out, but things must not be allowed to reach the point of tragedy. Military conflict was, in our view, inadmissible; it would be harmful to all the nations and nationalities involved and would drag out over a long period of time. As a result of the meeting in Moscow, both Tudjman [the Croatian leader] and Milosevic [the Serbian leader] signed a communiqué agreeing to stop military action and resolve the problems peacefully. But after the dissolution of the USSR, this initiative was not continued.

During that same final period of my activities as president of the USSR, on October 1, 1991, an international conference was held in Madrid to resolve the Middle East problem. The USSR and the United States jointly chaired the conference, following prolonged negotiations.

The Soviet Union had proposed such a conference for a long time, but the United States had taken a wait-and-see position. The United States finally agreed to that proposal only when relations between Moscow and Washington had entered a stage of real normalization, and after the Persian Gulf War had demonstrated that it was impossible to delay any longer the resolution of the Mideast problem.

The Madrid conference began the extremely complicated process of negotiating what was the most prolonged conflict of the era since World

War II. The negotiations have continued until the present day and have produced tangible results. Some setbacks have occurred, mainly through the fault of the Israelis, who reject the Palestinians' compromise proposals on the grounds that they fail to guarantee Israel's security. Still, I think the process will continue because the alternative—aggravation of the Palestinian-Israeli conflict and of relations with the Arab world in general—would threaten the security of both sides. Perhaps both sides would feel more confident if security guarantees included a system of security for the Mideast as a whole. New initiatives are needed, perhaps by the United States and Russia, the co-chairs of the Madrid conference.

Another special case concerns relations between the USSR and the countries of Central and Eastern Europe. To this day the question continues to be asked: Why did the USSR reconcile itself to "peaceful revolution" in those countries? Why did the Soviet Union not do everything it could to keep those countries within its sphere of influence?

Such questions reflect a failure to understand the policies of perestroika, or perhaps simply a reluctance or refusal to see the profound turnabout in world affairs that perestroika accomplished; in other words, a desire to hold on to the old imperial attitudes and policies, to refuse, as before, to recognize the right of all nations to freedom of choice.

The renewal of our foreign policy, as I have said, affected the entire spectrum of Soviet relations with other countries. The Soviet leadership understood that the content and nature of Soviet ties with the socialist countries would be the litmus test for demonstrating its intentions. It was not simply a matter of winning the West's (as well as the socialist countries') confidence in Soviet policies. It was a question primarily of winning the confidence of the Soviet people themselves in these new policies.

When we began perestroika, the meaning of which was to bring freedom to our own people, the Soviet leadership could not apply any other criteria to relations with the Central and Eastern European countries. Interference in the internal affairs of our neighbors was ended. No longer was advice given from Moscow, let alone orders. Although it was carrying out perestroika, and was convinced that it needed to free itself of the Stalinist legacy everywhere, the Soviet leadership nonetheless did not wish to export its own aims and intentions, its own experience.

The Soviet leadership made its plans and actions known during visits to the Warsaw Pact countries. But there was no hint of any kind of pressure. Sometimes certain politicians in those countries even took offense at this—

especially those who understood the need for change and wanted Moscow to push the leaders of other countries in that direction. But Moscow remained true to its position. When changes did begin in the Eastern European countries, the results of this manifestation of the people's will were immediately recognized as legitimate and as the expression of the freedom of any people to choose their own path of development.

The new principles and approach of Soviet foreign policy during perestroika played a decisive role in the unification of Germany. The Soviet Union understood the abnormality of having the German nation divided in two. More than once in the past, until 1959, the Soviet Union had submitted proposals for consideration by its Western partners that would provide for the unification of Germany. The West rejected these, considering them to be merely propaganda. To a certain extent, the proposals did have a propagandistic purpose. But our partners never once tried to take Moscow at its word.

In the first years of perestroika the question of German reunification did not arise as a specific problem. Subsequent developments were in large part determined by the situation in East Germany. This was a country where the people lived better in material terms than the population of other "socialist" countries of Central and Eastern Europe, but in terms of political freedom the situation was bad. The process of democratization in the Soviet Union made the East German citizens' unhappiness with the repressive regime in their country increasingly manifest.

Although the West German government never directly raised the question of reunification in discussions with Moscow, the leaders in Bonn, as a rule, did make a point of commenting on the abnormal division of their country. Our attitude was that the division of Germany was a product of history and that history itself would take care of it some day. Without categorically denying the possibility of reunification, the Soviet side suggested that time be allowed to solve the problem. This same idea was repeated during my visit to Bonn in June 1989.

In the fall of 1989, however, events began to develop at a quicker pace as a result of the mass exodus of East German citizens to West Germany, at first through Hungary and later through Czechoslovakia. Some left the country by any means available, even risking their lives by crossing the wall separating West Berlin from East Berlin. Within East Germany there were outbreaks of discontent and mass demonstrations. East German citizens understood at the time that the Soviet Union would not use force to prevent unification. This was a signal to them that their will to have unity could be realized. The pressure on the East German leadership grew, resulting in the resignation of the old leadership under Erich Honecker, the opening of the Brandenburg Gate, and the fall of the Berlin wall—that symbol not only of the division of Germany but of all Europe into East and West.

In the circumstances that developed, Moscow conducted itself optimally: It ruled out the use of force, including the use of Soviet troops deployed on East German territory. It did everything possible to allow the process to develop along peaceful lines, without violating the vital interests of the USSR or those of East Germany or West Germany, and without undermining peace in Europe.

In early November 1989, Moscow still hoped that the new East German leadership would be able to cope with the situation and, if there were to be reunification, would implement it in stages, preserving East Germany as long as possible. But events developed in a much more precipitous way. During November a process began in which the government structures of East Germany began to fall apart.

Under these conditions, at the end of November 1989 West German Chancellor Helmut Kohl presented his ten-point plan for the step-by-step reunification of Germany. At first Moscow rejected it, perceiving it as an improper attempt by the chancellor to take advantage of the situation and to act unilaterally. West Germany's allies also showed dissatisfaction. President Bush spoke of this directly to the Soviet leadership. The same response was evident from contacts with leaders of other countries, including France. But the new East German prime minister, Hans Modrow, by early 1990 proposed his own plan for advancing reunification.

At the end of January 1990 members of the Soviet leadership held a conference in Moscow on the German question. After an extensive and candid discussion (no report of this conference was published) the following position was formulated:

- The Soviet government would propose the formation of a six-member group (the four victors in World War II—the Soviet Union, the United States, Britain, and France—plus East and West Germany) to discuss all external aspects connected with unification.

- The policy toward West Germany would be oriented toward Kohl without ignoring the Social Democratic Party of West Germany.

- The new East German prime minister would be invited to Moscow along with the new leader of the East German Communist Party, Gregor Gysi.

- Closer contacts would be maintained with London and Paris on the German problem.
- Marshall Akhromeyev was to prepare the withdrawal of Soviet troops from East Germany.

At an "open skies" conference in Ottawa, in February 1990, agreement was reached on the formation of the six-member group, and three rounds of discussions were later held on the procedure to be followed.

Worth noting is that the new East German leaders began to act hastily without considering the possible results. On February 13 negotiations between East and West Germany began in Bonn on the formation of united financial and currency systems. After these negotiations were completed, Prime Minister Modrow of East Germany announced that the two states would soon unite, and on June 24 the so-called People's Chamber in East Germany quickly confirmed a hastily prepared draft treaty concerning economic, financial, and social union with West Germany. And on July 1 this treaty went into effect.

Meanwhile, during discussions on the six-member group and during bilateral negotiations between the Soviet Union and West Germany, the foreign policy aspects of German reunification were considered. Discussions included matters such as recognition by a united Germany of the existing borders (above all, with Poland), agreement that NATO troops would not be deployed on former East German territory after reunification (although a united Germany would be a member of NATO), the schedule for the withdrawal of Soviet troops from German territory, and assistance by West Germany (including financial) in the process of military withdrawal. The agreements reached were embodied in a treaty on the final normalization of relations with Germany. The treaty was signed in Moscow on September 12, 1990, and on October 3 German unification became a fact.

I confidently assert today that had the the unexploded mine of a divided Germany remained in the center of Europe, peace among the major European powers would have remained unstable and we could not have completely overcome the danger of East-West confrontation. Reunification proceeded calmly, without complications or disruption of European stability. This was one more proof of the fruitful and productive character of the new thinking and of the new Soviet approach to foreign policy in the perestroika era.

In discussing this new approach, we cannot fail to mention one more event that occurred in the early 1990s—the Persian Gulf crisis. Without going into the details of the well-known events, I would only make a few remarks: The Soviet Union had concluded a number of treaties and agreements with Iraq, making that country in effect our ally. Had the crisis occurred before the new thinking was adopted and confrontation ended, the Soviet Union would have been in a difficult position. But it was precisely our new foreign policy orientation that allowed us to take a principled position, to insist that aggression was unacceptable, no matter who the aggressor might be. From the beginning to the end of these events Moscow adhered firmly to this line.

The Persian Gulf crisis proved to be essentially the first serious experience with the new relations then being established between the Soviet Union and the United States. And we withstood the test of this experience, although the situation was not an ideal one.

Certain nuances of the Soviet position differed from those of the United States. They were only nuances, albeit important ones. Moscow did not think war should be waged against Iraq. We thought it was best to use peaceful political means to force Iraq to fulfill its obligations to the international community, first of all to withdraw from Kuwait. Appropriate diplomatic steps were taken to this end. But these steps were undermined by the position held by the Iraqi leadership, which miscalculated in its attempt to create a division of opinion both within the United Nations and in world public opinion.

As a result we did not succeed in preventing the Gulf War. We were not successful in upholding the political approach to ending this conflict, although evidently this approach could have been taken. However, the use of force had become the accepted way of resolving disputes during the Cold War. In the United States that approach persists to this very day. Still, it was a very important precedent in world politics that all actions aimed at stopping aggression and punishing the aggressor were taken with the approval and sanction of the United Nations and in line with Security Council resolutions.

At this point we should remind readers that the turnabout in foreign policy could not have been carried out had perestroika not achieved, within the Soviet Union, that level of democratization that ultimately led to the destruction of the totalitarian system, had our country not taken the road of openness and freedom.

On the one hand, without a domestic perestroika, changing foreign policy would not have been possible politically. On the other hand, perestroika convincingly proved to the rest of the world that the Soviet leadership had honest intentions. The destruction of the Soviet totalitarian system and the renunciation of Stalinist dogmas in theory and practice proved to the world that the new leadership sought peace.

Perestroika fundamentally democratized not only our foreign policy but also the methods by which policy was elaborated and decisions made. In this respect, the Nineteenth Party Conference played an important role when it proposed democratizing foreign policy decisions, ruling out actions conducted in secrecy (as in the decision to send Soviet troops into Afghanistan), and called for the active involvement of parliament in deciding foreign policy. At the same time, foreign policy became an arena of internal political struggle, especially as constraints were relaxed and internal political discussion and disagreement were permitted. The new spirit later extended to the open expression of different views and currents of opinion. This resulted in growing criticism of our foreign policy by both conservative forces—those of the Stalin school who held onto ideological orthodoxy—and radical democrats. Despite internal and external difficulties, however, the foreign policy of perestroika produced tangible and indisputably positive results based on the ideas of the new thinking.

The primary and fundamental result was that the Cold War was brought to an end thanks to perestroika and the new thinking. A prolonged and potentially deadly period in world history, in which the human race had lived under the constant threat of a nuclear disaster, had come to an end. For several years people have argued about who won and who lost the Cold War. In our view, the very question does nothing more than pay tribute to the past and to the old confrontational way of thinking. From the standpoint of reason it is obvious that all of humankind—every country, every human being—won. The threat of a nuclear holocaust became history—unless, of course, we backslide.

The end of the Cold War brought freedom of choice to many nations in Europe and the Third World and unleashed a worldwide democratic process that had been artificially restrained for decades. This is the second most important result of perestroika on the international level. The field of operations for totalitarianism has been sharply reduced. The field open to democratic development has been expanded.

The third result of perestroika on the international level was that perestroika contributed to the improvement and humanization of international relations.

Finally, the security of the USSR was fundamentally strengthened. Relations with other states, both East and West, became normal and nonconfrontational. The foundations were laid for equal partnership corresponding to the interests of all concerned. It became possible to substantially reduce arms production and thus arms spending. The decades-long threat of war had vanished and no longer troubled our citizens.

Yet vituperative criticism of our foreign policy in the 1985–91 period continues to this day and sometimes is simply slanderous. For example, critics in my country have said that when medium- and shorter-range missiles were being reduced in number, we acted too hastily and removed more missiles than, let us say, the Americans did. This last point is true. But wasn't it necessary to make reductions of any kind in order to avert a real and very great danger? High-precision American missiles aimed at us were capable of reaching our territory, all the way to the Urals, within minutes—while we would not have had time to take countermeasures. Wasn't it of primary importance to save the lives of our people? While sacrificing quantity, we gained immeasurably in quality. That was and remains the priority.

Critics at home have also charged that we lost our allies in Eastern Europe, that we surrendered these countries without compensation. But to whom did we surrender them? To their own people. The nations of Eastern Europe, in the course of a free expression of the will of the people, chose their own path of development based on their national needs. The system that existed in Eastern and Central Europe was condemned by history, as was the system in our own country. It had long since outlived itself and was a burden on the people. Any effort to preserve this system would have further weakened our country's positions, discrediting the Soviet Union in the eyes of our own people and the whole world. Moreover, this system could have been "saved" in only one way—by sending in tanks, as we did in Czechoslovakia in 1968. The consequences of such unjustified action could have included a general European war.

The folly of these criticisms is illustrated by the events leading to German reunification. Support for the East German regime was rapidly collapsing. Its citizens fled the country en masse, even at the risk of death. How was this regime to be saved? By revving up the tank motors once again? Given the importance of Germany to both East and West, given the concentration of armed forces stationed in Germany, any use of force to oppose the will of the German people for unification would have been fraught with the risk of war, perhaps world war.

As I have pointed out above, not everything in the perestroika era was ideal in the realm of foreign policy, not by any means. Certain things possibly could have been done more effectively or in a more sophisticated way. But I can say without hesitation: In all basic and decisive areas, the policies that we conceived and implemented were in the interests of our country and strengthened our security and position in the world. Last but not least, they contributed to consolidating the foundations of peace throughout the world.

CHAPTER 20

The Transitional World Order

NEW HORIZONS WERE opened up by the end of the Cold War and of military confrontation between the two camps, as well as by the limiting of the arms race in general, the complete cessation of the arms race in a number of areas, and the normalization of international affairs. It seemed possible that a new system of international relations could be created based on the principle of equality in all dealings among nations. Of course this would not rule out a certain degree of rivalry or conflict of interests, but it would allow for the resolution of all the main problems exclusively by civilized political methods. It also seemed possible that a new atmosphere for economic development could be created. The preconditions for truly free, open, and much more extensive exchange of cultural values were emerging. In short, the new situation was laying the basis for all countries to participate in truly worldwide development. To a significant degree it seemed that the prospects then emerging surpassed the opportunities that had arisen after 1945 in the post–World War II era, opportunities that had been missed.

After 1945, despite the ending of World War II, wars continued (or were revived) in several parts of the world, including wars involving the great powers. Many regional hot spots appeared. But in the perestroika era, when worldwide confrontation was ending, the process of eliminating such regional conflicts began. It is no accident that after 1989 an idea that began to be widely circulated in the world was the establishment of a new world order that would rule out war and confrontation and create peaceful cooperation among all nations.

But time has passed, and instead of the euphoria of 1989–90 pessimism has set in. The new world order is being considered either a myth or a utopian idea. What happened may be explained by several factors. Problems that had been suppressed or pushed into the background in the era of confrontation now came to the fore. New sources of tension emerged. Political leaders were confronted with new problems for which they were unprepared and had no solutions.

Further, the geopolitical map of the world had fundamentally changed. The confrontation of opposing blocs had ended, the Warsaw Pact organization had dissolved, and many new independent states had appeared. Consequently the bipolar structure of the international community disappeared. The world became truly pluralistic. It had lost the system of relations that had previously held it together and organized it, however defective that system was.

Freed from the threat of a nuclear nightmare that hung over everyone's head during the Cold War, and freed from the discipline imposed by each of the rival blocs during that time, every country found that it now possessed a new freedom of action. Each one sought to find its own place in the changing world and to identify its own true interests on a new basis.

To these factors of geopolitical change, one more factor must be added: the dissolution of the Soviet Union, which changed the "geometry" of relations, especially in Europe, but by no means in Europe alone. In the years of perestroika the Soviet Union had become a solid counterweight against any attempt to impose hegemony, but now it had disappeared. Accordingly, all those who in their hearts had been nurturing egoistic plans of whatever kind now had much greater scope for action. The world became less predictable, more uncertain.

The independent states, including Russia, that were formed in place of the Soviet Union became the objects of self-seeking plans and schemes by major foreign powers. This became evident essentially as soon as the Belovezh decisions had been made. A great chase began for possession of parts of the Soviet inheritance. This found expression in the selective policies pursued by Western governments in relation to each of the new states of the former USSR.

The dissolution of the USSR contributed to the revival of nationalistic and centrifugal forces in Europe and other regions. Western policies in a de facto way helped activate these forces, beginning with the hasty recognition of Slovenia and Croatia, which further propelled disintegration of the former Yugoslavia and ruined chances for a peaceful divorce among the former members of the Socialist Federated Republic of Yugoslavia (once this divorce had become inevitable).

All the processes and events referred to above undeniably complicated the international situation substantially. Still, as I see it, that was not the main problem. The main problem was that the policies and political leaders—both on the national and the world scale—failed to perceive or plan for the processes that unfolded or, still worse, had no program of action to neutralize the negative consequences of those processes and ensure a smooth transition to new relations, to that new world order people were talking so much about.

Was there a real possibility for us to find our way to a new world order after the end of the Cold War? Objective *prerequisites* for a transition to new world relations undoubtedly had taken shape by the end of the 1980s. But prerequisites alone do not constitute a real possibility.

The possibility of such a transition presupposes the subjective willingness of the main actors on the world political stage to carry through such a transition. Considering past history and the events that have unfolded quite recently, it can be said that the Soviet Union was willing to find a way to arrive at genuinely democratic and peaceful international relations. In the West, particularly in the United States, no such willingness existed. In the Soviet Union the new thinking and the foreign policy based on it had already put the new approaches into actual, material practice and had already applied the corresponding methods for resolving problems. In contrast, when the United States spoke about the new world order it essentially meant a continuation of its previous policy with some corrections in methodology. The United States viewed the end of the Cold War as the removal of many substantial obstacles on the road to achieving long-standing goals of American policy. The American conception was essentially limited only to making certain corrections in its international policies. The existing order in world economic affairs was essentially to Washington's liking. The strengthening of the free-trade system was considered desirable given America's solid position in relation to its competitors. Problems of civilization as a whole remained on a subsidiary or tertiary level as unpleasant matters that could be managed by taking measures of a partial nature that would not be burdensome for the United States.

The other Western powers had their own special interpretations of the conception of a new world order. Germany, for example, having achieved reunification, quite cautiously at first (and later more openly) adopted a policy aimed at reviving its former dominant influence in Central and Eastern Europe. This was reflected in other aspects of Bonn's foreign policy.

In other words, at the end of the Cold War, many, if not all, governments were in favor of a new world order, but there were different conceptions of what that order would be. Even if everything in the world had remained as before, these fundamentally different views would inevitably have resulted in disagreement and divergence among the world powers in a fairly short time. It is not just a matter of natural disparities in national interests among different countries—that is a constant factor in world politics, which can be taken into account in the course of finding a mutually acceptable balance of interests and reasonable ways of compromising. What was involved was an essential dissimilarity in the goals being set, in the very vision of the world and of its needs and prospects.

We must say, therefore, that along with the many unforeseen problems of world politics there were different strategic orientations and different political intentions.

The dominant conceptions, in fact, did not point toward the future but in many respects were anchored in the past; the past was their source of nourishment. In the best of cases, the question was how to renew or refurbish the traditional approaches. No new outlook really came to light, although that was exactly what was needed if we were to speak of a genuinely new world order.

Whatever the reason, in late 1991 and especially in early 1992 the course of world events began to flow along a different channel. In speaking of the events of recent years, what has become evident, above all, is that while the Cold War on the whole passed into history, its legacy and many of its elements have persisted, although in changed form. A certain estrangement between the former opponents, who now call themselves partners, still exists. It is expressed, for example, in the version of events that we have already mentioned and that is stubbornly repeated—namely, that the Western side was victorious and the East was defeated. This version of events is accompanied by a certain condescending attitude and sometimes even arrogance, as expressed in Western policies.

To a considerable extent the old image of the enemy no longer exists in its old form. But today, especially in recent times, attempts have been made here and there to create new variants of that old image in modified form. For example, the idea of various "dangers" coming from the East is expressed now and then in Western publications and sometimes in the speeches of Western political leaders.

In our view, there are three dangers today that pose the greatest threat. The first is the alarming signs of a new division of the world, the emergence of new trouble spots. These are apparent particularly in Europe, where there is an obvious attempt to consolidate what is supposed to be recognized as Western. Granted, the dividing line is now drawn in new areas. Still, we cannot help but view with concern the attempts to construct on European soil a new system of security exclusively based on NATO, including Eastern European and Central European states in this alliance, while in effect ostracizing Russia. It is true that at the same time there is a lot of rhetorical recognition that European security is unthinkable without Russia.

Another fairly evident danger is what may be termed *a new arms race*. The most dangerous types of military technology continue to spread throughout the world. There is a creeping expansion of the technological capability for the production of nuclear weapons and other weapons of mass destruction. What happened in India and Pakistan should oblige the international community and the UN Security Council to take action. Military technology is being refined and perfected, and conventional weapons are acquiring the capacity to function as "absolute weapons." In the more developed countries, new techniques for killing or paralyzing the enemy are being developed, including psychotropic, electronic, and laser weapons.

The disastrous consequences of the arms race that was part of the Cold War are well known. That arms race not only oppressed everyone with its state of mutual fear and terrible tension; it also drained the economic potential of the participating states. It had extremely negative political and psychological consequences as well, strengthening the positions of the most military-minded elements in society who are well known for their intolerance and cruelty.

A third element has become evident in recent years—a notable revival of traditional power politics, a preference for military methods in solving problems. The most striking examples in recent years (although they are by far not the only ones) are in Yugoslavia and the second Persian Gulf crisis. In both cases the political behavior of the parties to the conflicts and of some other countries showed that they saw the resort to arms as the only way of resolving problems. These events constitute a serious warning.

Along with these relapses into the power politics of the past, which are especially dangerous in today's new conditions, other phenomena exist that can be regarded as the early shoots of a future renewal of the world. For example, world public opinion has been activated to some degree to infuse universal human values and principles of morality into world affairs and the resolution of major problems. An example was the conference of government leaders on environment and development held in Brazil in 1992, and subsequent conferences on demographics and women's rights. Another example may be seen in actions the United Nations has taken since the end of the Cold War in which for the first time it played the role of peacemaker and defender of the peace, the role for which it was originally intended. Another sign of things to come may be seen in the enhanced role played in international relations by a new element in politics—major nongovernmental organizations which in generalized form reflect the sentiments of world public opinion.

These new phenomena have a meager influence in world affairs, but even so they are quite important. In the light of everything said above, can we assert that the trend toward eliminating confrontation is powerful enough now to be irreversible? Unfortunately we can only answer that confrontational elements are still very much woven into the fabric of world politics. The grounds for this view are especially compelling in light of the fact that the confrontational approach is consistent with political traditions having deep historical roots, traditions based on the notion of a world balance of power, the desire to assert hegemony, to establish spheres of influence, to identify one's own interests with those of the world as a whole. These tendencies continue to exist, although often in disguised form.

In view of all this, how do we see the world today? Is there a "Cold Peace," so to speak? Or has there been a reversion to confrontation, granted that it is not full-fledged?

In my view, what we see now is a unique period in world development that can only be described as transitional. It has its own special features and distinguishing characteristics. What is involved, apparently, is not just a transitional period but a special kind of transitional world order, one that could exist for a long time, one that is characterized by instability, conflict, and the predominance of uncontrolled spontaneous forces in world relations.

How long this transitional period lasts will be determined by the interaction of many factors. One factor is the choice that the more advanced countries will make—whether they will favor equal cooperation or domination in international relations. This in turn will affect the resolution of problems related to the elimination of the socioeconomic and technological gap between North and South, between the rich and backward countries.

Another factor will be the direction taken by developments in several major regions of the world. These are Europe, particularly the post-Soviet space; the Asian-Pacific region, particularly China; and the Arab world and the Mideast. Developments in the United States and on the American continent as a whole will be of essential importance, particularly the success or failure of Pan-American integration processes. The countries of sub-Sahara Africa represent the biggest unknown factor in the overall equation.

Another important factor will be the way that worldwide problems are solved given that military power will play a reduced role and economic power will have an increased role, along with competitiveness on the world market and a change in the correlation of forces in the world community.

A great deal, of course, will depend on the internal development of the Western countries as a whole.

Much will depend on whether individual countries and the international community display the necessary understanding of the importance of global problems. The issue is not only that the deepening of these problems would create increasing elements of tension in society but also that it could cause new conflicts between states, such as a struggle for natural resources, beginning with oil and gas and ending with water and problems of uncontrolled migration.

This list is by no means exhaustive. It is a deliberately incomplete listing of the circumstances that will determine the duration of the transitional world order and the emergence of a truly new and genuinely peaceful world order. But basing our expectations on what we know today, we can assume that this time frame will be fairly prolonged.

What must not be forgotten is that the preconditions for the absolutely necessary changes in the future will not take shape only in the realm of world politics and economics. The decisive role ultimately will be played by fundamental processes that affect the very foundations of existence of the worldwide human community.

CHAPTER 21

The New Thinking in the Post-Confrontational World

In drawing a political balance sheet on the first post-confrontational years, we can arrive at the following conclusions:

- The world has entered a new phase in its development—a transitional order that will lead it to some new state of existence whose contours are still undefined.

- The world has entered this new phase, as before, in a politically fragmented condition, although this fragmentation has taken on a new configuration, and in fact the nature of international relations on the whole has changed.

- The world is gradually moving through an arc of crisis—partially conscious of this, yet partially unaware. The potential for crisis in all spheres of existence, all regions of the world, is accumulating. Scientists in the Department of Research on Problems of Peace and Conflict at Uppsala University in Sweden have calculated that over the past five years ninety conflicts of varying intensity have been recorded around the globe and forty-seven of them continue to this day.

- The constructive potential in world politics has diminished notably. Both international policies and those of individual countries have not only made no effort to counter disorganizing developments but have often displayed impotence or indifference in the face of dangerous chaotic processes. Policy making has trailed along in the wake of events but has neither foreseen nor attempted to prevent their occurrence.

Once again, the world is facing a serious, if not critical, choice. Either it will allow the processes we now observe to continue to develop or it will try, through the collective efforts of governments and peoples, to influence their evolution in a direction favorable for everyone. Thus far no one has resolved how to arrive at the second, more salutary alternative. The situation seems insoluble.

Yet in the mid-1980s, as hopeless as the prospects for curbing the arms race and ending the Cold War appeared, those things were actually accomplished! The understanding on both sides that continued confrontation represented a mortal danger gradually took root and played an important role in this accomplishment. What was needed as well was the political will to put an end to the situation. The decisive role in this was played by the new thinking and the policies of the Soviet Union, based on that thinking. Thus both sides were able to break through the seemingly impregnable wall of old ideas and the policies of hatred, intolerance, and mutual rejection that corresponded to those ideas.

Essentially the same factors that succeeded in the past are needed today: first, an understanding that the policies being pursued have no prospects for resolving today's problems; second, the political will to change the direction and orientation of these policies; and, third, a conception that accurately reflects the needs of today's world and corresponds to the challenges of the time.

Further, the experience of the past few years, the overcoming of the Cold War, has not yet been entirely squandered. And we still benefit from the assets created at that time, for example, the treaties reducing nuclear and conventional weapons, and several agreements setting limits on actions harmful to the environment.

How, then, should we relate to the new thinking, which served as the conceptual basis for overcoming the Cold War and which retains its significance today? Is the new thinking just a part of history? Does it no longer reflect the needs and interests of worldwide development? Or is it only that certain people would like to consign this philosophy to oblivion? I believe the latter is the case and that underlying that attitude are narrowly egoistic interests, a desire to maintain the status quo in international relations at all costs.

The point of departure for the new thinking was the concept of the wholeness of the world, its interconnectedness and interdependence. Is this idea really outdated? On the contrary, the world's interdependence makes itself felt ever more strongly with each passing year. Everyone today, it seems, is talking about globalization.

And is the proposition no longer relevant today that universal human interests must take priority? Again, just the opposite is true. Today, as researchers and international forums point with alarm to the current dangers threatening the survival of the human race, this proposition is more solidly grounded than ever. It is precisely today that joint efforts aimed at saving the human race must become the backbone of world politics.

The new thinking asserts the principle of freedom of choice and recognizes pluralism regarding the interests of different countries and the right of each to defend its interests; at the same time it demands that politics find a balance among the interests of all countries as the basis for making mutually acceptable decisions. This also reflects a realistic understanding of today's increasingly diverse world.

The new thinking rejected brute force as an instrument of world politics. Can it be that recent events have refuted the correctness of this requirement? Of course not. Something else troubles us, however: A process is under way in which people are gradually growing accustomed to the use of force. Politics is becoming immoral, and permanently aggressive, even in solving domestic problems. Is it not time to place limits on this barbarization of politics?

Finally, the new thinking calls for political methods to be used in solving problems, and it is oriented toward patience and tolerance. This approach is unquestionably justified—it is the lack of dialogue, of trying to find political solutions, that often results in bloodshed.

It is my profound conviction that the principles of the new thinking have not become outdated but indeed still apply today. Further, as confrontation has been overcome thanks to these principles (although they are by no means used consistently by the West), it means that the present backward trend has occurred to a large extent because these principles have been forgotten. They have fallen victim to self-seeking, egoistic intentions and actions.

Thus one of the most important prerequisites for improving world affairs and passing beyond the present complicated transitional order is a return to the principles of the new thinking and to finding ways of solving the world's political problems that correspond to these principles. This is not to say that we should simply repeat the methods of the past, even of the recent past, even those that have been successful. No, the world is developing and evolving and the new thinking must also evolve.

The efforts of our team at the Gorbachev Foundation since it was established on March 3, 1992, have focused precisely on analyzing ongoing developments in world affairs so as to enrich the new thinking.

Naturally, the course of worldwide development has in itself forced us to pay significant attention to changes occurring in the geo-political realm. These changes are truly significant: In place of the bipolar structure in the world, a new multipolar, pluralistic structure has arisen with fundamental changes in the balances of forces among nation-states and groups of states. Along with that, the relative weight and influence of certain states in world politics have also undergone change. Economic, scientific, and technological factors are becoming increasingly important. It is no accident that today more and more discussion is heard about the increased role of geo-economics alongside geo-politics.

As our analysis has deepened, it has become clear that we cannot limit ourselves to geo-political and geo-economic problems. Although these problems must be studied, that alone will not enable us to penetrate to the primary causes of existing problems and difficulties or find ways of resolving and overcoming them.

The development of the entire world organism has a complex structure, which minimally is twofold. This "double-layered" quality is to some extent inseparable from world history. But in certain periods it becomes particularly obvious and is often the cause of sharp contradictions.

The first, upper layer (the surface layer) comprises the multiple relations among nation-states and peoples. Here a decisive role is played by the subjective factor—politics, politicians, and political forces working in different directions—and the interests of governments, peoples, and social and national communities are interwoven. Typical of processes in this sphere are mobility, changeability, and frequent shifting of coordinates.

The second, deeper layer involves immanent, objective shifts in the basic nature of civilization, beginning with the constant renewal of means and methods of economic progress and ending with the constant and unstoppable evolution in the way of life of the millions of people in the world. In the final analysis, these shifts determine the dynamics and direction of world development.

Take economic development, for example. During the twentieth century the developed countries passed from classical industrial production, characterized by widespread manual labor, to assembly-line production. Automated production emerged later and was followed by cybernetics and information systems. A new society has begun to emerge from industrial society. It is often defined as the postindustrial, or information, society (although neither of these terms is entirely accurate).

These processes, of course, are connected with those developing in the upper layer, but the link is of a special kind. Scientific and technical progress to a significant degree has been impelled by the requirements of politics, by the "struggle of each against all." In the twentieth century, a venerable law of history has been fully confirmed: Wars have been the most reliable consumer and most efficient accelerating mechanism for economic and industrial progress.

If the surface processes, mainly the political ones, have influenced the more profound processes of economics and revolutionary changes in production, then the more profound processes have had very little practical effect on the superficial processes. The deeper processes have actually strengthened the various attempts to divide the world on the basis of force; those who master the secrets of technology earlier and more efficiently for military purposes can exploit these abilities in military conflicts or in bloodless trade wars.

Scientific and technological progress has changed not only the economy but also the world's social structure and its consumption patterns, as well as the way of life and the thinking of millions of people. These changes, of course, have not always been consistent with the real needs of normal development. Here again, the influence of the surface layer, with its confrontational political culture and the self-seeking nature of individualist society, has had its effect.

Finally, the more profound processes in the scientific and technological realm, mainly the computer and information revolution, have significantly accelerated a tendency lodged in the very nature of our civilization—the tendency toward internationalization and subsequent globalization of world development.

We have referred to only a few modern trends, but they are sufficient for us to say that these objective shifts in our civilization obviously need to be adequately considered on the level of politics. As a rule, however, this has not happened.

In the past, when the pace of such shifts was still fairly slow and had only local effects, the contradiction between the two layers of world existence did not produce catastrophic consequences. Policy making lagged behind, but it was able, so to speak, to get away with it, although the consequences even then were quite negative. During the past few decades, however, as these processes basic to our civilization have sharply accelerated and acquired an unprecedentedly profound and genuinely global character, the situation has changed. We urgently need to define new parameters of economic, social, political, and spiritual development in society and develop policies for managing the new challenges before us. Once again, however, this has not happened.

In short, an extremely dangerous *gap* exists between politics and the development of objective processes. Over time this gap has grown into an antagonism capable of blowing up the world.

The end of Cold War confrontation represented a partial defusing of the contradiction I have described above and averted a nuclear war. As I have said, however, in recent times we have regressed, granted not toward nuclear war but possibly toward the rise of new tensions. The end of Cold War confrontation, moreover, normalized the situation only in the upper, or surface, layer of world development; it did not touch the second, deeper layer and did not represent a resolution of the contradiction between the two layers.

Yet the intensification of the contradiction between the two levels, the inability of politics to take into account the more profound changes in the very fundamentals of existence, cause us to characterize the situation as a crisis of contemporary civilization. Our resources are obviously nearing an end, and the customary forms of development are being exhausted.

A crisis in the model of technogenic development is making itself felt. This is quite obvious. Modern technology-based civilization has placed tremendous possibilities in human hands, but at the same time it has created conflict fraught with catastrophic consequences, a disharmony in the relations between human beings and the rest of nature.

A crisis in the forms of social life is at hand everywhere in the world. The character of political activity even in democratic systems seems to be increasingly less democratic. Contradictions between the individual and society, between government and the individual, are not being resolved but are accumulating. Increasing tension is noticeable even in relations among individuals.

We find that world relations are in serious crisis because they do not meet the requirements of today's interdependent world. The political culture inherited from the past does not allow the international community to concentrate sufficiently on the task of overcoming global threats.

The world economy is shaken now and again by spontaneous eruptions and unexpected crises that threaten people the world over. According to an opinion fairly often expressed at international conferences, attempts are being made to use the global economy in general and finance in particular to destabilize the economy of one or another country. There are indications that economic power centers are coordinating activities aimed at pushing Russia off to the sidelines in relation to the world economy and holding back China's modernization process.

An extremely unhealthy symptom of our times is the moral degradation of the individual and of society, which has grown to tragic proportions in some places. Fundamental spiritual values are being lost. Terrorism, the spread of organized crime, and especially drug trafficking are dangers in and of themselves and also create a breeding ground for the criminalization of politics.

Lastly, there is an ideological crisis. The dominant ideologies have proven incapable of explaining what is happening or proposing any rational way out of the existing situation.

In short, we are talking about a global crisis in all areas.

The research we have conducted at the Gorbachev Foundation has led us to conclude that it is impossible to find a way out of the present transitional period by attempting to resolve only the current ongoing political problems—however important they may be. It is essential to move forward decisively toward finding answers to the new challenges on the global level of civilization as a whole. It is necessary, in other words, to find roads leading to a new civilization.

It is difficult to foresee what this new civilization would be like. What is undeniable, however, is that it should ensure a harmonious or at least nonconfrontational coexistence between humankind and the rest of nature; it would ensure peaceful, democratic co-development of all nations and nationalities; it should be more kind and humane in relation to individuals, protecting their rights and ensuring the well-rounded development of each individual.

We understand that building such a civilization is a long-term task (although on the scale of history a task that cannot be postponed). Few people in the world are ready for the profound, fundamental changes required for the creation of this civilization. What, then, should be done?

We should not try to effect immediate all-embracing changes; rather, we should move toward such change step by step, finding urgent solutions where they are absolutely necessary and partial solutions where nothing else can yet be done. Solutions will gradually enlarge the field of agreement and the range of possibilities for later, more substantial measures.

Absolutely unacceptable, however, are measures that would introduce instant revolutionary change in one or another sphere of international relations or domestic circumstances. In today's fragile world, sudden change is terribly painful and would be self-destructive. Evolution, reform, and carefully thought-out change—these are the optimal roads to take.

In our view, the new thinking can assure gradual but sure movement forward without infringing on anyone's interests, but respecting freedom of choice and preserving the unique characteristics of national or regional cultures.

As I have stated above, new conclusions and new ways of posing questions are necessary today. Above all, it is important to focus on the challenges of the new millennium. These are challenges to life itself, to the very existence not only of the human race but of all living things on earth. These are the challenges of (1) globalization, (2) diversity, (3) global problems, (4) power politics, (5) democracy, and (6) universal human values. We will deal with each of these six challenges in the following six chapters.

These are well-known challenges that we have all become accustomed to discussing. But familiarity dulls our perceptions and weakens our awareness of danger. It reduces our energy for thought and action aimed at overcoming these challenges. This is a problem especially because some political leaders and scientists console themselves by suggesting that these challenges have been exaggerated and, in any case, may solve themselves. After all, they argue, not all the predictions have come true so far.

But let us ask a simple but grave question: can we really ignore these challenges? The answer is clear, at least for anyone who seriously thinks about the prospects of the future. No, it is not possible to avoid these challenges or avoid seeking to manage them effectively. We do not have the right to do that. Avoiding these challenges would mean signing a death warrant for future generations.

I believe that humanity is capable of dealing with these challenges.

CHAPTER 22

The Challenge of Globalization

THE PROCESS THROUGH which the world is becoming an increasingly many-sided integrated whole has roots that go back to as far as the fifteenth century, according to scholars in Russia and other countries. The trend toward integration has been manifested in the most varied forms—from empire building, colonial conquests, and trading companies operating across several continents to the emergence of worldwide transportation systems, the rise of multinational corporations, and the growth of new worldwide communications systems.

As early as the 1970s and 1980s, some scholars used the term *mondialization* (from the French term *mondiale*, meaning "worldwide") in referring to the internationalization of the processes of production and exchange. The powerful flow of capital from one country to another has also been noted, along with an increase in trade that has exceeded the pace of growth in industrial production.

Today the term *globalization* is more commonly used to describe these world processes. It reflects the fact that the processes of internationalization have essentially embraced all spheres of existence of the human community worldwide and also that the interdependence of the various countries and peoples has acquired a qualitatively different character and become a real factor of great magnitude.

The globalization process is, in many respects, internally contradictory. On the one hand it opens up for all the world and for each country new and previously unheard-of chances to accelerate development, to link up with the most advanced forms and methods of production, and to participate in the exchange of cultural and intellectual values. On the other hand—on a much broader scale than previously—it gives those nations and giant monopolies that are economically, technically, and politically more power-

ful the ability to exploit other countries and populations and extract enormous profits from the uneven development of the various regions of the
world.

Considering both the positive and negative potential of these processes,
globalization poses a challenge in that it requires a new quality of human
activity to adapt to new conditions. Thus it requires a new quality of politics in the broadest sense of the word.

Globalization has received a further impetus as a result of changes that
have occurred since the end of the Cold War. In the wake of those changes,
the world market truly became a worldwide phenomenon after dozens of
countries began to make a transition to the market economy and to pluralistic democracy. For the first time in decades a global field for worldwide competition emerged with all its advantages and deficiencies. This is an important step toward greater interdependence and interconnectedness among the
countries and peoples of the world.

Another qualitative change that has become especially noticeable in
recent years is the swift expansion of the information revolution, whose
effects are felt throughout the world economy, above all, in the world financial and banking systems. The world economy has become more dynamic;
the interconnections (and competition as well) between national economies
has increased substantially. Transnational corporations have acquired an
ever increasing degree of independence from national economies and operate on a world scale without consideration for the interests of those
economies.

Especially striking changes have taken place in the realm of finance. It
was noted at a session of the Interaction Council, in May 1995, that a dramatic increase had occurred in the mobility of capital based on modern
communications and information systems. Capital movement has become
separated from the movement of goods and services. This course of events
is fraught with grave dangers. For example: as shown by the turbulence on
the stock markets as a result of the Asian crisis in 1997–98.

New developments in the realm of universal security also provide cause
for serious concern. The global threat of nuclear catastrophe has become
more remote, although it has not been entirely eliminated. But today it is
evident that global security is fragile.

The world is full of scattered conflicts that have drawn into their orbit
significant numbers of people and have involved an increasing number of
countries in the process of trying to overcome these conflicts. What is

worse, the conflicts directly affect the most varied interests, from nationalistic to religious.

There is a global expansion of terrorism, drug trafficking, corruption, and organized crime involving Mafia-type organizations.

Environmental problems are mounting. A shortage of food resources, sources of energy, and potable water is beginning to be felt. The area covered by forests and cultivated land is shrinking, and the earth's oceans and atmosphere are being polluted. All these phenomena have arisen or become more acute in recent years because they are unique manifestations or consequences of the quickening pace of globalization and the growth of universal interdependence.

On a theoretical and political level, a significant problem is the correlation between worldwide, global interests and those of national states. This problem had previously attracted attention and became the subject of debates, which sometimes led to misunderstandings. But now it has become an especially acute problem.

The realm of universal human interests continues to expand. All the phenomena described above give added weight to the question of the interests of humanity as a whole.

There is one other theoretical and political question that must be considered as the new thinking develops: A kind of inversion has occurred in the way domestic and international processes (and policies) are affecting each other.

In the era of confrontation and even in the period that brought it to an end, international processes increasingly affected domestic conditions in various nations. The Cold War forced all countries to subordinate their domestic actions to its requirements and interfered with normal domestic development. In recent years, however, there has been a shift: decisions in a given country regarding domestic problems, economics, the ecology, and so on, have tangibly affected life in other countries. Recall, for example, how in the post-confrontational period military conflicts erupted mostly within the boundaries of one country, but then often, though not always, became internationalized. At the root of these conflicts have been incorrect or unsuccessful domestic political decisions, above all those involving nationalities.

Thus each country now has a greater degree of responsibility for its domestic actions insofar as they affect the international community. Thus, too, the very great necessity for every government and political force to consider the needs of the international community, both its problems and concerns, when making internal decisions. Unfortunately, in the practical activities of national governments this increased interconnection between domestic and foreign affairs is not being taken into account to the extent necessary. But without such consideration, political decisions may not only be erroneous; they may be quite harmful as well. They may well end up hurting the governments that initially made the decisions.

All this taken together—the new manifestations of globalization and its consequences—requires that the kind of international dialogue that played an irreplaceable role in ending the Cold War must be raised to a qualitatively new level. It must be understood that at this new stage it is no longer enough that only the great powers engage in a dialogue to determine the general trends of world political development. Instead, the efforts, experience, and intellectual capacities of most of the world's nations must be brought together. We should be talking about laying the basis for mechanisms to establish some kind of regulation or management of worldwide processes.

In previous stages of social development, national societies and governments had their own political and juridical frameworks, their own "rules of the game," limited by their national boundaries. But in a world that is quickly becoming globalized, the rules are becoming obsolete. Problems are not being solved but are becoming more acute. Politics today is called upon to enrich itself with a truly philosophical view of a world that is simultaneously united and contradictory. If politics fails to adopt this view, the task of managing or regulating global processes will remain unresolved.

It is recognized more and more widely that certain rules of the game must be established if the new world is to establish some form of administration or management of worldwide processes. Certain groups have attempted to provide for such management—for example, the so-called Group of Seven [the seven richest and most powerful countries, whose top officials meet regularly to discuss world problems—the United States, Canada, Britain, France, Germany, Italy, and Japan]. The United States, in statements by its highest officials, has more than once voiced a claim to "American leadership of the world." The pretensions of the G-7 or of the United States alone are not well founded, however. Today's world of free, independent, sovereign states is by no means willing to accept leadership only from one direction. This becomes increasingly evident with each passing year.

The idea of creating a world government has come up many times and is frequently found in the pages of both scholarly and political publications. But it is unrealizable, at least for the time being. Other issues that have taken center stage in today's political thinking include self-determination, self-identification, and self-government. Accordingly, on the eve of the twenty-first century the idea of administering world processes can be realized only as the idea of coordinating the efforts of national governments and unifying those efforts for the sake of solving specific common problems.

Of course this is an extremely complicated task. For centuries people have been accustomed to isolated actions by various countries. Each nation has been concerned about itself and has viewed other nations as only temporary allies or fellow travelers. Fairly often, nations tried to solve their own problems at the expense of others. In today's conditions such approaches can only worsen the difficulties for each country. Anyone who would try to play a zero-sum game is bound to lose. But in order for this to be understood and, even more important, to be put into practice, a genuine psychological revolution is necessary.

Obviously the goals of global management cannot be achieved all at once, in a single leap. Even with a "great leap forward," we could not coordinate the efforts of the international community and establish some form of management or administration of worldwide processes. Thus it is necessary to approach this goal step by step, to try to enhance the role of existing institutions and encourage coordination of the efforts of various governments.

Above all, we are thinking about the United Nations. In 1995 this organization was fifty years old. The half century that has gone by has demonstrated both the enormous potential and, to a certain extent, the limited nature of this organization. Practice has shown that the UN has functioned most efficiently when *all* its members—certainly not just the permanent members of the Security Council—demonstrated unity of will and intention, and sought to achieve specific, realistic goals. This is exactly what we should strive for today.

In recent times, however, the UN has evidently been in danger of playing a reduced role. Proposals are being made to restrict the scope of its functioning, and attempts to manipulate UN resolutions have become evident.

The need for specifying and refining anew the functions and role of the United Nations has been felt for a long time. It must become an organization that takes into account to the fullest extent the challenges and real needs of the new world that has come into existence.

Many plans for reforming the UN have been proposed. Thus far none have achieved the necessary consensus among members. The Agenda for

Peace and Agenda for Development worked out by the UN general secretary in the first half of the 1990s, although quite useful, have to a large extent remained only on paper.

Of course the UN needs a general conception of action, an integrated strategy of global partnership. Perhaps it is also worth trying to carry out specific measures for improving the UN. Obviously security has many different aspects today—economic, environmental, and social—that need to be taken into account, including in the UN Charter and in the structure and composition of various UN agencies and bodies. For example, the creation of an Economic Security Council has been requested. An authoritative body for environmental monitoring and coordination of actions by national governments in this area is obviously necessary. There is also a growing need for a coordinating center to combat terrorism, organized crime, and drug trafficking.

The rights and powers of the UN General Assembly may need to be revised. Perhaps a certain category of decisions or resolutions by the Assembly (where life-or-death global problems are involved) should become binding on all members.

Clearly an important task of the UN and its institutions is to improve the current international legal system. The system now represents an uncodified set of juridical standards that partly contradict one another and do not by any means cover all the "legal space," so to speak, in international relations. As a rule, new problems that have arisen in recent decades have not been taken into account in this system of international law.

Urgently needed is a new interpretation of the principle of national sovereignty. This is, of course, a very delicate subject in an era witnessing the tempestuous rebirth of national feelings. Still, all nations have recognized to varying degrees that the principle of absolute sovereignty is no longer functional in certain spheres. The number of international agreements having to do with resolving the most varied kinds of problems—from arms reduction to environmental measures—and the rapidly multiplying number of such agreements are graphic evidence of the need to redefine national sovereignty. Today many nations have delegated some of their sovereign rights to the international community. Such practices will apparently expand, necessitating an appropriate legal form for them.

Still another problem, no less delicate, is that existing norms and standards of international law are not, as a rule, reinforced by monitoring to determine whether members of the international community are abiding by these standards. Globalization produces new demands for a kind of international responsibility or, if you will, discipline. What can be undertaken in this respect and in what way is another question requiring attention.

Other areas in which UN functions could be improved may undoubtedly be suggested, but the chief need today is to reaffirm and strengthen the UN's role in the world. Of course, no matter what improvements in the functioning and structure of this organization may be introduced, there also needs to be an understanding that , without an attentive and respectful attitude by all nations toward the work and decisions of the UN, it cannot be an effective body. This includes the financing of UN activities in a timely way worthy of the role the UN plays. A special session of the UN, it seems, ought to be devoted to this topic.

In addition to the United Nations, almost every continent has various regional or continent-wide organizations. Their functions are political and often economic. The emergence of these organizations is essentially a manifestation of the trend toward globalization, a reflection of the need for international coordination in making decisions affecting peace, security, and cooperation on a regional scale.

The regionalization of the world, in some respects, contradicts its globalization, creating the danger of intensified economic and political rivalry between regional organizations.

Considering all aspects of the matter, it seems essential to establish effective collaboration between regional organizations and the UN, its Security Council and its other institutions. This would allow the creation of a kind of unified system of world and regional decision-making bodies and would ensure coordination (rather than rivalry) among regional organizations.

Economic rivalry among regional organizations, as among individual nations, is of course inevitable. It can be kept within necessary limits, however, with the help of international economic and financial organizations—for example, the World Trade Organization (on the condition that it become an instrument for establishing equality and mutual respect for all interests). It seems evident that with the changes occurring in the world currency markets, especially with worldwide expansion of the market economy, the time has come for reform of the appropriate international organizations brought into existence half a century ago at Bretton Woods.

It should be noted that regional organizations for peace, security, and cooperation can be exceedingly useful—but only if they have the necessary powers and instruments to conduct their activities. The importance of these necessary powers is illustrated by the ineffectiveness of the Organization for Security and Cooperation in Europe (OSCE). The very existence of this institution exemplifies how the lack of clearly defined powers—particularly the right to make decisions that are binding on all members—as well as the weakness of its agencies—which, at best, are merely consultative bodies or have only observer status—prevents this organization from being an effective instrument for security and cooperation.

One may argue that the OSCE has not yet emerged from its initial, formative stage. However, the fact is that a number of its influential members prefer the organization to be ineffective for reasons that include a desire either to avoid the "burden" of carrying out the OSCE's decisions or to preserve NATO at all costs as the chief instrument for European security.

A last point: The search for answers to the challenge of globalization in our times is by no means solely the precinct of professional politicians. Particularly the last ten years have shown that the forces of civil society play an enormous role in this sphere. The activism of scientists, physicians, writers, and representatives of the business world were also essential in overcoming the Cold War, primarily by pointing up the real dangers of East-West conflict and creating a spiritual climate for policies of détente, reconciliation, and retreat from confrontation.

The forces of civil society can play a similar role today. Therefore we should reiterate a proposal advanced earlier: Let us establish, under UN auspices, a kind of permanent worldwide brain trust (or "council of the wise"). This would consist of people having no government duties and who are free of any ideological or other preconceptions or prejudices, people who are capable of objectively evaluating the new phenomena in world developments and translating their conclusions into practical recommendations. The experience and authority of Nobel Prize winners could be utilized in this connection.

A similar council or forum could be established in each major region, perhaps on every continent. Drawing on the inexhaustible potential of the world of science and culture, these institutions could enrich political thought in a fundamental way and initiate decisions or recommendations that would truly serve universal human interests as well as regional and national interests.

CHAPTER 23

The Challenge of Diversity

VIEWED IN THE long term, globalization is simply a process in which a new worldwide civilization is taking shape, brought about as the result (judging by the experience so far) of the global spread of advanced science and technology, and the deepening of genuine economic and social interdependence among all nations.

Unfortunately, this process is often viewed as some kind of worldwide standardization of life, as if everyone would be living in a drably uniform way. It seems to me that such standardization will not happen, that the different nations and nationalities will not be boiled down in a single melting pot. Nor will the specific qualities of each nation and nationality be obliterated. No uniform primitive mentality will arise to take the place of the various kinds of psychology, ways of thinking, inner soul, and character of the various nations and nationalities that have been formed historically. In the words of one of our outstanding Russian historians and thinkers, Mikhail Gefter:

> I am convinced that the world that the twentieth century will pass on as a legacy to the twenty-first will not be the world of a single humanity toward whose creation the previous centuries have striven in one way or another. It will be a *world of worlds*, living side by side and interacting, with a mutual interest in preserving life-giving differences. Differences will become the meaning and purpose of human activity, if you will, a decisive factor in the survival of the species *Homo* . . . This is new. This is untested. But really there can be no other way.

The dialectical process by which world unity is coming about while diversity is simultaneously increasing is one of the most complicated but real and urgent subjects for research concerning global development. We cannot fail to point out that, in parallel with expanding globalization, the number of independent states is multiplying before our eyes. An ever increasing number of nations and nationalities are expressing the desire for independence, up to and including the formation of new states—as if to say: Granted it's small and weak, but it's our own country.

Usually this contradictory tendency is explained by the democratization of life in the international community, the emancipation of nations initially from the fetters of colonialism, later from the chains of ignominious dependence on other countries, and finally from the oppressive burden of confrontation and general Cold War loyalties that placed a tight rein on national aspirations. The peoples of the world are seeking self-identity and independence.

As time passes, will this process end? The World Congress of Geographers predicted in 1992 that the number of new independent states would continue to grow in the future. Independent study of this phenomenon is beyond the scope of this work, but it is already clear that the multiplication of independent states is an inevitable result of the globalization process. This is because globalization, which brings about assimilation, coordination, and interdependence among nations and nationalities also forces each entity in this process to defend its own cultural characteristics, its own values and way of life. The process of interdependence, therefore, gives rise to both mutual attraction and repulsion. Just as there is interconnectedness, so too there is a certain mutual drawing of lines of demarcation.

The movement of the human community toward interdependence requires each participant to correct certain unique behaviors, adapt to the requirements of global markets, and subordinate themselves to certain universal imperatives. This means that the familiar conditions of existence are rapidly evolving. Participants are forced to change long-established customs and traditions and to revise their value systems. Of course this pressure is perceived or responded to differently. Some people become accustomed to the flood of change, whereas others feel they have fallen into the clutches of outside forces, even hostile forces, forces that threaten to tear them away from centuries-old cultural traditions. These forces seem to encroach on what is most precious—the identity of a national group, nation, or country. The perception of this threat leads to an instinctive opposition to globalization processes—or, more exactly, to their concrete manifestations. From this also arises a desire to take refuge from these oncoming changes by withdrawing into one's traditional niche, whether national, religious, or other.

In these times the phenomenon of aggressive nationalism has been triggered by a combination of the reaction against globalization and the desire of nations and nationalities to defend their rights and overcome injustices and restrictions of their rights—a desire that greatly intensified after the end of the Cold War.

The very concept of nationalism varies in different countries and among different nationalities. Often it is interpreted positively—as a desire to preserve and strengthen the uniqueness of one's own nation or nationality, and in such cases this is not objectionable.

However, the new breed of aggressive nationalism has a quite different content. Involved here is speculation by essentially antidemocratic forces that would like to achieve power, influence, and dominance by exploiting national sentiments and to create a kind of nationalist "paradise"—something far removed from the ideals of peace and humanism. It is a paradise that, for most normal people, would be a hell.

Aggressively nationalist forces exploit the idea of defending the rights and sovereignty of their nations, but in fact they prevent their own people's full enjoyment of their rights and sovereignty. Under present conditions, and especially under the conditions that will exist in the future, it will be possible to realize national rights and sovereignty only by considering the interdependence of nations and the absolute necessity of cooperation with other countries and with a world that rules out hostility and intolerance.

Another often troublesome trend, apart from aggressive nationalism, is "hyper-ethnicism." This harmful trend may combine with aggressive nationalism, but it can also be entirely "benign" (although that makes it no less dangerous). It is expressed in the desire to eliminate the multinational states that have taken shape historically and to create "ethnically pure" states. In discussing this phenomenon, it should be emphasized that the right of nations to self-determination is a natural right recognized by the international community. The International Covenant on economic, social, and cultural rights adopted by the United Nations on December 16, 1966, states in its first article: "All nations have the right to self-determination. By virtue of this right they freely establish their own political status and freely decide their own economic, social, and cultural development."

In other words, the right of nations to self-determination is no different from the right to freedom of choice, which is defended by the new thinking.

And when a nation unambiguously expresses its desire to exercise this right to self-determination, it is immoral—to say the least—to try to hinder it. For any nation, however, it is in that nation's own interests, when determining the ways and means for implementing this right, to consider a fairly broad range of circumstances that would be disastrous to ignore. Above all, few nations, and even fewer small administrative territories, are ethnically homogeneous. So when one ethnic community exercises its right to self-determination, it is very easy for this action to restrict the rights of another ethnic community. This is soil in which conflicts grow, conflicts that can become extremely severe and cause instability.

Furthermore, in cases where exercising the right to self-determination leads to the dissolution of a traditionally multinational state, the heirs of this state encounter a great many problems in "dividing up the inheritance," in addition to purely ethnic problems—so many problems that only in exceptional cases are they solved painlessly. Most often they cause relations between the separating parties to become clouded or embittered not just for years but for many decades.

The splitting of existing state structures into new states inevitably results in economic instability. To ensure the viability of the new structures is not a simple task—after all, economic complexes that had been built up over a long time are being torn apart. Often the new states fall into the orbit of other larger, more powerful states that treat them as loot to be plundered.

All these considerations, derived from historical experience, have been tragically and convincingly confirmed in recent years in the former Yugoslavia. All the negative consequences of hasty, poorly thought-out decisions that were supported no less hastily by foreign governments have appeared there. The common result of these decisions has been a long, drawn-out war that has brought countless catastrophes to the nations and nationalities of that country.

The fate of the Soviet Union is another example; its fragmentation into fifteen independent states was not preceded by the necessary planning and well thought-out measures and led to many negative consequences. Among them was the appearance in all cases of new national minorities although, properly speaking, *minority* may not be the proper term, because in some cases millions of people were involved and were comparable in number to the native population. There have also been attempts at "ethnic cleansing," violations of human rights, and so forth.

The problem is not limited to these two examples. No part of the world is free of "hyper-ethnic" tendencies in one form or another—for example, ethnic disruptions have occurred in China, India, Turkey, Spain, Canada, and Belgium. It is difficult to imagine the chaos that would erupt in the world if the desire for ethnic (or ethno-religious) isolation—the wish to separate one or another minority from an existing state structure—were to take the form of real measures to redraw the borders of existing states. This would not be a path toward better organization but a step backward toward universal disorganization of the human community.

The way out of this situation might be a carefully considered application of the principle of *federalism* in the broadest sense of the term. This principle offers the possibility of ensuring the rights and interests of individual nations, nationalities, and ethnic groups and also preserves all the advantages of the existing larger state structures. For example, the preservation of the Soviet Union in the form of a renewed federation (even with elements of a confederated structure) undoubtedly would have given each of the component nations the possibility of ensuring its own rights and would also have preserved the advantages of a large economic, legal, cultural, and military space. A federation would have helped avoid all the major difficulties and losses that all the components of the former Soviet Union are encountering today.

In certain cases—if conditions allowed—positive results might be achieved by applying the principle of national-cultural autonomy.

Generally, then, the right of nations to self-determination is indisputable, but it should not be incontrovertible. The question of the forms and methods by which self-determination is achieved deserve the closest attention, as well as flexible, cautious, and historically justified approaches.

Of course a question with still no generally accepted answer is how to balance universally recognized human rights with the rights of minorities, the rights of nations to self-determination, and the sovereignty of nations.

Considering the new legal standards that have emerged, the existence of unified structures embracing many nations, and both the interdependence and the growing multiplicity of the international community, we must contemplate a substantial revision of the concepts currently operating in the world. This, of course, can be accomplished only by collective efforts, and the results must be recognized by the entire international community.

Thus the simultaneous emergence of globalization and increased diversity in the international community, as well as the interdependence and mutual influences of these processes, are facts of life that cause many highly complicated problems. The problems occur in the domestic life of various nations, often impacting a nation's very destiny, as well as on the international level. Naturally opinions vary regarding this matter. For example, Francis Fukuyama, in his book *The End of History*, advances an idea that is popular in the West, namely, that liberalism was victorious in the Cold War and that the socialist idea was completely defeated; he then envisages the most extreme form of liberal values and the liberal mentality extended to the whole world. The ideal liberal model for him, of course, is American society and its values. This fairly clear assertion allows no alternative to the inevitable subordination of all nations to a single model with a monopoly on the truth, that is, melting all of humanity in the same old liberal pot.

History has already known attempts to act on the basis of a monopoly on the truth—such as the attempt to ordain for all of humanity a transition to socialism based on the Soviet totalitarian model. It is well known how that ended. And no doubt Fukuyama's pretensions will end in the same kind of grand finale. Indeed, even the Western world, in its present form, rejects any kind of single model—more exactly, the American model—as the only one. In advanced Western society each country has its own forms and methods for carrying out liberal ideas and using the mechanisms of the market economy and pluralist democracy. This alone refutes Fukuyama's predictions.

In his subsequent major work, *Trust*, he presents additional arguments in support of his basic thesis; for example, he asserts that all countries in the twenty-first century that do not renounce their own national traditions and characteristics, who do not "get married" or at least "become engaged" to what he calls "democratic liberalism" or "capitalism without borders," are doomed to vegetate.

Fukuyama's theoretical construct also collapses when tested against reality. Most countries since World War II have achieved impressive economic and cultural advances precisely by relying on their own traditions and psychological outlooks, while bowing to the demands of modernization. In some respects, these very countries—for example, Japan, South Korea, and Singapore—have already shown their ability to give the older industrial powers, beginning with the United States, a run for their money. The Asian financial crisis of 1997-98 dealt a substantial blow to these countries but by no means eliminated their potential for the future.

As for the countries of Central and Eastern Europe, including those of the former Soviet Union, the application of market mechanisms and pluralist democracy has also been carried out in quite different forms, taking into account specific national features. Attempts simply to impose ready-made models have ended in blind alleys and have complicated the process of reorganizing society. The people of Russia, in particular, have rejected these attempts as alien to their culture.

Another variation on predictions about development under conditions of globalization and the simultaneous growth of diversity comes from the pen of Samuel P. Huntington. In his work entitled *Clash of Civilizations* he advances the hypothesis of an inevitable conflict in the twenty-first century, an irreconcilable struggle between different civilizations. Essentially he seems to suggest that differences among civilizations inevitably lead to a universal struggle of each against all. A great deal of discussion, mainly critical, has been directed at Huntington's work. Without repeating what others have said on this topic, I believe that certain contradictions and even conflicts between various regions or cultures undoubtedly have occurred over the course of history. But although such problems cannot be ruled out in the future as well, they are hardly as explosive today as Huntington indicates.

The most serious and dangerous clashes today take place not so much between civilizations as within them. This is not surprising: The increased diversity in the international community has led to a unique result—a certain rise in pluralism within regional civilizations and the appearance of new contradictions among different segments of those civilizations. It is enough merely to cite the clashes between certain Arab countries or among differing political currents within each country, as well as bloody conflicts on the African continent and the complicated developments in Southeast Asia.

Another circumstance that cannot be ignored is that the current conflicts between different civilizations have resulted not so much from differences among them as from social factors, including the legacy of the colonial past, the widening gap in levels of development between countries or groups of countries, and the unequal legal status of immigrants (especially immigrants who went from developing countries to developed countries). This latter factor could, in the coming century, be a detonator of many conflicts.

Thus neither the hypothesis of a universal leveling out to meet the standards of liberalism nor an inevitable conflict of civilizations can be considered indisputable. Does this mean, then, that the dialectics of globalization and diversity, the challenge of diversity itself, will not entail complications? Absolutely not! But the factors underlying these complications are more subjective than objective and seek either to exploit objective differences or speculate on them.

I am mainly referring here to policies that ignore regional differences among civilizations, ignore national interests, and disregard specific national features of countries and populations. After all, any variant of hegemonism [policies aimed at imposing the hegemony of one country or bloc], any relapse into colonialism, any attempt to impose a particular model on all other countries or to establish worldwide "leadership" by any one power discounts the national interests of other countries. Thus far, only certain American politicians have expressed pretensions to the role of leadership on a world scale, but there are proponents of such ideas on the regional level.

The conclusion is obvious: Any policy that seeks to be democratic, humane, and responsive to the interests both of the country pursuing that policy and the world as a whole must carefully consider the specific features of world regions and regional civilizations as well as the national interests and specific features of each country and each nation.

There is no need to demonstrate that the interests of various countries and peoples differ, sometimes quite substantially; this is normal and natural. In this connection, one of the principle of the new thinking must show the way: the search for a balance of interests, a balance that establishes the extent to which one or another country may be able to take a certain action.

An important aspect of this problem is the interpretation of the term *national interests*. Surely the national interests of a country are often interpreted incorrectly. History—including modern history—reveals many cases in which the desire for unlimited hegemony has been presented as being in a country's "national interest." Or a desire to dominate a certain region, or to declare another sovereign state or group of states to be in one's "zone of strategic interest." Such an approach reveals a lack of moderation and is impermissible.

Clearly a particular region's situation might affect the interests of a neighboring country, even a distant country, and force that country to pay close attention to the state of affairs in that region and possibly take measures to defend its own interests. But in no case should it violate the sovereignty of its partners or its neighbors.

Another erroneous interpretation of a country's national interests may be expressed in a desire for isolation, for a kind of economic, political, or spiritual autarchy. In an interdependent world, the genuine interests of any country—as I have said—depend on its using the advantages of international intercourse in the broadest sense.

Essentially any inaccurate approach, any kind of distortion—either exaggeration or underestimation—in the interpretation of one's national interests, ultimately ends in failure in both domestic and foreign policy.

An obvious question, however, is who should act as judge. Who has the right to decide whether a particular country's national interests have been defined correctly? I think the judge in this case must be the country's own people. It is in their sense of responsibility and wisdom that the correct interpretation lies. And even though people may be influenced and misled, eventually they become aware of their true interests.

The Italian scholar and politician Sergio Romano, in his book *The Factory of Wars*, expresses the profound thought that conflicts and wars, as a rule, have erupted when one or more states have mistakenly interpreted their own national interests, including, and this is often primary, the interests of their own national security.

Today such mistaken interpretations are especially dangerous. In an interconnected world, any error, especially one made by a great power, can resonate throughout the world and create crises far more damaging than ever occurred in the past.

CHAPTER 24

The Challenge of Global Problems

A GREAT DEAL has been spoken and written about global problems. There is no need to repeat it. My aim is different: to approach global problems as one of the major challenges facing humanity on the verge of the twenty-first century and to ask, above all, what demands this challenge places on world politics.

First, we should call attention to the fact that global problems have a quality that differs from other challenges humankind faces. Delay or refusal to search for answers to the challenge of global problems could lead to the gradual extinction of humanity.

Prognoses differ regarding the number of years remaining before worsening global problems, especially environmental problems, become catastrophic. Understandably, not all such predictions can be accurate since the mechanisms in the evolution of global problems have not been studied thoroughly, and various factors as yet unknown may exist that will influence our present course. Therefore I will not repeat predictions that have already been made or make new ones. One thing is clear, though: The human race has only decades, not centuries, to resolve its global problems. Historically this time frame is minuscule. But for the practical needs of science and politics it is fairly substantial. In these years much can be thought through and undertaken.

The discussion about resolving, even if only partially, our global problems, which we know are a matter of life and death, has entered a new stage, with both positive and negative characteristics. On the positive side is the increasing awareness of the dangers of continuing along our current path and the growing understanding that measures must be taken regarding relations between human beings and the rest of nature in order to improve the situation. Scientists have recently focused their attention on anthropogenic changes in the earth's climate that are exhausting our natural resources and affecting the ability of humankind to provide itself with basic needs, including food.

Many works have been devoted to the topic of globalization. Two recent ones are worth mentioning: Alvin and Heidi Toffler's *War and Anti-War* and Erwin Laszlo's *The Third Millennium—Challenge and Prognosis*. These two books examine the entire range of problems facing the international community and the relation between those problems and the evolution of population patterns, as well as natural evolution, and the close connection between these processes.

It should be noted that in the business world increasing attention is being paid to global issues. Many large and small companies have been working seriously and sometimes effectively to reduce the consumption of energy and natural resources in production and have taken steps to minimize or eliminate the environmentally harmful consequences of production. Of course these efforts so far have been insufficient. As a rule, they follow the traditional path of merely refining the very technological processes that are essentially incapable of ensuring a radical improvement in the environment. At the same time the operations of these very same companies in the developing countries often proceed entirely along the old lines, engaging in fairly dirty production. Still, it is necessary to take note of a certain shift in business activity regarding this matter.

All this represents something positive, but what about the negative side? The greatest negative aspect is that politics continues to lag significantly behind science. It is true that after the Rio de Janeiro Conference in 1992 several world conferences on global problems were held as well as various meetings of government ministers of both developed and developing countries. But although the subject has not been forgotten, the practical consequences of all these measures so far have not amounted to much.

One gets the impression that economic egoism, the pursuit of profits at all costs, as well as national ambitions (above all, those of the developed countries) have thus far taken precedence over considerations not only of human solidarity but even the interests of one's own future. The world continues to live at the expense of future generations. We are living on borrowed time, with the risk that we will never repay the loan. This failure could ruin our descendants' lives, the lives of coming generations.

The general situation in the world continues to worsen. The proposition cannot be made that the root of this is someone's ill intentions. We cannot imagine that someone is deliberately trying to make the world situation worse and bring us all closer to catastrophe. On the other hand, not everything can be written off by attributing it to sloppiness, carelessness, or irrational action.

The root of the evil, it seems to me, is found in the very paradigm of development, the very concept of progress, and the incentives to progress that developed over many centuries and still persist today. This boils down to the fact that for centuries progress for society has been equated with continual technical advances—the instruments for maintaining the necessary domination of human beings over the forces of nature, the concept of "man as the king of creation." This approach has led, on the one hand, to an unlimited expansion of the demands placed on natural resources—which are largely nonrenewable—and, on the other, to the depletion and poisoning of the biosphere, including disruption of its internal balance and capacity for self-renewal.

Further, we are talking about a concept of progress that constantly encourages consumption on a larger scale, the unlimited expansion of the needs of society. A significant proportion of these needs—and with the passage of time this has become an irrationally large proportion—is artificially created and serves exclusively to extract additional profit. Thus the measure of progress and the driving forces behind growth have been material consumption and unlimited consumerism.

Essentially profit and money have become the only "reliable" incentives for the development of society, but by their very nature these incentives ignore fundamentally important human needs, including education, culture, and spiritual growth, which are the factors of real progress. In *Megamachine*, the French writer Serge Latouche concluded that in a purely market-based economy nothing that could be done will be done unless it is profitable.

Extreme inequality is seen in the distribution of production and consumption; this is not an age-old feature but a comparatively new one in our present stage of development. A handful of developed countries representing about one-fourth of the population of the earth disposes of more than 80 percent of all income, while the remaining three-quarters account for 19 percent. Approximately 45 percent of the world's scientific research is carried out in the industrially developed countries. "Progress" today for the bulk of the world's population can be equated, at best, with stagnation and, at worst, outright regression. I could go on in the same vein, but the preceding discussion is sufficient for us to conclude that the modern concept of progress is deficient and dangerous. A change is needed in the very essence of this concept if we are to find a way out of the existing impasse.

To make such a change we need a radical turnaround in our thinking, one that is global, historically long-lasting, and humanist in the fullest and truest sense of the word. What is needed is a revolution in consciousness that would provide the grounds for and ensure a new approach to the basic way of life and forms of behavior of human beings in today's world.

But the process of changing consciousness is a prolonged and difficult one. And it is made even more difficult by the fact that at the present stage of history humanity is required to make a transition from unthinking wastefulness to rational self-restraint and yet maintain the level of consumption necessary for the harmonious development of human beings. Meanwhile attention must be given to our individual spiritual values and to the spiritual reconstruction of social consciousness. Improvement of social consciousness is the task of a politics based on a sober, sensible, and carefully thought-out approach to the problems I have listed—a politics based on the consideration that all global problems are interconnected.

So then, population growth brings about increasing consumption of energy and natural resources and thus worsens the environmental crisis and threatens the viability of life on earth. Like population growth, the environmental crisis deepens divisions between developing and developed countries, between North and South, and makes it more difficult to overcome the sharp contradictions that arise in this connection. The deepening of this division, in turn, creates new obstacles on the path toward resolving environmental problems.

The task of world politics is to understand the systemic nature and interconnectedness of global problems. As of now this mind-set does not exist. Only at the Rio de Janeiro Conference were global problems examined in their totality, although of course the depth and extent to which this was done varied greatly. The search for an answer to the challenge of global problems must be comprehensive, but cannot exclude special emphasis on particular problems, depending on their urgency and importance.

Today it seems that the environmental crisis is the most urgent and important one. This worsening crisis is perceptibly affecting people's health. The World Health Organization in the 1980s determined that an individual's health depends 20 percent on genetics, 20 percent on environmental conditions, 50 percent on lifestyle, and 10 percent on medicine. (Medicine plays an enormous role in saving the lives of those who are seriously ill, but on the level of maintaining health in general its effect has proved insufficient thus far.) These proportions are changing: The negative effect of environmental factors is increasing and, as a corollary, genetic factors are playing a greater role as a result of genetic changes brought about by environment pollutants. The remaining percentages, in contrast, are decreasing.

Two Russian scientists, Yu. M. Gorsky and V. V. Lavshuk, have estimated that if the environmental crisis in Russia continues to worsen, by the year 2005 we can expect the contribution of environmental factors to people's health to rise to 40 percent and the genetic factors to 30 percent, while lifestyle factors will decrease to 25 percent and medicine to 5 percent. This will represent a serious danger for subsequent generations in Russia. Resolving the environmental crisis presents itself more and more as a matter of saving the human race and its gene pool.

Another problem is the population explosion. When people first started talking seriously about the environmental disaster and the need to reduce the burden we are imposing on nature, little was said about the demographic problem. Today, in the opinion of the most serious researchers, the population explosion could become the decisive factor impelling us toward disaster. Since 1955, the earth's population has doubled and now numbers approximately 6 billion. If present trends continue, by the middle of the next century the population could grow to 12.5 billion, and, according to some estimates, to as much as 20 billion. Some argue, however, that by that time population size will stabilize. But at what point will that occur? The United Nations Fund for Population Activities (UNFPA) has developed a program to keep population from rising beyond 7.8 billion by the year 2050. If the necessary efforts are made, it would then be possible to provide everyone on earth with the necessary food and other resources. This would be difficult to achieve but, as the specialists assert, it would be possible.

In the past the question of population growth caused serious tensions between developed and developing countries. Today, according to the UNFPA, this conflict has largely been overcome. The developing countries agree, in principle, on limiting population growth, as this is a necessary precondition for their normal environmental and social development, The demographic problem, of course, is bound to produce many disputes, including those connected with the views of major religions, as was confirmed at the 1994 Cairo Conference on population problems. But there is no alternative. Each country, keeping in mind its own responsibility for the future, must itself decide what measures to take. As worldwide experience has shown, population growth tends to decline or even stop (and then stabilize) as the standard of living and of culture in everyday life rises and as general and medical education increase.

At the initiative of UNESCO's director general, Frederico Mayor, programs for increasing education and training, including medical training in the developing countries, are already being carried out. Ultimately the economic development of the countries of the so-called South will be of decisive importance. In other words, the enormous gap between South and North must be bridged, not only for the sake of the South but for the world as well. If the situation in the South continues to deteriorate, as it has until now, no success can be expected from efforts aimed at restoring environmental health or preventing the spread of dangerous diseases. Even the world economy will be unable to develop normally unless the problem of the less-developed South is resolved.

Another important issue is that development of the South is not a quantitative problem but a qualitative one. Thus solutions cannot be approached, as is often done, from a purely technical-economic standpoint.

The current problems in the countries of the South are a legacy of the colonial era, when the natural development of these countries was slowed, and also a result of continuing exploitation by the North, although in new forms and with new techniques.

A provocative study, entitled *The Debt of the West*, by economist and sociologist Hafez Sabet, scrupulously examines various aspects of the relations between South and North. Sabet calculates that if all aspects of the debt are taken into account, it is not the South that is in debt to the North (or more exactly to the West) by the amount of $1.3 trillion, but it is the North that is in debt to the South by a figure forty times larger, approximately $50 trillion. This figure is disputed by Western experts. But even if it is exaggerated, that does not change the essence of the matter.

Today we may be at a turning point in historical development. The elimination of colonial empires has given the countries of the South the possibility of returning to the sources of their own centuries-old civilizations. Disillusioned with initial attempts to mechanically copy Western civilization, and later disillusioned by what was called "a socialist orientation," the countries of the South are seeking new paths. They are reviving many traditions, values, and customs that had been lost in the past and at the same time are assimilating the most interesting and appropriate elements of worldwide experience.

Several Asian and Latin American countries with lagging development in the past have moved rapidly ahead in a relatively short time. Other countries are still seeking their roads to progress. In this process we observe inevitable distortions and excesses. But on the whole it is a healthy phenomenon. One cannot help respecting and supporting this process. It is particularly unacceptable to see in the South's new self-assertion a hostile challenge to other countries or to oppose this self-assertion at all costs and involuntarily fall back on dogmas of the colonialist era. Whether existing contradictions will become a threat for the entire world or whether matters will be arranged satisfactorily so that there will be co-development of different civilizations of a kind that will assure a less painful entry by all humanity into the twenty-first century—this will depend on mutual understanding and a serious approach toward the search for mutually acceptable solutions.

Of course many Western countries are aiding various developing countries. The European Union has such aid programs, but the resources being allocated are pitifully small compared to the needs. Moreover, the aid is by no means always used effectively.

The United Nations recommends that 0.7 percent of the gross domestic product in the advanced countries be allocated for aid to developing countries. But in fact only Denmark, Norway, Sweden, and Holland have met this target. France is close behind them, with 0.63 percent. The United States spends only 0.15 percent for these purposes, Japan 0.26 percent, and Germany 0.37 percent. Alongside this aid, however, massive amounts of resources are still being extracted from countries of the South, primarily in the form of repayment of debts.

In the recent past and within the framework of the new thinking, the Soviet government proposed that the problem of development as a whole, particularly the North-South problem, be internationalized, that is, become a subject of constant concern and attention by the international community. At the summit meeting in Rio de Janeiro a statement was made about the need to coordinate efforts in this direction. But thus far only good intentions remain. I should note that it seems unrealistic and against their interests for developing countries to orient themselves toward the creation of a consumer society. This would hardly produce solid results but would only worsen the problems existing in the world, primarily the environmental crisis. It seems to me that the optimal goal is to make a transition to postindustrial conditions emphasizing people's cultural and spiritual needs, as well as their health.

Countries of the South would be substantially assisted by international efforts to end local or regional conflicts and, of course, prevent new conflicts both within countries and between them. After all, internal and external conflicts have been one of the main reasons for the ruination and economic dislocation that afflict countries of the South. Today the arms spending of these countries exceeds the amount they receive each year in the form of aid. These conflicts not only devour resources but retard development and contribute to the persistence of poverty and backwardness.

The challenge of global problems is a new phenomenon in human history. For the first time in millennia it is possible that the human race will perish because of progress. Preventing such an outcome depends on people themselves. It is impossible not to agree with Erwin Laszlo, a founder of the Club of Rome and head of the Budapest Club, when he states: "*Homo sapiens* (literally, the intelligent human being) has lived to see the time when his or her existence increasingly depends on his or her intelligence."

CHAPTER 25

The Challenge of Power Politics

"A WORLD WITHOUT armaments, a world without wars"—this was the attractive slogan Nikita Khrushchev advanced at one time. It expresses the aspirations of the foremost thinkers in history. But so far it has never been realized. If it were, of course, the entire international community would benefit in every way.

Perestroika, taking into account the new realities, returned to this exceptionally important subject. The new thinking approached it from two angles. It emphasized, on the one hand, the inadmissibility of a nuclear war and its deadly consequences as well as the need to renounce military methods in general as a means of resolving conflicts. On the other hand, it acknowledged that rational goals could not be achieved by the use of force but only by renouncing power politics. In a word, a transition had to be made to a nuclear-free world and a world without violence, as the leaders of the Soviet Union and India stated in the celebrated New Delhi declaration of November 1986.

We know that other viewpoints exist, up to and including outright justification of war as an inevitable evil rooted in the very depths of human nature—an evil that the human race can never eliminate.

This assumption may seem to be confirmed by history. The facts are well known, testifying that over thousands of years the earth has known only a few that were completely free of war. And why even speak of thousands of years? The period from 1945 to 1991 alone saw approximately 150 different wars and armed conflicts (depending on how these calculations are made). Approximately 7.2 million soldiers died in these conflicts. That ignores civilian casualties, the wounded and the crippled. Of the approximately twenty-four hundred weeks after 1945, when World War II ended, only three weeks have been completely free of war.

The parade of wars has not ended to this very day. Does that mean, though, that things will always be this way? It is not a simple question; the tradition of power politics and of solving problems by armed force is deeply rooted in the consciousness of individuals and entire nations. It is impossible to uproot these traditions all at once.

Nevertheless, there is hope based on real facts, the same facts that underlie the new thinking. They are as follows:

- There is an ever wider recognition of the exceptionally destructive nature of modern warfare (especially when nuclear weapons or other weapons of mass destruction are used), and that modern weapons can cause irreparable damage not only to the defeated side but to the victorious side as well.

- There is the fact that the ideological-political and military-political division of the world into opposing blocs has been overcome. It is this division that has continually fed the danger of nuclear holocaust.

- Although the rivalry between the great powers was a major factor in the outbreak of two world wars, today economic differences between countries are being resolved by political as well as economic means. The rivalry continues but remains on the level of technology, productivity, and the capacity to be competitive on the world market.

- With the elimination of colonial empires, the struggle between the colonizers and the colonies has been removed as a source of military conflicts. Disputes between the colonizers and the former colonies continue and are sometimes quite sharp (as we have discussed). Here, too, the former colonial masters tend to use economic and political methods of compulsion rather than arms.

- The last several decades have seen gradually accumulating experience in peacefully resolving conflicts. Efforts in this area have proceeded with difficulty, but there is increasing understanding of the need to extend this experience and persistently use it.

These factors are the basis for hope that traditional power politics can be uprooted. Countervailing trends are also apparent, however. One trend is the revival of aggressive nationalism, the sharpening of national and ethnic conflicts, as discussed above. Although they usually begin within the borders of a particular country (thus far at any rate), they potentially can spread across borders and become conflicts between nations. It is not impossible that large-scale social conflicts could arise, especially in developing countries (for example, Mexico). John Kenneth Galbraith does not exclude the possibility of such conflicts breaking out in the developed countries as well. What is involved here are potential conflicts between marginalized elements in society—the "underclass," as Galbraith calls them—and those who are employed or well-to-do. Such conflicts can begin within national borders but cause international complications.

In a number of cases, including in Europe, certain territorial or national claims have been made by one country against another. The greater number of such conflicts have emerged in the developing world. Let us recall, as one example, the border war between Peru and Ecuador.

A number of political scientists and politicians suggest that the intensifying contradiction between the wealthy countries of the North and the poor countries of the South can lead to military conflicts. In this connection, they point to the danger of the spread of nuclear weapons slipping out of control and to the number of countries on the verge of gaining nuclear capability or already making nuclear weapons. Recent events in India and Pakistan illustrate this point.

Still another factor that may tend to provoke or increase the danger of new wars is the unceasing arms race in the South. Many poor countries, in contrast to the developed countries, have increased military spending in recent years, instead of reducing it. Iran, for example, according to SIPRI statistics, increased its spending for military purposes between 1992 and 1995 by 42.5 percent—Pakistan by 19.5 percent and Saudi Arabia by 12.92 percent. These military buildups are encouraged by the North's efforts to expand arms sales, which are motivated, in turn, by commercial interests and sometimes by political considerations as well.

In the most advanced countries, beginning with the United States, efforts are under way to develop new kinds of weapons, including electronic, psychotropic, and others, based on principles that differ fundamentally from "classic" models. "There remain fewer and fewer chances for an era of disarmament to set in after the Cold War," the German magazine *Stern* wrote recently. "For the weapons manufacturers, the years of stagnation are coming to an end, when military budgets and arms exports were shrinking."

Thus humanity is approaching the beginning of the twenty-first century under conditions in which wars still occur, the sources of wars persist, and the arms race continues, although it has cooled somewhat since the termination of the East-West conflict. At the same time the chances of preventing wars are increasing.

In short, the challenges of power politics and potential warfare persist—and so does the life-and-death importance of these challenges.

Under these conditions, the question of universal security is becoming increasingly important, along with ways and means of assuring it. The approaches to this question worked out by the new thinking retain their significance. They also require further development, taking into account changes in the situation that have occurred and are emerging. Given the current interdependence between nations, security can only be thought of as security in common. Economic, ecological, and social aspects have become extremely important organic components of the general conception of security. Guaranteeing security is closely linked today with the maintenance of stability both within nations and within regions.

Of course what we have said here does not exhaust the complex subject of security and the particular features this problem has acquired in our time. The need for strengthening universal security and maintaining peace makes it highly desirable and important that a whole range of measures be carried out.

First, the threat of nuclear military conflict must be completely eliminated. The removal of this danger would strike a substantial blow against power politics in general and against the widespread power politics mentality. The measures necessary to achieve this goal in general are well known. But it is worth restating the main measures and in some cases adding to them on the basis of recent experience. What is primarily involved, it seems, are the following measures:

- It is necessary to continue the actual reduction of the nuclear capability of the United States and Russia, both countries having begun this process. But in the near future the other nuclear powers—China, Britain, and France—should be urged to join in this process; a special agreement should be concluded among the five nuclear powers on procedures for reducing and eliminating nuclear weapons.

- The complete cessation of nuclear testing, which began in 1996, should be accompanied by measures to make more rigorous the system preventing proliferation of nuclear weapons, up to and including tough sanctions carried out through the United Nations against violators.

- It is important to create, under UN supervision and with participation by the International Atomic Energy Agency, an effective worldwide system on the earth's surface, in the atmosphere, and in outer space for monitoring preparations for the military use of nuclear power.

Certain agreements that have already been reached must be implemented under strict international supervision. These are agreements on the prohibition and destruction of chemical and bacteriological (biological) weapons. The possibility exists that these agreements may be violated—that is, some countries may produce such weapons of mass destruction and even attempt to use them. The problem of how to implement strict monitoring and sanctions in cases of violation is still a significant one.

Conventional weapons represent a special problem. The modern forms of these weapons have achieved such qualities that they are comparable to weapons of mass destruction (although on a territorial scale they do not inflict comparable damage). There are other kinds of weapons being produced that have been termed *nonlethal* in American military terminology. Some of them, for example, jamming or putting out of commission the opponent's means of communication and information, the development of substances taking the form of a lather or foam that interferes with the movement of enemy military equipment, and electronic and electromagnetic devices that interrupt enemy communications or power supplies, can truly be called nonlethal. Other so-called nonlethal weapons do significant damage to human health or incapacitate people altogether. All this requires, it seems, new approaches to the problem of conventional weapons. It would probably be appropriate to begin a worldwide dialogue on setting qualitative limits for further improvement or refinement of conventional weapons, however difficult this might be to achieve.

In Europe a treaty is in effect for reducing the number of troops and weapons. Experience regarding this treaty, despite all the difficulties that have arisen, is quite positive. If it were extended to other regions or continents, such a step could only be welcomed.

Perhaps it would be expedient in cases where neighboring states were agreeable to try to establish zones—even of limited extent at first—in which the number of weapons permitted would be lowered or reduced to a minimum. Examples of countries that have taken this road include New Zealand and Costa Rica. They get along quite well without being armed to the teeth and maintain only a minimum number of instruments of destruction. Their example is an object lesson and a model for others to follow.

Arms exports, especially to the developing countries, constitute a serious problem. It is understood that such exports bring large profits to the arms manufacturers as well as to the governments of the exporting countries. It is hard to relinquish large profits. But the export of arms consistently feeds the danger of new conflicts and nourishes the activity of extremists of all kinds, including international terrorists, not to mention the effect this has on the economic development of countries spending large sums to purchase these arms.

In the long term it would be important in general to stop arms exports or at least to reduce them to a certain level established by international agreement. As for arms exports to regions where armed conflicts are under way, they should be banned outright. Illegal arms exports should be made the equivalent of international terrorism and drug trafficking. I would support in every way the initiative taken by the former president of Costa Rica, Oscar Arias, regarding the establishment of a system to control the arms trade.

Considering recent political trends and the world situation, it would be entirely possible to coordinate the intelligence services of permanent members of the UN Security Council (and over the long term possibly include other democratic governments) to combat terrorism, drug trafficking, and the illegal arms trade. Arms manufacturers understandably would not agree to this proposal. The international community, it would seem, has the necessary level of maturity to take up the long-term task of conversion from military to civilian production, the reorganization of a substantial part of military industry for civilian production (and later the overwhelming majority of military plants). In the twenty-first century the human race should not live armed to the teeth. It should prepare to live peacefully, to use the money that formerly went to military spending in order to respond to such challenges of our times as the environmental, energy, and food crises.

From a dispassionate study of the experience of recent times in the Mideast, Africa, Southeast Asia, the former Yugoslavia, and the Caucasus region, we should conclude that special agencies can be established under the UN and regional organizations for security and cooperation to prevent or stop regional conflicts through diplomacy but also, if necessary, by economic and military means.

An important task is to establish mutual understanding and cooperation in regions of the world that could be called border regions between civilizations—for example, the Balkans, the Mediterranean, and the Mideast. It is especially in these areas that conflicts have arisen in the past and present. It is not excluded that such conflicts will continue to arise in these areas over the long term. Special efforts by the European and international communities are required in these areas, along with an especially attentive attitude and effective preventive diplomacy. In the long term, what is needed is the energetic development of peaceful interaction of all kinds among the peoples and countries in these border regions between civilizations.

These are absolutely necessary steps in my opinion, and if they are taken, the accent can be shifted from forceful methods of conducting policy to peaceable and civilized methods. Thus far, unfortunately, no desire to move in this direction is noticeable. That is why today we observe a kind of backward movement, a regression into an atmosphere more typical of the past.

Concerned about this, the International Foundation for Socioeconomic and Political Science Studies in Moscow, the Rajiv Gandhi Foundation in New Delhi, and the Gorbachev Foundation in the United States (San Francisco) have jointly submitted to the UN a program of global security. The program has four parts: nuclear disarmament, reduction of conventional weapons under reliable supervision, strengthening regional security structures, and the prevention and resolution of conflicts (with the participation of special groups from the general public, a commission of the General Assembly, and a proposed body of political observers and intermediaries, as well as the participation of an institution for the study and prevention of conflicts).

A topic I cannot avoid touching on is security in Europe. It hardly needs to be demonstrated how important peace on this continent is for global security—history itself is ample evidence of this. But the present situation in Europe cannot be considered favorable. Not too long ago Europe faced a dramatic choice: to continue along the fatal path of confrontation or to radically change course and move toward new, good neighborly relations among the countries of Europe. This choice was made collectively, and a historic turning point was reached. A summit conference in Paris in November 1990, it seemed, had laid the basis for new relationships and a new European policy and formulated its principles.

Today Europe once again faces a choice: to continue to pursue the course outlined in Paris or for each country to withdraw to its own regional neighborhood and return to some extent to the fragmentation characteristic of the past. In other words, will there be a greater Europe that is truly united, whose interests are becoming increasingly integrated, or will it be a sum total of smaller Europes, weakly connected with and even hostile to one another?

It is true that in recent years much has changed in Europe, especially since the end of the East-West confrontation. Europe's political geography has undergone a significant evolution, as has the situation in various other regions. But in our view, these changes do not in any way cancel the principles defined in Paris.

But these principles are not really working. Or if they are, it is only to a slight degree, since we still see military conflicts within Europe (in the former Yugoslavia and in the Caucasus region). The danger of a new division of the continent has arisen with NATO's expansion to the East, which will inevitably encourage military preparations in a number of countries on the continent.

The Paris principles require continent-wide cooperation, along with improvement of existing mechanisms and the creation of new ones for policies applying to Europe as a whole.

There is already a continent-wide organization in Europe—the OSCE (Organization for Security and Cooperation in Europe), which continues to perform the functions for which it was founded in 1975. But it has not yet fully adapted to Europe's needs or to the new situation in which it finds itself. Many useful passages are found in the documents adopted by this organization, but some are ignored and others simply cannot be implemented as the organization does not have the necessary institutional means.

A further institutionalization of the OSCE is obviously needed, particularly the establishment of a Security Council. I have argued for this idea for many years. The council would be concerned with preventing conflicts and extinguishing them when they break out. How to establish such a council and what functions to assign it is a matter for all the member states of the organization to decide. But such an agency must exist. And it must exist as a Europe-wide agency closely linked with the UN Security Council.

As long as no such body exists, NATO will keep trying to assume its functions. But NATO is incapable of performing those functions in view of the aims and purposes for which it was created. It is true, as I have said, that certain changes have taken place in NATO. A council for cooperation in which most European countries participate has been established. A document concerning mutual relations, cooperation, and security has been signed between

Russia and NATO. The Berlin session of the NATO Council devoted special attention to enhancing the role of all the countries of Europe within the framework of NATO's structure (although no noticeable results are apparent along these lines). NATO's functions are being politicized, but this is happening very slowly and the process of NATO's transformation is far from complete. If NATO were transformed in accordance with the new conditions, it could perform certain useful functions in Europe without conflicting with the OSCE or genuine Europe-wide cooperation in one form or another.

Unfortunately, events in spring 1999 showed that NATO, for the time being, is following quite a different course. The war it unleashed against Yugoslavia in March 1999 means, first of all, that this alliance, which was established as a *defensive organization* for the protection of its members, according to the treaty signed in Washington in 1949, has gone over to offensive operations beyond the bounds set by that founding treaty.

Second, this war provides evidence that the United States, which plays a commanding role in NATO, is willing not only to disregard the norms of international law but also to impose on the world its own agenda in international relations and, in fact, to be guided in world relations solely by its own "national interests," taking the United Nations into account only if UN decisions and actions serve U.S. interests.

Third, NATO policy, as in the Cold War years, is placing primary emphasis on supremacy in military power, as well as the threat of employing that power and the actual use of superior military force.

In April 1999 NATO adopted a new strategic conception. It speaks, to be sure, about the role of the UN, along with other international organizations. But at the same time declarations were made at the highest level that NATO was prepared to act wherever it wished and however it wished, if it considered that necessary, without any UN resolutions.

NATO's new strategic conception, approved at the NATO summit meeting in Washington, as well as NATO's actual conduct in the Balkan crisis, showed that the decisive role in determining the destinies of the European continent would be assigned to NATO, rather than to the OSCE.

The war against Yugoslavia—the first war in Europe since World War II—sets a significant precedent indicating the direction of the new American strategy. The war began with a great deal of fanfare about preventing a humanitarian catastrophe in Kosovo. There is no question that the policies and actions of President Milosevic toward the Albanian minority in

Yugoslavia deserve condemnation and a response on the part of the international community.

But this should be done only with the knowledge and consent of the United Nations and under UN auspices. In violation of this generally recognized principle of international law, NATO engaged in a massive armed assault on a sovereign country. The heavily concentrated bombing of Serbia created, on top of the Kosovo catastrophe, a humanitarian, ecological, and social catastrophe throughout Yugoslavia, a European country of long standing. Such neighboring countries as Albania and Macedonia, and perhaps others, are being drawn into the orbit of this tragedy. The situation in the region as a whole is explosive.

It will hardly be possible to restore Europe and the world to the status quo that existed before March 23, 1999. The actions of the United States and NATO prompt everyone—and Europeans, first of all—to reflect deeply on American policy on the eve of the new century. It has become evident that Washington has not been able to elaborate a strategy that is adequate to the challenges of our time or to the position of the United States itself in a world that has been renewed.

The viability and future of the North Atlantic alliance itself have been called into question. Without NATO the United States could hardly carry out its highly dangerous and destructive new course, either in the world arena or in Europe alone. NATO consists above all of the European countries—with their more profoundly democratic and humanistic culture. This culture, together with a very rich experience of many centuries of dramatic and sometimes bloody history, especially in the twentieth century, is incompatible with policies involving the crass and unceremonious use of force. The grumbling, the stir of dissent against the actions of the United States, which can be heard in European circles of the most varied kind, as well as in other countries of the Americas, is a symptom that the White House would do well to think about seriously.

The war in Yugoslavia will inevitably force Europeans to return to the idea of having a Europe-wide strategy of their own for the twenty-first century. The need for this has long since come of age. It was on this basis that the *Charter of Paris for a New Europe* came into existence in 1990. Some dismissed this document with light-minded scorn, but no one has proposed any ideas or principles better than the ones embodied in the Paris charter. The present Yugoslav tragedy is partly a result of the fact that the charter was not adopted as the basis for actual policy by the governments that endorsed it.

Renewed consideration is being given to this matter. Let me cite as an example the remarks of former Chancellor Helmut Schmidt of Germany: "Alliance between Europe and North America remains desirable as never before. But Europe should not become a strategic satellite of Washington. . . . NATO cannot guarantee peace on the entire planet, let alone resolve the enormous problems of a nonmilitary character that humanity will encounter in the twenty-first century."

The "Green Cross International" Statement

[Translator's note: After the Milosevic government agreed to withdraw its forces from Kosovo and permit an international force, primarily NATO troops, but now under UN authorization, to take control of the province, Mikhail Gorbachev issued the following statement dated June 18, 1999.]

Now that the air strikes against Yugoslavia have stopped, the world community will have to assess the damage and draw lessons from the events of these past months. We should not allow this misguided and unwarranted action to be followed by the wrong conclusions. Faced with the plight of the Kosovars, the destruction of much of the essential infrastructure in the rest of Yugoslavia, and the tremendous damage to international relations, triumphant statements sound hollow. What is really needed now is responsible analysis.

As president of Green Cross International, a nongovernmental environmental organization that was among the first to sound the alarm about the environmental consequences of NATO's military action, I feel duty bound to continue the discussion. A region-wide environmental catastrophe may have been avoided, though only time and an unbiased assessment will tell. Some might now ask: "Was the threat exaggerated? Could nature be much more resilient to the impact of war than we thought?" Such complacency is dangerous.

Let us recall the effects of the hostilities that followed Saddam Hussein's aggression against Kuwait. Data cited at an international conference on the environmental consequences of war held in Washington in June 1998 indicate that these consequences are long-term. Green Cross experts estimate that 40 percent of Kuwait's strategic water resources have been irreversibly polluted with oil. The reports of health problems among US and British soldiers who fought in that war—problems that now also affect their children—are alarming. The environmental and medical consequences of the war in Iraq itself are, for reasons that are well known, not widely covered by the media or studied by scientists.

Military action against Yugoslavia included use of weapons containing depleted uranium (DU). Such weapons burn at high temperatures, producing poisonous clouds of uranium oxide that dissolve in the pulmonary and bronchial fluids. Anyone within the radius of 300 meters from the epicenter of the explosion inhales large amounts of such particles. Although radiation levels produced by the external source are quite low, the internal radiation source damages various types of cells in the human body, destroys chromosomes, and affects the reproductive system.

We are told that depleted uranium components are harmless and that DU weapons are therefore a legitimate means of warfare. Many military and political leaders believed—and some seem to believe even now—that nuclear weapons too are quite "conventional," albeit a more powerful kind of weaponry.

I am calling for a comprehensive analysis of the environmental situation in Yugoslavia and other countries in the region and in the Danube basin. This should be a priority. But we must do more than that. That military conflicts in our time can cause both a human and an environmental catastrophe makes the task of preventing them even more important. Prevention must be foremost in our thinking and our actions. But if hostilities break out despite all our efforts, they must be constrained by certain legal limits. Such constraints have been laid down by the Geneva conventions and their protocols. They should be supplemented by provisions to limit the environmental damage caused by warfare.

Specifically, I believe that strikes against certain industries and infrastructure, such as nuclear power stations and some chemical and petrochemical plants, must be prohibited. We should prohibit weapons whose use may have particularly dangerous, long-term environmental and medical consequences. In my view, weapons containing depleted uranium should be among the first to be banned.

The time has come to convene a second conference on the environmental consequences of war in order to discuss issues of this kind. The conference should also address the need for an emergency fund to finance measures to deal with the aftermath of environmental catastrophes. Recent events underscore the urgency of this proposal.

Environmentalists, political leaders, and public opinion should now demonstrate that we can learn the right lessons from the tragedies of the twentieth century. The human drama and the drama of nature should be of equal concern to us. They should sound a call to responsible action.

To summarize briefly, then, peace and security in Europe require new efforts. The European political structure has not yet undertaken such efforts, or it has done so to an insufficient degree. The following must be kept in mind, however:

- The peaceful future of Europe can only be a joint future, or peace will not exist at all.

- A joint future and continent-wide security require, above all, profound and widely ramified cooperation on a Europe-wide basis in all the main spheres of life.

- A reliable basis for such cooperation exists in the common roots of European culture and a common history, as well as an undeniable common interest in peace and stability.

CHAPTER 26

The Challenge of Democracy

IN HIS BOOK *1984*, George Orwell predicted that the 1980s would be marked by the dehumanization of society and the implantation of authoritarian or totalitarian tendencies throughout the world. Orwell's "anti-utopia" was a powerful portrayal of an inhuman, oppressive system. But he was mistaken. It was exactly the 1980s that revealed a powerful tendency toward democratization in many countries and in the international community. The zone dominated by totalitarian regimes was substantially reduced. A decisive role in this trend was played both by perestroika in the Soviet Union and by the processes of change in Central and Eastern Europe. All these essentially revolutionary changes had a stimulating effect on democratic values in general, turning them into an effective factor for promoting mutual understanding among most countries and peoples. This was true almost everywhere, from Latin America to South Africa. Unfortunately, thus far we cannot say that overcoming totalitarianism in the Soviet Union has resulted in the genuine democratization of either Russian society or the other former republics of the Soviet Union. The freedom of choice provided by perestroika has by no means resulted in the choice of genuine freedom.

The regime in Russia today can be called democratic only in part. Outward forms and institutions characteristic of democracy do exist, but their content remains authoritarian in many respects. Moreover, in Russia and other countries of the former Soviet Union forces continue to exist that long for a return to the essentially totalitarian past (although a complete return to that past is simply not possible). All in all, it is highly significant for Europe and the world that Russia should take the road of deepening and expanding the basis for genuine democracy. Without exaggeration, the future development of both the European community and the world largely depends on this effort.

At the same time, a political crisis has arisen in most Western countries that have had democratic regimes for decades, if not centuries. The problem is that the traditional political systems that took shape in the West over the past few centuries (primarily during the nineteenth century)—based on parliamentary democracy and numerous political parties—are facing a crisis. The democratic institutions in these countries always were limited (especially in the first stages of their development) and have begun to wither noticeably under the new conditions. Is this a paradox? Not at all. In fact the contrary is true! This crisis, too, has essentially become an illustration and manifestation of the general worldwide tendency toward democratization.

Civil society in the Western countries has become stronger. Practically universal literacy, broader professionalism at all levels, an increased percentage of the population involved in intellectual labor both in production and services—all this has produced a natural desire among people for a fuller realization of their rights, for a more active part in resolving social problems, for self-rule and self-management.

Western society today increasingly rejects bureaucratic centralism in political systems, along with corruption and excessive formalism. Political parties proclaiming that they represent this or that stratum of society have in fact become, to a considerable extent, the unwitting tools of an elite; thus they have ceased to express the interests of their constituents and are losing ground. Existing electoral systems by no means guarantee genuine representation for the majority in government bodies. As a result of growing abstention from voting and fragmentation of the vote, many parties are unable to get a sufficient percentage of the vote to gain a seat in parliament; thus the current parliamentary forms of government have in fact come to represent only a minority of the population. This is also true for the top leaders—the presidents, for example.

One of the most striking examples of the antidemocratic nature of these existing political systems is that government bodies pay very little attention to social problems, even in what seem to be the most democratic countries. These problems primarily involve marginalized people, such as the elderly, the unemployed, the homeless, and the poor in general. Yet there is a growing population of these "superfluous" people and, with few exceptions, they are increasingly viewed as pariahs whom society can ignore.

Correspondingly, an ever widening discussion is taking place in many countries as well about the role of government in meeting social needs. So-called classical liberalism, which demands that government be "freed" from social spending, in fact represents nothing but a refusal to be concerned with the have-nots in society. Evidently this kind of approach reflects a concept of democracy that has outlived its historical usefulness. But this concept is stubbornly promoted and in many cases applied. Russia is no exception to this view of the government's role in social problems.

Waves of social discontent, however, have forced governments—even those inclined to promote "absolute liberalism"—to concern themselves with social problems and, accordingly, make corrections in their domestic policies.

Added to all this is the incapacity of present political systems to find an optimal solution to the problem of nationalities and national minorities. In this sphere, antidemocratic principles and practices are increasingly evident in the present structure and functioning of political institutions.

The alienation of citizens from government power—which is the quintessence of the present crisis of democracy—is a dangerous trend. It strengthens antidemocratic forces and opens the way for authoritarian trends.

The twentieth century has provided irrefutable evidence of the dangers of authoritarian and especially dictatorial systems of government. The seeming efficiency of such governments and their high level of organization ultimately leads society into a blind alley, producing chaos and confronting people with insoluble problems. It is not accidental that the end of our present century has been marked by powerful antiauthoritarian, antidictatorial movements and by the downfall of many regimes of that nature. Authoritarian trends still exist, however, and play a role in quite a few countries.

All this generally aggravates the problems involved in implementing democracy, making it one of the most important challenges for the coming decades.

This challenge is not just a domestic political challenge. The nature and direction of domestic policy also determines the nature and direction of foreign policy—this truth has long been known. Democratic political systems make a government more openly visible to the outside world and thus create preconditions for mutual trust and understanding with other equally democratic societies. On the other hand—and this has been shown by numerous examples—an authoritarian or totalitarian system results in closed, secretive behavior relative to the outside world. For such regimes, confrontation turns out to be the most comfortable foreign policy, allowing the regime to tighten the reins on its own population and use any form of coercion it desires. An invariable attribute of the foreign policy of any totalitarian system is to support analogous regimes in other countries.

We in the Soviet Union knew this very well from our own experience. The so-called Brezhnev doctrine, whose most glaring expression was the invasion of Czechoslovakia in 1968, had domestic political as well as foreign policy aims. Among the motives for suppression of the Prague Spring was the desire to strengthen a domestic policy line aimed at preserving the existing authoritarian system in the USSR. It is no accident that as a consequence of that action, repression was intensified against loyal critics of the existing defects and shortcomings of the Soviet Union's policies.

To promote democracy throughout the world it is necessary to overcome the present crisis of democracy in the Western countries as well as work for true democratization of life in Russia and the other former Soviet countries. Political power must spread down to the people by means of decentralization of power and enhancement of the role of local self-government. Here, of course, it is important not to cross over the boundary beyond which decentralization becomes disintegration. And naturally in each country this process will have its own variations corresponding to the particular features of that society.

The democratization of international relations implies first of all recognition of and unconditional respect for the rights and interests of all countries and peoples, for genuine equality among them, ruling out any form of *diktat* in the day-to-day practice of international politics.

At the same time all countries must respect existing international organizations, starting with the UN, and must strictly fulfill all obligations to these institutions on an equal basis as well as to the world community as a whole. The role of international organizations must be recognized as a direct expression of the equality of all entities active in international relations.

In this connection, it must be noted that the United States' declared desire to establish democratic governments throughout the world (which by itself can only be welcomed) is by no means compatible with its attempts to impose on other governments its own forms of democracy. Even worse is the United States' declared intention to assert American leadership over the whole world. Support for democracy is necessary, yes, but only in genuine democratic forms. Otherwise the very desire to promote the spread of democracy is called into question.

Similarly, Washington's disregard for the UN and its decisions, which has been demonstrated many times, is out of keeping with its proclaimed adherence to democracy. The same is true of U.S. attempts to bypass the UN in resolving problems that come directly under UN jurisdiction, and of course Washington's failure to meet its financial obligations to the UN. The United States is not alone as far as the violation of democratic principles in world affairs is concerned. Unfortunately the world in general is still a long way from genuine equality among governments, and some countries do not in practice abide by the principle of nonintervention, a principle that also forbids covert interference in the internal affairs of other countries. Examples of such violations can be found on every continent.

It is understandable that the larger, more powerful states can make a larger contribution to the solving of international problems. But this can only be done if the rights of all nations are recognized and respected. The major powers do not essentially have greater rights than other countries. They have a greater responsibility to the world in general. And that includes the establishment of genuinely democratic principles in international relations.

The major powers have a duty to make sure that small and medium-sized countries, no matter where they are located, should have the real possibility of making their contribution to the world community.

During the years of Cold War confrontation the major powers used small and medium-sized countries as pieces on the chessboard of world politics. After the Cold War ended the situation ought to have changed. Although some manifestations of change are observable, on the whole the situation has remained the same.

Perhaps, considering both the increased need for democratization of world relations and the complications arising on the road toward such democratization, it may be desirable to develop a special code of rights and responsibilities for governments within the framework of the world community as a whole. This might prove to be a very difficult task. Not all governments (including those that declare democracy to be their fundamental principle) are ready or willing to acknowledge in an international document certain rules of behavior that all must observe. Such rules could prove to be awkward and restrictive—especially for those who are used to operating unilaterally, doing as they please. It is difficult to state with assurance that these rules would be observed even were they signed and ratified (but that would be a necessary condition for their effectiveness). Nonetheless, such rules could have a certain restraining effect on potential violators of the democratic norms of the world community.

Another important aspect of the democratization of international relations to which all governments must adhere without deviation is respect for human rights in their domestic policies; they must also support respect for such rights by other members of the world community. Governments must consider both the principle of respect for human rights (UN documents contain sufficiently clear substantiation of those rights) and the specific ways in which governments or nations perceive this principle.

The problem is that although international treaties on human rights have been signed and ratified by most governments in the world, evident nuances emerge in the way they are interpreted or implemented. A fairly large number of cases are known in which certain governments have not recognized obvious violations of human rights as such. Usually national traditions are cited in these cases.

An even greater lack of agreement arises when other countries demand that a country charged with violating UN-specified human rights take measures to correct the situation. Such demands are often viewed as violations of the sovereignty of the state involved.

Of course a major problem is the absence of internationally recognized legal definitions of the limits of international jurisdiction and the right of the world community to insist on observance of the principle of inviolable human rights. But that is not the only problem.

The concept of human rights—especially the possibility of outside intervention to ensure that these rights are observed—is a relatively new phenomenon. It is the result of a gradual development in political culture that included the awareness of these rights, which arose primarily in Europe and North America. In Europe, for example, the universality of human rights is recognized by all governments. This implies acceptance of international intervention in the name of preserving human rights. However, a special tribunal concerned with these problems exists only within the framework of the European Union and the Council of Europe, which have special conventions ratified by all the members.

A number of other governments that have recognized the universality of human rights do not by any means adhere to the appropriate rules in all cases. We do not have to go far to find examples. A commission on the observance of human rights in Russia every year records numerous, flagrant violations of those rights, ranging from restrictions on journalists to torture by agencies within the Ministry of Internal Affairs. But this has not put an end to such violations.

Nations that only recently obtained independence are suspicious about international demands for respect for human rights. For them sovereignty is of such overriding importance that they are ready to interpret any action by foreign powers as a violation of sovereignty even when that is not intended. Their attitude is fully understandable, however. The history of these countries has seen so many forms of overt and covert intervention in their internal affairs (sometimes under seemingly plausible pretexts) that today they have the right to question and be hesitant.

Countries where authoritarian regimes exist, or where holdovers from an authoritarian past persist, also are quite often reluctant to implement human rights on their territory. The very history of the Soviet Union is a reminder. For many long years the Soviet Union considered human rights as some sort of false issue that had been manufactured artificially (even the phrase *human rights* was published in our country only in quotation marks preceded by the word *so-called*). For a totalitarian system, the very posing of the question of human rights is a challenge, a vicious assault on the very essence of its policies. And only perestroika brought this to an end. I believe, that the democratization of international relations will not fully develop unless some way is found to guarantee human rights on a global scale.

It is possible that ultimately the UN, along with regional organizations for security and cooperation, will create special structures empowered not only to monitor the observance of human rights but also to impose sanctions and use other enforcement measures, especially in cases of flagrant violation of human rights. This would include violations of the rights of national minorities or other groups subjected to violence, discrimination, or denial of legal rights.

In any case, the democratization of international relations has become a pressing need. It is a preventive measure to ensure that world peace is not violated and that no government engages in arbitrary actions in the world arena; it would also be important for the democratization of life in all the countries of the world. Finally, without democratization of international relations we cannot arrive at a new, genuinely peaceful world order.

CHAPTER 27

The Challenge of Universal Human Values

THE HISTORY OF humanity is to a large extent the history of its values. These have served as a source for the moral precepts that in the final analysis govern the actions of any given human community. At every major historical turning point, values have changed—they have been enriched or impoverished. But they have always had a common basis, and that is what makes human beings human.

Values have been embodied in world religions. They have inspired both individuals and large groups, and have nourished various ideologies and mass movements. These ideologies and movements have varied quite widely in outlook and in the results they achieved. Many were defeated and disappeared from history's stage without accomplishing much. But the basic values they upheld survived them. These values retained their significance and will do so in the future, because without values human beings are doomed to moral "brutalization" (*odichanie*). "The denial or destruction of values (religious, spiritual, moral, civil, political)," as the great Florentine humanist Georgio La Pira has written, "inevitably results in injustice, persecution, and oppression."

Today many philosophers and representatives of various religions speak about the crisis of values. Works by outstanding writers are devoted to this subject. Even politicians frequently refer to it. But the situation remains the same. Ancient, universal moral principles, the only basis on which human life can develop, have in many ways been consigned to oblivion or hypocritically used to conceal actions that conflict with those values. Many so-called new values are more like justifications for egoism and self-serving behavior, for pride and ambition, for money-grubbing and unrestrained consumption; they do not seem to be rational principles corresponding to the essence of human nature.

The dilemma formulated by wise men of old—to be or to have?—has taken on new and threatening meaning today. That is because human life is increasingly subordinated to this very desire to have. Consumerism and the desire for things, originating from the negative aspects of the market economy, have pushed into the background any desire for spiritual enrichment or cultural progress, the desire for improving or perfecting human thinking and consciousness. The "freedom to have" is regarded as the highest achievement of history, as its grand finale. Yet this is nothing more than the renunciation of all higher aspirations for a better, a genuinely humane future.

If society enters the future with these current false and distorted values, then it will have no future. It would mean the degeneration of *Homo sapiens*, God's highest creation.

A return to age-old, spiritual, moral, life-affirming values, to a humanist and genuinely optimistic worldview is one of the decisive tasks of our era. It is a universal human task. A global one. Without the great store of values that have been accumulated over millennia, people will be unable to cope with the dangers threatening them, will be unable to solve problems that have become such serious challenges for them.

As a result of the globalization of society and the increased integration of the world in our time, the entire human race has acquired common global interests, beginning with survival itself. Under these conditions, primordial human values have taken on a special meaning that can be decisive for our entire existence. At the same time, those primordial values have become more inclusive, so to speak. Because the human race has acquired the ability to destroy itself through nuclear war or an ecological catastrophe, the value of life has acquired a certain tragic quality. For the first time in history we face the challenge of defending human existence itself, not just saving the lives of individuals or nations.

The protection of the natural environment has become a high priority for the human community. The task of preventing an ecological catastrophe is undeniably a universal one. This means that moral values must find material expression in world politics. In the final analysis, a system for collective management of worldwide processes must be created, an effective form of collaboration based on equality among nations and peoples. We must know how to combine and jointly subordinate national interests and actions for the sake of worldwide interests and actions. From this value-based viewpoint, we must once again talk about the need for a new politics capable of leading the human race out of its present impasse.

Unfortunately, up to the present time universal human values have too often seemed to exist in isolation, while politics pursued its own course far removed from those values.

In 1995 the world celebrated the fiftieth anniversary of the victory over fascism. The history of fascism is probably the most vivid and convincing example of the total and ignominious failure of policies based on suppressing universal human values and breaking with fundamental moral principles.

Examples of similar experiences are also known in Soviet history. I refer, above all, to Stalinism and its consequences, but also to the post-Stalin era when Soviet troops were sent into Hungary, Czechoslovakia, and Afghanistan. These actions contradicted the values and principles of the general human community and dealt painful blows to the Soviet Union.

Today, in the new conditions that have arisen it is not enough simply to appeal to history to condemn the breach between politics and universal human values. It is necessary to think about something else altogether: What are the needs that must be met in this era when no one's fate is separate but rather the fates of all are interconnected? Do not the needs arising from this situation make it imperative that we observe and abide by universal human values? I note with satisfaction that these questions are answered in the affirmative by representatives of the most diverse ideological tendencies and religious faiths, and by scientists of different schools.

But, as ever, politics is lagging behind. Is this not the most profound source of many of the misfortunes we encounter in our times? At this point it should be emphasized that for international politics certain values have acquired especially great significance today. Among these values is tolerance. Given the great multiplicity and diversity of the world, its viability and the viability of its component parts largely depend on how much tolerance there is for differences.

The UN declared the year 1995 to be the Year of Tolerance. The UN Charter states that the display of tolerance is an indispensable principle that must be applied in order to prevent war and maintain peace. This is undeniably correct, but this thought must be carried further: Tolerance has now become one of the most decisive universal human values.

The twentieth century as a whole proved to be a century of intolerance in human relations, social relations, and international politics. The governing principle was intolerance, inspired by nationalism, racism, and an insatiable lust for profits, territory, sources of raw materials, and new markets for one's products. In our times intolerance has caused many bloody conflicts, from the republics of former Yugoslavia to Somalia, from Rwanda to Sri Lanka, from Afghanistan to Chechnya. This is one phenomenon of history and of the present day that has not spared any of the spheres of human relations nor any region on earth.

The affirmation of tolerance in relations between people, between communities, and between countries, as called for by the UN, is a guarantee that the inherent value of human beings will be recognized, along with freedom of choice for every nation and every minority or nationality.

In the broadest sense, tolerance is respect for the views of others, which rules out any attempt to impose one's own views and convictions by force. It is an appeal for dialogue, a search for ways to prevent conflicts and resolve disputes.

In the realm of international politics proper, tolerance means behavior that seeks mutually acceptable solutions based on a balance between disparate interests. It means painstaking work and negotiations to find compromise solutions in order to resolve the most difficult problems.

Tolerance does not mean an all-forgiving attitude, as many would argue, nor does it mean ignoring differences. It means recognizing differences as the source of ideological, political, and moral enrichment, and thus is a road toward mutual understanding and respect.

All the major positive shifts that have taken place in recent years were possible, above all, because countries that had been enemies were able to arrive at a mutual understanding. They were able to consider one another's disparate interests and find a balance among them.

Mutual understanding is also one of the universal human values. It does not mean ignoring disparate interests; that is, it does not exclude a variety of intentions by different sides in the course of jointly resolving some problem. It does, however, presuppose reaching agreements honestly, examining questions concretely, and of course subsequently carrying out these agreements fairly. If obligations are not accepted and carried out with honesty, there can be no mutual understanding.

To arrive at mutual understanding it is necessary first to know one another better, to understand the concerns of one's partners and the constraints on their actions. This is true not only on the level of political leadership or among politicians in general; genuine mutual understanding can be reached in the best possible way if the populations of the corresponding countries establish relations of mutual trust among each other. Hence the continuing importance of unprejudiced communication between countries, peoples, and citizens.

The experience of recent years confirms all this. Extensive communication between the citizens of the Soviet Union and of the United States allowed both nations to change their attitudes toward each other, and this became an important political factor.

Tolerance, mutual understanding, and trust are inseparably connected with one more fundamental, universal human value—solidarity. There needs to be solidarity of all people with one another, with the closest and most distant citizens on earth, with the poor and the impoverished, with the suffering and the deprived.

In recent years the world has frequently encountered moving examples of humanistic solidarity. Let me recall, if nothing else, the touching wave of sympathy and support shown for our citizens after the disaster at Chernobyl and the earthquakes in Armenia and on the island of Sakhalin. The world community, many social organizations, and ordinary citizens have displayed genuine solidarity with the victims of wars, especially on the territory of the former Yugoslavia, and with those who have suffered from natural disasters. It seems we can affirm that the spirit of solidarity in the world is rooting itself ever more deeply.

Despite all this, a lack of solidarity can still be felt, mainly in politics at the international level. Instead of solidarity, alienation and indifference toward the sufferings of others often enters in. This applies both to domestic politics and to international politics. A cynical, calculating egoism and even a desire to profit at the expense of the suffering of others is unfortunately present.

In particular, there is an absence of genuine and effective solidarity with the Third World. The need for close cooperation with Third World peoples is being ignored. This creates conditions in which dictatorial regimes can arise, regimes that conduct themselves unpredictably in international relations. It also creates preconditions for countless internal conflicts, resulting in enormous casualties.

The twenty-first century and the entire coming millennium will be an era of universal tragedy if human solidarity does not gain the upper hand over the widespread contempt for the human race itself and the indifference to the fates of millions.

Voltaire once said that the history of preceding centuries had been the history of fanaticism. It can be said that the history of the two centuries since

Voltaire has been the history of ideology or, more precisely, of ideological politics. With the passage of time there has been a steady decrease in the "efficiency factor" with respect to accumulated wisdom. There has been a refusal to recognize the great insights of certain scholars, thinkers, and natural scientists. This was the case, for example, with Malthus in the late eighteenth and early nineteenth centuries and Einstein in the twentieth. On the other hand, people's capacity for self-destruction has increased.

Fanaticism and ideology have not disappeared in our times, but they have lost many of the positions they formerly held. And they are changing their outward appearances, adapting to the new conditions. Today, however—not because of anyone's wishing it but as a result of objective processes—humanity has entered a world of different proportions, a world in which universal human values have acquired life-or-death significance. To preserve these values, which are the achievement of all human history over many centuries, and put them into operation in daily life is no easy task. It requires, above all, a high level of understanding of today's problems and no less high a level of commitment to moral values. Neither of these can be achieved without purposeful effort. Such effort must be oriented primarily toward intellectual development and creating cultural preconditions for the solution of emerging problems. This means raising, educating, and training young people properly and emphasizing the role of spiritual principles in everyday life. From this it follows that humanity's intellectual and spiritual forces have an enormous responsibility.

The development of global thinking for all humanity is now on the agenda. Having roots in common with individual thinking, such global thinking can take shape as a logical result of developing and refining individual thinking. All intellectual history essentially has been the history of the broadening of horizons and boundaries. The time has come when our entire planet must be the horizon.

Today, in fact, human beings are becoming increasingly accustomed to a broader perception of the world. Even without realizing it, we are being drawn into a whirlpool of global events, receiving information from the most varied sources, above all, television, radio, and the press, sharing a vast store of information from the most remote parts of the earth. Today, by the very logic of events, we are being pushed toward an understanding of the need for interaction and cooperation among all nations of the world, toward an acceptance of today's global realities.

Amid the diversity of human existence, universal features are increasingly coming to the fore. People of varying cultures are being drawn closer together to engage in a dialogue. Barriers are being destroyed, revealing the human essence common to all individuals who belong to different branches of a common tree: world civilization. Human beings, while asserting their sense of self, at the same time are becoming universal entities, beings who strongly feel their ties with all others on the earth. Through this very process a global way of thinking is taking shape.

So then, universal civilizational processes are giving rise to an urgent need for the assimilation and practical application of universal human values. Here, too, politics is lagging behind. But people are becoming increasingly aware of the need for political leadership.

CHAPTER 28

The Beginning of History?

THE NEW THINKING and its application in the late 1980s and early 1990s had practical results of considerable importance. Substantial changes took place in the everyday life of the world community: It was freed from confrontation and Cold War, and the danger of nuclear catastrophe was removed from center stage. A fundamental renewal of the geo-political and geo-economic landscape had begun. At the same time and by the same token, we observed a consolidation of universal civilizing processes.

Recent years have witnessed criticism of the new thinking and of the results of its practical applications. It is true that despite substantial achievements and the undeniably positive shift that occurred in the world thanks to the new thinking, not everything we planned has succeeded. Much was not carried through to completion, to a great extent because the dissolution of the Soviet Union in December 1991 prevented continuation of the changes that had begun. Later on, the changes we had implemented were even declared to be unsuitable and unnecessary.

In recent times Russian foreign policy in some respects has returned to the kind of approach typical of the new thinking and to ideas we had initiated. In this way the new thinking has proven that it corresponds to the spirit of our times and that it flows from the objective needs and trends of the modern era. But life moves forward, raising new demands and posing new tasks. Naturally the new thinking, too, must continually evolve and progress.

If we were to attempt to make a concise generalization of everything set forth in this book, we might propose the following formula: Humanity cannot be simply a community constantly seeking to survive; sooner or later this approach will lead to catastrophe. It must become a community of progress for everyone—for North and South, East and West, for countries that are now highly developed as well as those that are relatively deprived.

As I have said, the idea of progress itself needs to progress. For humanity to realize the meaning and purpose of its own history, it must do so without irreparable harm to itself and to the rest of nature, without exploitation of some groups of people or entire nations, and without irreversible moral and spiritual losses. We must advance through worldwide cooperation based on complete equality, without any use of force, and with peaceful co-development of all nations.

This necessitates a profound change in the course of history itself, a change in the present paradigm, in the human community's very way of existence. In the history of the human race such changes are known to have occurred. They have varied in depth and extent, but they have occurred more than once and changed the foundations of existence, the means of existence, indeed humanity's basic way of life.

The pace of historical development has increased with the passage of time, and the intervals between epochal changes have grown smaller. The transition from a consuming economy to a producing economy (the Neolithic revolution) took several thousand years. Many centuries were required before the stage of small handicraft production had exhausted its potential and industrial production came into existence. But only a single century was needed to pass from industrial society to so-called postindustrial society, to the information economy.

An urgent need has arisen for a new transition in which societies would be organized according to principles that would allow elimination of the unparalleled threats endangering the very existence of humanity: We need to replace a civilization that produces without thinking, that is exhausting the natural resources on which its existence depends, with a civilization that constantly reproduces the conditions required for its existence, accumulating and not destroying the potential for future development. We need a civilization that aims not merely to survive but to live to the fullest and provide a full life for present and future generations.

This transition naturally will depend on the domestic policies of states and of the world community as a whole, and on the way that each country or community disposes of its worldly goods. It will depend on the paths they choose for domestic development.

The new thinking does not limit its horizons to international and global problems and processes. It is directly concerned with domestic policies and links these policies to the actions of governments in the international arena. Properly speaking, perestroika in the Soviet Union was an application of the principles of the new thinking to the solution of domestic problems that our country was then facing. I emphasize the international-political aspect of the new thinking because global problems are among the most important problems humanity will face in the transition to a new form of existence.

Another task of the new thinking is to search for answers to new problems that may be posed by changing times and that will face the entire world community. The intention of the new thinking is to call for joint efforts worldwide to find answers because it is impossible to impose on humanity some predigested answers thought up by only a few people. The only effective answers will be collective ones that make collective action possible. This presupposes the understanding that no one has a monopoly on the truth but that by generalizing the entire collective experience that has accumulated and that reflects the input of all ideological tendencies, we can arrive at truly joint conclusions and decisions.

The modern world can no longer be built on the basis of an endless confrontation of ideologies. Differences of opinion cannot be eradicated, but while they will continue to exist, it is possible to find a synthesis for the collective solution of problems and the construction of a platform on which we can work jointly.

The means of advancing to a new way of life can and must vary from country to country, from continent to continent. This is only natural. The forms in which decisions are made, the modes of operation, are bound to be multiple and diverse. What is important is that everyone must pursue the common goal: a genuine renewal of the life of the entire world community in order to arrive at new conditions of existence for the human race.

Various answers to current challenges have been proposed in the sphere of international politics and relations. Unfortunately these variations too often turn out to be new only in their outward manifestation. Their actual content leaves old methods and approaches untouched.

The changes that began in 1985, first in the Soviet Union and then in other countries (and all countries have changed in the past ten years, regardless of the different ways the results may be evaluated) reflected objective needs, the needs of the future, the need for a new world civilization. These changes have sometimes been described as the end of history. It has been asserted that with the worldwide spread of market relations the end of history has arrived. In recent times, this point of view has most prominently been expressed, as we have said, by Francis Fukuyama. But it is not an original idea. Walter W. Rostow, much earlier than Fukuyama, expressed the view that the consumer society is the "highest stage of progress."

The idea of the end of history contradicts the actual course of history. Essentially it represents a denial of any further forward movement in history, or it oversimplifies to an extreme degree the meaning and purpose of history by reducing it to a mere accumulation of wealth and expanding consumption. History has not stood still and will not. Its evolution, of course, does not follow a straight line. History constantly rises to new heights and multiplies its own characteristics both qualitatively and quantitatively.

A serious evolution in all aspects of the life of the world community is predetermined by the profound and unstoppable processes that have begun in the world. I am convinced that a necessary stage on humanity's path toward a new state of being must be, and cannot help but be, a renewal of its thinking. It is an insistent need of our times that this kind of thinking be given its rightful place and developed further, that the new thinking be enriched, for it has already proven capable of overcoming impasses and opening the way for breakthroughs in politics where it had seemed no breakthrough was possible.

INDEX

Index compiled by Fred Leise